DATE DUE

DEC - 6 2000	

CRISIS IN THE FAMILY

CRISIS IN THE FAMILY

THREE APPROACHES

by Roseann F. Umana, M.S.
Steven Jay Gross, Ph.D.
Marcia Turner McConville, ACSW

GARDNER PRESS, INC., New York
Distributed by Halsted Press
Division of John Wiley & Sons, Inc.
New York • Toronto • London • Sydney

GARDNER PRESS, INC.
19 Union Square West
New York 10003

Distributed solely by the Halsted Press Division
of John Wiley & Sons, Inc., New York

Library of Congress Cataloging in Publication Data
Umana, Roseann F
Crisis in the family.

Includes index.
1. Family psychotherapy.   2. Crisis intervention (Psychiatry)
3. Psychoanalysis.   4. Behavior therapy.   5. Social systems.
I. Gross, Steven Jay, joint author.   II. McConville, Marcia Turner,
joint author.   III. Title.
RC488.5.U48   616.8'9'156   78-14945
ISBN0-470-26506-x

Printed in the United States of America

CONTENTS

Foreword   vii

Introduction   ix

1. Family Crisis Intervention   1

2. Psychoanalytic Model of Family Crisis Intervention   35

3. Problem-Oriented Model of Family Crisis
Intervention   43

4. Systems Model of Family Crisis Intervention   53

5. Crisis Intervention   57

6. Individual Crisis Intervention   71

7. Behavioral Crisis Intervention   77

8. Systems Crisis Intervention   83

9. Psychoanalytic Model of Family Therapy   89

10. Behavioral Model of Family Therapy   99

11. Systems Model of Family Therapy   115

12. Evaluative Research   131

13. Comparative Analyses: Three Therapeutic
Frameworks and Three Models of Human Behavior   171

References   179

Index   195

FOREWORD

This volume by research-oriented and innovative family therapists compares and contrasts the basic concepts and approaches of various "schools" of professionals who deal with crises in families and who develop techniques for dealing with them. Each approach reflects its own historical antecedents as sociology of knowledge would lead us to expect. Psychoanalytic approaches developed out of the study and treatment of individuals and continue to reflect that origin. Behavioristic approaches have grown out of interests in applying learning theory. Some systems approaches emerged from studies of communication and general systems by persons who initially had been trained psychoanalytically or who approached families as small cultural units, each with its own set of shared meanings, beliefs, and norms about feelings and their expression.

Various concepts of crisis are widely employed these days. They are used to describe social systems whose ordinary functioning or survival may be threatened by events and processes that can, on the one hand, overwhelm their decision and coping mechanisms or, on the other, their perceptions of, and abilities to cope with, reality. Psychologists have developed explanatory theories and techniques for dealing with crises of dyads, families, communities, organizations, and nations. Different psychotherapists, as experts in dealing with reality and nonreality, not only describe and explain crises in some of our basic social systems, but also treat and prescribe treatments for dealing with events and processes which their participants perceive as ranging from merely painful to horrendous. These different approaches to crisis in families both describe the salient aspects of these processes and prescribe ways to treat them. Therapists after all consume the results of, as well as produce, scientific, theory-oriented investigations. They are interveners in social processes who have been invited by their clientele to apply psychological knowledge. Therapists and their clientele contract with one another, though often tentatively, reluctantly, and ambivalently for the roles they will take in dealing with one another. Ambivalence plays only a somewhat smaller role in intense crises than in less oppressive situations. So therapists face the twin problems of understanding and helping. They need theories of crisis to enable them to understand and explain what is going on and to prescribe what to do next with their patients. Their approaches must intrigue and involve their clientele who must trust their therapist-educators sufficiently to continue to work with them.

I have gotten to know the second author of this volume well over the past five years and have found our discussions of these topics interesting and often exciting. We both have been intrigued by their consonance with work on analogous topics at more macro-levels of social complexity as studied by social psychologists, sociologists, and political scientists.

Some of the ideas mentioned in this volume seem clearly applicable to other fields. One is the notion that a crisis calls for third-party intervention and the application of new skills or fresh resources because ordinary modes of coping or routine procedures have proved limited and inadequate. In many situations such circumstances would mean a call for mediators or arbitrators. Another is the idea that the tension so often associated with situations considered to be crises ought more properly and usefully be designated a result or consequence rather than be considered a defining characteristic. From a phenomenological point of view, crises are self-defined times of trouble and effort to cope, decide, and act.

It is my feeling that a basic monograph of the sort presented here which can provide the verbal underpinnings of the comparative insights of the theoretically and empirically oriented therapist, has been due for some time. It is thus very satisfying to see this volume appear in a form that can make it widely useful. I recommend it to all who deal with crises and especially to those who wish to learn how to help more effectively in crises.

Thomas W. Milburn
PROFESSOR OF PSYCHOLOGY AND PUBLIC POLICY
OHIO STATE UNIVERSITY

INTRODUCTION

Our major goal in writing this text evolved as we attempted to make sense of what appeared to be a hodgepodge of models and practices in the fields of family crisis intervention, family therapy, and crisis intervention. As clinicians we were concerned that many of our colleagues were in the same dilemma as ourselves—practicing in a field that lacked clear conceptual boundaries.

In writing the book we found a need for common dimensions from which we would make sense of the numerous approaches and models. As we became more capable of making these classifications, we were pleased to find that the development of our textbook allowed us to perceive more clearly the range and the boundaries of our field. We hope that this knowledge will aid both the reader and ourselves in our current clinical practice, and will also serve to facilitate the development of more effective intervention strategies.

This text examines the relationship among three major, popular movements in mental health: family crisis intervention, family therapy, and crisis intervention. Family crisis intervention, drawing on the premises of family therapy and crisis intervention, presents a framework for dealing with crisis stimuli in the context of the social system, usually the family. Intervention aims to change interactions within the system (family) in order to potentiate a positive, growth-enhancing resolution of crisis. Its link with family therapy is that it defines behavior in a social context, attributing dysfunctional behavior to ineffective rules of interaction, and explaining behavior in terms of its impact on others— or its message value. In other words, maladaptive behavior is viewed by adherents of the family therapy framework as "functional" in maintaining the current interactional system. Treatment then focuses on changing the rules of interaction which are maintaining the dysfunctional behavior.

Crisis intervention elevates change to the forefront, demanding that mental health professionals acknowledge the modern human condition as a series of rapidly changing experiences. The ability of the family to cope with these changes has strained the family's capacity for tolerating stress and creatively coping with a rapidly changing society. Likewise the capacity of the individual to cope with a rapidly changing society has led to renewed interest in crisis intervention. Crisis intervention theorists explore the issue of individual adaptability to sudden stressful events. The premise of these theorists is that change and crisis normally occur in the process of living and provide the opportunity both for personal growth and for dysfunction and stagnation. Intervention aims to assist (teach) people to gain the skills needed in order to resolve crises more effectively.

In retrospect it appears inevitable that these two intervention frameworks would be combined. Their product, family crisis intervention, views man as being a social being who is confronted by change. Like any offspring, family crisis intervention integrates the common values of the two parent frameworks while highlighting their areas of discord. It is the purpose of this book to examine all three approaches individually and as they interact.

We shall discuss the three frameworks from a cognitive, theoretical, rather than an applied, perspective. Our aim is to make explicit the underlying assumptions of each framework by clarifying and classifying as much as possible the models of human behavior involved. In this context, three models of personality are investigated: psychoanalytic, behavioral, and systems. The psychoanalytic model emphasizes inner man and the motivations underlying his behavior. The behavioral model focuses on behaviors, their antecedents, and consequents. The systems model highlights the social context (outer man) and its determination of the individual's behavior. It is the authors' contention that each of these models—psychoanalytic, behavioral, and systems—and each of these frameworks—family crisis intervention, family therapy, and crisis intervention—would yield a different definition of the problem, a different intervention strategy and a different role for both therapist and the client. This text will discuss each of the frameworks within the context of each of the three personality models (see Table 1).

It is our hope that the reader will gain an appreciation of the three modes of intervention from this model. The reader should also understand what the translation of these modes into three models of man yields in terms of the goals

Table 1
Intervention Frameworks and Theoretical Perspectives

Intervention Frameworks	THEORETICAL PERSPECTIVES		
	Psychoanalytic	Behavioral	Systems
Family Therapy	Psychoanalytic family therapy	Behavioral family therapy	Systems family therapy
Crisis Intervention	Individual crisis intervention	Generic crisis intervention	Systems crisis intervention
Family Crisis Intervention	Psychoanalytic family crisis intervention	Problem-oriented family crisis intervention	Systems family crisis intervention

of therapy, the role of the therapist and client, and most critically, the underlying assumptions which guide both assessment and treatment.

The format and style of each chapter will include a discussion of both the model of man (i.e., psychoanalytic, behavioral, system) and the intervention being examined (family crisis, family therapy, or crisis). The reader will note that in order of detail, the family therapy chapters come first, the crisis chapters next, and the section on family crisis, last. This represents the state of the field. Family therapy is the major shaper of family crisis intervention and, to some extent, of crisis intervention.

As authors we have definite biases. Gross and McConville have developed their own model, which is described in the chapter on systems approaches to family therapy. Umana and also favors a systems model. Interestingly, the model developed by Gross and McConville incorporates key ingredients from each of the three approaches to human behavior.

We have attempted to describe all approaches fairly, though if any are misrepresented, it is our error. To those people whose work we have omitted, we apologize. To those whose work we have included, we trust that it has been represented fairly and accurately. Finally, it is our hope that readers will find this text interesting and useful.

Roseann F. Umana, Ph.D.
Steven J. Gross, Ph.D. ABPP
Marcia T. McConville ACSW

CRISIS IN THE FAMILY

1

Family
Crisis
Intervention

Basic Premises

FAMILY CRISIS

According to Caplan (1961, 1964, 1970), a crisis occurs when an individual is confronted with a problematic situation for which his typical way of operating in the world and his usual supports are not sufficient. That is, the individual's problem-solving behavior is not adequate to produce a satisfactory solution to the difficulty at hand (Rapoport, 1965). A crisis effects a temporary disruption of an individual's normal patterns of living, and is characterized by high levels of tension.

A family crisis refers to the same process, but focuses on the family as the locus of the problem. In a family crisis, then, the interactional patterns are in a temporary state of disequilibrium or flux caused by the introduction of a stimulus that is novel to the family. Examples of stimuli that may lead to a family crisis include the sudden exhibition by a family member of acute psychiatric symptomatology (such as suicidal attempts or threats, or bizarre behaviors). Other events that can function as precipitating factors or crisis stimuli are loss of housing or employment, and the addition, loss, or sudden severe illness of a family member.

It must be noted that only some familites will experience a crisis as a result of any one of these events. What, therefore, are the necessary conditions of a family crisis? One requirement, according to Caplan (1964) and Hill (1958) is that the stimulus must be a novel one. In addition, according to Caplan, a crisis is a situation in which the family's normal problem-solving skills are not sufficient. Caplan also contends that lack of a sufficiently strong support system or network within the family can be a causal factor in crisis induction.

Clearly, what is implied here is that what may constitute a crisis for one family may not be so perceived by another family which has the resources to resolve it. Thus there can be no simple listing for all families of events that define family crisis. Perhaps a better way to approach the problem would be to ask what kinds of precipitating events will interact with what kinds of families, under what kinds of circumstances, to effect a crisis.

In this regard, a number of articles have been written describing normal crises in family life (Rapoport, 1963; Warkentin & Whitaker, 1966; Hill, 1958). Such articles are concerned with identifying specific points in family life where crises may occur due to a shift in family responsibilities or family membership; as, for example, the birth of a child, loss of income, or a death in the family. Additionally, several researchers have explored family patterns of dealing with these and other crisis situations, such as disaster (Drabek & Boggs, 1968), a child's terminal illness (Kaplan, Smith, Grobstein, & Fischman, 1973), and the addition or loss of a family member (Hadley, Jakob, Milliones, Caplan, & Spitz, 1974). For example, Raush, Barry, Hertel, and Swain (1974) assume that over the course of the life cycle, couples must pass through specific stages (newlyweds, new parents, and so on) in which particular concerns or events becomes the focus of attention. During each stage, new tasks (such as caring for the baby) must be learned, and the partners must develop new modes of relating to each other as well as to persons outside the marital relationship. Raush et al. (1974) argue that couples who interact in a way which limits the satisfactory solutions available to them in new situations are likely to experience emotional stress and increase the probability that the family will experience a crisis. Although Raush et al. do not specifically make predictions about family crisis onset, it seems reasonable that the conditions they describe (that is, the inability to develop new modes of relating when confronted with a new stage [stimulus] because their information is limited) are both necessary and probably sufficient for crisis onset. (Glick, 1974).

However, in a recent study examining conflict resolution and self-esteem (Glick, Gross, & Pepinsky, 1979) it was reported that a couple's level of self-esteem was related to the way they handled conflict. Specifically, self-esteem seemed to function as a trait affecting all situations, regardless of the developmental stage of the couple. Thus this study did not support Raush's view that greater conflict exists in low self-esteem couples when they are dealing with a specific developmental problem. The study was more supportive of Satir's view that couples low in self-esteem would experience any expression of disagreement with the partner as negative. It also is likely that these couples are more prone to crises.

DEALING WITH FAMILY CRISIS

Bolman (1968) described ways to approach families in crisis. Either one attempts to cope with their crises before they occur (primary prevention), or tries to lessen their impact after they occur (secondary prevention). He categorized these methods in three ways: as communitywide intervention, milestone approaches, and high-risk approaches.

Communitywide intervention. Communitywide intervention aims to improve the state of community organization both at the level of environmental quality and by increasing the effective provision of family supportive services. The idea is essentially to better the community so that families will face fewer crises, and so that those crises that do occur will have less of an impact.

Milestone Approach. This type of family crisis intervention attempts to make contact directly with families at those points in its life where normal crises are likely to occur. Such programs obviously are limited to those publicly visible family crisis points such as school entry, childbirth, and death. Some examples include free clinics for prenatal and early infant care, teaching parents basic child rearing skills, and so forth.

High-risk Approaches. Intervention with high-risk families is oriented toward those families identified through clinical and epidemiologic studies to have the highest risk of crisis or of failure to successfully achieve crisis resolution. While Bolman (1968) occasionally points to high-risk subpopulations in the middle socioeconomic class, he concludes that the major portion of high-risk populations is defined by poverty.

> They are more apt than not to be poor, underemployed, undereducated, under 16 or over 65, of a minority group, and having a different life style. In addition, they are more likely to have come in contact with the community's police and welfare functions and are apt to view and be viewed by the community in stereotyped ways. The net result is the existence of a sizeable social and communicative distance that requires specific attention when planning high-risk family-oriented programs. (p. 461)

Although any family given the right set of circumstances may experience a family crisis, it is more likely that those with the least resources—families that are poor and/or isolated—will have a greater incidence of such crises.

THE EFFECT OF CRISIS ON FAMILY FUNCTIONING

While it is not possible to state that in all cases a specific type of event will lead to crisis for all families, it is possible to identify the characteristics of a crisis for any family experiencing it. This follows from a basic tenet of crisis theory; namely, that regardless of the specific nature of the crisis stimulus, crises are dealt with in a predictable and patterned way. According to Caplan (1964), this process of crisis resolution proceeds through four typical phases. In Phase 1, the initial rise in tension due to the crisis stimulus provokes habitual problem-solving responses. That is, the family attempts to resolve the problem as it has resolved problems in the past. If these typical responses do not lead to resolution, the family enters Phase 2. This phase is characterized by lack of success and the continuation of the problematic stimulus. This in turn leads to increasing tension, distress, and feelings of ineffectuality. Continuation of the crisis stimulus results in a further rise in tension, which Caplan defines as Phase 3. According to Caplan, this tension acts as a "powerful internal stimulus to the mobilization of internal and external resources" (p.40). This phase would typically be characterized by the family's utilization of novel problem-solving methods, attempts to redefine the problem, a reexamination of the problem and perhaps an awareness of its neglected aspects, or perhaps an active resignation to the present state of affairs, and a use of trial and error. It is suggested by Caplan that it is the third stage at which the family is most likely to consider outside assistance as part of the seeking out of new or previously unidentified resources.

According to Caplan, in Phase 4 the crisis continues and can neither be solved nor avoided. Tension mounts further, and leads to major disorganization, which may manifest itself either in family dysfunction or in the dysfunction of one of its members (e.g., manifestation of psychiatric symptomatology). Therefore one of the implied assumptions of crisis theory is that crisis is a time-limited, temporary state of being that resolves itself in one way or another in a short time. According to Caplan, this resolution, whether it results in solution of the problem accompanied by a return to former levels of effective functioning, or in a movement toward equilibrium at a more dysfunctional level, will occur within approximately six weeks (See Figure 1-1)

Caplan's description of the process of crisis resolution also suggests how family functioning might be altered by the introduction of a crisis stimulus and by repeated, unsuccessful attempts to resolve it. In observing a family in crisis, one would expect to see the family functioning in ways that become increasingly chaotic, with a large number of random, trial-and-error attempts to deal with the crisis stimulus, and with mounting tension and increased levels of family conflict. A common error made in the diagnosis of family problems is to characterize a family seen in the midst of such a crisis as normatively chaotic, disorganized, and dysfunctional. What must be remembered in evaluating the functioning of such a family is that much of the confusion, hostility, and tension may be a temporary characteristic of the crisis situation, one which, if

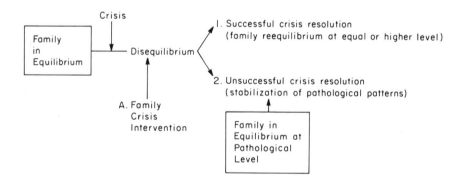

Figure 1-1.
Process of crisis resolution.

the crisis is resolved, will disappear. Thus a family described as disorganized and dysfunctional during a crisis episode may be observed to function in a much more effective manner within a few weeks time.

SEEKING HELP IN A FAMILY CRISIS

Some crisis intervention programs focus primary and secondary preventive efforts on such known crisis points as contacting a family when they are about to have a child, or when they are about to send a child to school. These programs, which we earlier called milestone approaches, (Bolman, 1968) are designed to prevent the occurrence of a crisis or to lessen its impact if it does occur.

Families who experience a crisis generally come to the attention of interveners in one of two ways. First, in looking for new ways to resolve the crisis (Caplan's Phase 3), the family may voluntarily seek outside assistance. In this case the practices of the clinic or practitioner determine whether the family will receive help with the crisis. For example, if in seeking help the family approaches an agency with a no-waiting-list policy, the family probably will receive help during the crisis period. If, however, the family approaches sources of help that delay help giving for as short a period as a few weeks, the result may be detrimental. In the time limited world of crisis such a delay becomes simply one more unsuccessful attempt to resolve the crisis. Such help sources will see only families that have failed to resolve the crisis (Phase 4) and have therefore begun to stabilize at a dysfunctional level (see the discussion of differences between family therapy and family crisis intervention in section 4 of this chapter).

As a result of current practices in mental health it is more likely that lower- and lower-middle-class families will receive help from mental health sources during the crisis period, while families from higher socio-economic levels are more likely to receive help only after crisis resolution failure. Since mental health outpatient clinics tend to draw clients from the lower end of the socio-economic spectrum, and since such clinics frequently see people on a walk-in basis, their programs often provide crisis intervention services as part of their repertoire. Middle- and upper-class families tend to seek out private practition-ers, who are likely to set up appointments for treatment a week or more in advance. This suggests that such families probably receive crisis intervention services from societal agents who are not a part of the mental health community (e.g., clergy and family physicians).

Families in crisis also come to the attention of outside interveners when the family crisis either takes place in the public view or in some manner comes to the attention of societal agents. Examples would include a family argument in which neighbors call the police, a suicide attempt by a family member in which a hospital emergency-room staff becomes involved, or a school counselor's or teacher's observation that a child is acting different than usual. In each of these ways someone outside the family may be in a position to observe change in family behavior, and is therefore in a position to suggest, encourage, or force the family to seek outside help.

GOALS OF FAMILY CRISIS INTERVENTION

Based on the assumption that the family in crisis is in a temporary state of disequilibrium, the family crisis intervener has as his major, albeit minimal, goal to help the family return at least to the level of effective functioning that it had prior to the onset of the crisis. A more optimal goal espoused by family crisis interveners is to increase the level of effectiveness of the family beyond its precrisis functioning level in order that the family may be more resilient in future crises. In other words, beyond the minimal goal of resolving the crisis and returning the family to its previous ongoing norms, the crisis intervener may desire to help the family discover and add to its repertoire of behaviors some new problem-solving skills which would enable the family to resolve without crisis a larger range of problematic novel situations.

BASIC ASSUMPTIONS OF FAMILY CRISIS INTERVENTION

Family crisis intervention essentially espouses the basic assumptions developed in crisis theory. They can be attributed primarily to Caplan's notions of the nature of crisis and crisis resolution, and are defined as follows:

1. human functioning requires the maintenance of an ongoing homeostasis or equilibrium not only within the organism but in relationship to the environment.

2. any disruption of this equilibrium is followed by attempts to restore it or to achieve a new adaptive balance.

3. certain disruptive periods can, by their characteristics, be identified as crisis states.

4. behaving organisms are more susceptible to external influence during a period of disruption than during one of stable equilibrium.

5. the period of disruption is self-limited and may be followed by a new adaptation which is qualitatively different from the one which preceded it.

6. equilibrium can be restored by changing features of the environment, changing modes of coping, or both (Kalis, 1970, p. 73).

7. the outcome of any crisis can be predicted, based on the success of the family's crisis resolution attempts.

Beyond these basic tenets of crisis theory, family crisis intervention also assumes that the family is the most influential context in which crisis occurs. Specifically, the family is viewed as having the greatest impact on the production, maintenance, and resolution of a particular crisis. Family crisis intervention, then, differs from crisis intervention in that it maximizes the active role of the family in crisis management. Thus the family crisis intervener defines the family rather than the individual as the unit in crisis.

Additional assumptions about family crisis and intervention methods depend on the intervener's particular theoretical notions of individual and family functioning. For this reason a major portion of this book examines three disparate approaches to family crisis intervention based on three different theories of human functioning. In succeeding chapters we will examine the psychoanalytic (Chapter 2), problem-oriented (Chapter 3), and systems (Chapter 4) approaches to family crisis. Additional assumptions of family crisis interveners will be described as they relate to each of these three theories of human functioning. Throughout the remainder of this chapter, we will focus only on those elements which are common to family crisis intervention as a therapeutic field; that is, elements that are shared by family crisis interveners regardless of theoretical orientation.

ASSESSMENT IN FAMILY CRISIS INTERVENTION

In terms of assessment, the first concern of the family crisis intervener is to identify the crisis stimulus, the perceptions and reactions of family members to the onset of the stimulus, and the attempts made by the family to resolve it. The intervener will seek answers to questions such as:

What particular event, within or outside of the nuclear family, provoked the crisis (e.g., what is the precipitating event, the crisis stimulus)?
How did the crisis occur?
When did it occur?
What has the family done to date to resolve it?
What is there about the family and about the event that is forestalling resolution? What is it that is keeping this family from resolving this problem?

TREATMENT METHODS IN FAMILY CRISIS INTERVENTION

Based on the assumption that a family crisis is both a time-limited event and one during which the family is more susceptible to external influence (e.g., more willing and able to seek advice and help), the family crisis intervener typically offers a more intense and rapid provision of services than do adherents of more typical treatment approaches. For example, it would be much more likely in family crisis intervention that the treatment team would (a) be available on a twenty-four basis, (b) make home visits, (c) not use a waiting list, and (d) see families as soon as possible in cases of referral.

In terms of frequency and length of sessions, family crisis interveners are likely to see families for extended sessions (perhaps two to four hours in length) on a high-frequency schedule (perhaps daily at first, then biweekly and weekly as the family moves toward termination). Further, family crisis interveners expect duration of contact to be limited to five to ten sessions over a one- to two-month period (Langsley et al., 1968a).

The use of psychotropic medications also is typical of family crisis intervention. Psychotropic medications are prescribed liberally to reduce anxieties in order that family members can work more effectively on problem resolution. An additional treatment objective of family crisis interveners is to achieve the active involvement of family members as rapidly as possible. Thus, if an individual family member approached a family crisis intervener for assistance, a home or office visit would generally be scheduled as rapidly as possible, with all family members encouraged to attend.

The emphasis of family crisis treatment is on the current life situation, with minimal exploration of the history of the family. Family crisis interveners make extensive use of time-limited treatment contracts, as we have mentioned, offering to see a family for a maximum number of sessions, usually not more than ten. Use of a team approach in which two or more therapists are assigned to the family also is common. Interveners generally use multiple therapy modalities and do not limit themselves to a specific set of techniques.

THE ROLE OF THE INTERVENER IN FAMILY CRISIS INTERVENTION

The emphasis on rapidity and intensity of service provision suggests a much more intense, active role for the family crisis intervener than for therapists in more traditional modalities. In family crisis intervention the intervener is very active, offering numerous suggestions about what ought to be done. The family crisis intervener acts not only within the session but also by being available on a twenty-four hour basis and setting up emergency sessions as needed. The intervener may act as a mediator between the family and outside systems (between the family and the school, between the family and the employer).

An important attitudinal difference between family crisis interveners and adherents of more traditional approaches appears to be that the latter frequently focus on the family as "sick" or as containing a "sick" individual, while the former perceive the family as in need of learning skills to solve their problems. Based on the assumption tht the family is acting in a dysfunctional way only temporarily and in direct response to a stimulus, the family crisis intervener focuses on those relevant skills that the family lacks and that can be taught quickly and intensively to return the family to a functional state.

HELP GIVERS IN FAMILY CRISIS INTERVENTION

Help givers in family crisis intervention cover a wide spectrum. Who treats the family in crisis depends in part on the theoretical outlook of the organization or crisis center that is contacted. Therapeutic agents in the family crisis intervention field consist of mental health professionals from the medical (Becker & Weiner, 1966), educational (Rapoport, 1965), and systems orientations (Langsley et al., 1968b), nonprofessional volunteers (McGee, 1974), and natural help givers (Bard & Berkowitz, 1969).

A natural help giver is someone who does not ordinarily define himself as a mental health professional, but who, because of his job or the location of his dwelling, is a natural part of the environment of the family in crisis, and who may act as an intervener in times of crisis (police, lawyer, family physician). For example, there have been a number of programs around the country that have trained police officers to act as family crisis interveners (Bard, 1970; Phelps, Schwartz, & Liebman, 1971).

Two major approaches have been utilized in training police officers to function in this role. The first type, commonly termed the specialist-generalist model, is one in which a subgroup of patrolmen is selected for intensive training. These police officers are assigned to patrol units as specialists taking primary responsibility for handling domestic disturbances in addition to normal patrol duties. Three major projects have been conducted within this model, in New York City (Bard, 1970; Bard & Zacker, 1971), in Louisville, Kentucky (Driscoll, Meyer, & Schanie, 1971; 1973), and in Oakland, California (Radelet, 1973; Oakland Police Department, 1971).

The second approach to such police training is the generalist model, in which all patrolmen assigned to a particular precinct or area are given training in family crisis intervention techniques. Following completion of training, these officers return to their normal tour of duty and handle domestic disputes as a part of their normal work. Two major projects utilizing the generalist model have been conducted, one in Richmond, California (Phelps, Schwartz, & Liebman, 1971), and the other in Columbus, Ohio (McGee et al., 1975). The generalist approach is based on the broader notion that a natural part of the police function is to act as a mental health resource, sometimes called a frontline screener, for psychiatric and other social problems (Liberman, 1969).

FAMILIES RECEIVING FAMILY CRISIS INTERVENTION SERVICES

There are no accurate statistics concerning the kinds of families that become engaged in family crisis intervention services. But the emphasis, as described earlier, tends to be on those families that have the greatest likelihood of crisis involvement; that is, lower-class families. A number of factors, including the fewer resources available to lower-class families and the greater extent to which their lives are conducted in the public view, have resulted in the location of crisis centers in lower-class neighborhoods.

TYPICAL SETTINGS FOR FAMILY CRISIS INTERVENTION

The typical setting of a family crisis intervention service is the walk-in crisis center, a special kind of outpatient clinic in which services are available around the clock. Other settings include mobile response units, admitting offices of psychiatric hospitals, and emergency rooms of general hospitals. The least likely settings are private offices and outpatient facilities that have waiting lists.

Roots of Family Crisis Intervention:
Family Therapy

Family crisis intervention essentially developed during the 1960s. During that period a large number of programs provided mental health services to families in crisis (Becker & Weiner, 1966; Cameron & Walters, 1965; Langsley et al., 1968a). The 1970s have seen the further development of such programs (Gwaltney, 1974; Goldstein & Giddings, 1973; Mcgee, 1974; Bard, 1970).

Writings in the family crisis intervention field have been primarily reports about service, and have paid minimal attention to theoretical underpinnings or to the development of a cohesive intervention framework. As such, the field until now has presented a wide diversity of unintegrated exploratory approaches. This diversity is exemplified in such areas as the types of manpower employed, kinds of intervention settings utilized, number and length of therapeutic contacts, and goals of intervention. Though one can infer from various reports that a number of theories of behavior change and intervention methodology are being employed by family crisis interveners, those active in the field have, with few exceptions, failed to tie program reports to underlying theoretical constructs. Thus the literature of family crisis intervention is a hodgepodge of disjointed, nonparallel experiments in intervention.

This book provides an integrated theoretical base for family crisis intervention by exploring both the most relevant frameworks for intervention from related fields, and the most commonly used theoretical models of therapeutic intervention. Although reports of family crisis intervention programs lack any discussion of their theoretical and historical roots, we have concluded that family crisis intervention is essentially a hybrid of two distinct modes of intervention, both of which developed in this century. These two modes are family therapy and crisis intervention. Both are of fairly recent origin (approximately from the 1950s) and have currently achieved some popularity as therapeutic frameworks.

In order to give the reader a clear understanding of the origins of family crisis intervention, the remainder of this chapter will examine the two related fields from which family crisis intervention essentially took its basic assumptions about treatment and family crisis. We will examine the family therapy and crisis intervention fields in terms of their origins, treatment goals, assumptions, methods of assessment and treatment, traditional help givers and help receivers, and the settings typically utilized in intervention. We begin with family therapy.

HISTORICAL DEVELOPMENT

The most important concept in family therapy is the premise that the family constitutes a system (Foley, 1974). Hall and Fagen (1956) have defined a system as a "set of objects together with the relationships between the objects and between their attributes. The objects are the component parts of the system, the attributes are the properties of objects and the relationships tie the system together" (p. 18). From this perspective, the pathological behavior of an individual family member is seen as purposeful in maintaining the present family system. From this vantage point, family therapists "subscribe to the proposition that altering the family system, and hence the transactions between the persons (sub-systems) who are part of that larger system, result in changes in the individual. Therefore, change at *any* point in the system may well affect any or all of its components" (Sager & Kaplan, 1972, p. 256). Family therapy, then, involves changing the patterns of interaction among family members such that the pathological behavior of a family member is no longer necessary to maintain the family system. When such a change has been effected, the pathological behavior will cease.

The basic premises of family therapy have developed over the last two decades both as a result of studies of families with a schizophrenic member (or as some family therapists would contend, schizophrenic families) and as a result of therapists' frustrations with individual treatment approaches. By the early 1950s, a number of researchers had pointed to the importance of the family in the development of schizophrenia. There were several key individuals and groups who helped to define the field of family therapy: Bateson and his communications project, which included Jackson, Weakland and Haley; Bowen and his study of mother/child "symbiosis" with schizophrenic and normal families; Lidz and his work with schizophrenic families; Whitaker and Malone, and their work using cotherapy teams; and Ackerman, who introduced the concept of working with families within a psychoanalytic framework. There were numerous others who also had a major impact on the field, but these individuals should be considered the pioneers (Guerin, 1976).

During the 1950s there was much research that examined the parental patterns in the families of schizophrenics. For example, Reichard and Tillman (1950) examined patterns of parent-child relationships in schizophrenia. Wahl (1954) examined histories of 392 schizophrenics hospitalized while in the military service, and concluded that antecedent family events were significant in the development of schizophrenia. While these and other such studies concluded that the family was influential in the development of schizophrenia, they did not of themselves lead to the conclusion that the family itself was the unit to be treated. However, in the mid-1950s the relationship of schizophrenic symptomatology to the family was examined from an interaction perspective. In 1954 Jackson published a paper entitled "The Question of Homeostatis," in which he described some psychological upsets occurring in other family members when the identified patient improved. In addition, he tentatively related parental interaction patterns to specific symptoms of the identified patient. In 1957 Bowen reported the results of an in-depth study of five hospitalized families, each of which included a schizophrenic member. His findings supported those of Jackson (1954), Lidz et al. (1957) and others, who reported the fluctuating nature of symptoms from one family member to another as changes in family interaction took place. Bowen (1966) further reported that the nature and kind of symptom observed reflected the content and nature of the total family interaction. In 1958 Weakland and Jackson reported that acute upsets in schizophrenic patients coincided with covert disagreements among family members.

These studies went beyond the earlier notion that events in the patient's family predisposed him to schizophrenia, and concluded that current family interaction directly influenced symptomatology. Also, the finding that other family members demonstrated distress when the identified patient's symptoms abated suggested that the pathological behavior of the identified patient was somehow advantageous to and being maintained by the family system. These studies suggested that the schizophrenic family member was acting as the symptom bearer for the entire family, which led to the notion that the most appropriate unit of treatment was not the schizophrenic family member, but the family itself. As a result, researchers in the field developed an interpersonal theory of schizophrenia and experimented with various approaches to family treatment.

These developments in family treatment occurred at a time when individually oriented treatment was the predominant approach within the mental health field. Emphasis on the individual—his early development, his current experience of the world based on developmental factors, and his change based on insight into these processes—was the major focus of theory development, therapeutic intervention, and research (Haley, 1971). At the same time, however, therapists were finding that when patients effectively treated in a hospital setting returned home, they often regressed. Sometimes another family member began to show symptoms of emotion distress instead. Ackerman (1954) observed the same phenomenon in outpatient treatment, reporting that "It is by no means rare . . . that as one member of the [marital] pair gets better, the other gets worse . . . Or, as the child responds to psychotherapy, the parental conflict becomes drastically intensified" (p. 360). Therapists examining this phenomenon consistently reported that the patient usually came from a disturbed family, and this led to the theory that a problem child was a symptom of a problem family. As a result, therapists began to experiment by including additional family members in the treatment session. Further, they began to consider models that emphasized the interpersonal aspects of behavior as more useful than models that were primarily focused on the individual.

In developing family oriented, interpersonal approaches to schizophrenia, researchers began to incorporate ideas developed in fields outside of mental health. Specifically, general systems theory (von Bertalanffy, 1968), developed in the physical sciences, emphasized the systemic properties of the family group. General systems theory focuses on the function and relationship of objects within a circular (interdependent, rather than linear, cause and effect) relationship. Likewise family researchers drew on theoretical premises, including information and communications theories, developed in the field of cybernetics. (There is some debate as to whether family therapists developed a systems approach first and then became aware of general systems theory, or whether both were developed concurrently [Bowen, 1966]). By 1956, Bateson and others (Bateson, Jackson, Haley, & Weakland, 1956) had begun to develop a communication theory of schizophrenia based on conjoint therapy with schizophrenic patients and their families. Since that time, the focus of additional research has been greatly broadened to include a wide range of dysfunctional behaviors, and has led to the conclusion that such behaviors are functional when observed within the context of a particular family system.

Various theoretical models have been employed by researchers and therapists in an attempt both to explain family behavior and to provide a framework for family intervention. These models have included role theory, information theory, games theory, psychoanalytic theory, and learning theory. Currently there is no consensus about using any one theory as a base for the study of family interaction, although systems theory remains the most influential (Olson, 1970; Sager & Kaplan, 1972). This model represents the movement away from a linear-based conception of cause and effect toward a circular feedback model in which the behaviors of family members are interdependent.

In an extensive review of the family therapy field, Olson (1970) concluded that family therapy has made three significant contributions to the understanding of human behavior. First, notions developed in family therapy have contributed "to the understanding and treatment of schizophrenia and other emotional disorders." Secondly, by its use of a systems approach "to understanding the family, it has challenged many assumptions regarding the causal determinants of individual psychopathology." Finally, it has "developed innovative ways to treat such problems" (p. 504).

In summary, the movement toward treating the family rather than the individual represents an alternative perspective of psychopathology, in which such behavior is viewed as functional within the context of a family system.

THEORETICAL FRAMEWORK

Three major models of family therapy are in wide use today: psychoanalytic, behavioral, and systems. These focus respectively on the way the individual experiences the interpersonal dynamics of his family, on the manner in which problems are presented within the family, and on the transactions among its members. Although they differ in focus as well as in methods of intervention and criteria of effectiveness, all three models share the view that individual behavior is developed and maintained within a social context. Further, the three models assume that the social context having the most influence on an individual's behavior is his nuclear family. Ackerman (1954) argues the importance of a family orientation in therapy by pointing out that "although psychiatrists have traditionally concerned themselves with the problems of the individual, they have long recognized that there is usually a second person in the family involved in the patient's pathology" (p. 361).

Beels and Ferber (1969) point out four major differences between family therapy and individual therapy. First, therapeutic intervention aims at changing the family system of interaction rather than directly altering the behavior of the individual, while individual change is viewed as a by-product of changes in family patterns. Indeed, as Beels and Ferber point out, the focus in treatment on the system of interaction rather than on the behavior of the individual patient is the most fundamental difference between the two modes of therapy.

A second difference between family and individual therapy is that the former is often of shorter duration than traditional individual therapy. While there exist wide variations in treatment length within each of these two fields, usually depending on the theoretical model employed, it is likely that if we combined all models of family therapy and all those of individual therapy, family therapy generally would be of shorter duration.

The third major difference is the primary importance attributed by family therapists to nonverbal interaction, as opposed to the basically verbal focus of individual therapy. In general it seems that concern with nonverbal behavior has been maximized by family therapists partly because of theoretical notions about the impact of nonverbal communication on the behavior of family members, and partly because seeing the entire family presents the therapist with a greater opportunity to focus on nonverbal interaction. We should note that some models of individual therapy, such as Gestalt, do focus on nonverbal behaviors, but this is not the norm.

The final point of difference mentioned by Beels and Ferber is the nonconfidentiality of family therapy. This means that while individual therapy sessions involve only two people (therapist and client), family therapy includes other members.

It is the authors' view that a more significant difference distinguishes family, individual, and group therapy. This is the presence of additional persons with whom the identified client has a special ongoing relationship with a shared history. The element of an ongoing relationship among the client group is, in our view, a more specific and unique characteristic of family therapy. It is this element of the family therapy that provides the therapist the opportunity for direct observation and intervention in intrafamilial dynamics.

SUMMARY

The most basic assumption of family therapy is that interpersonal transactions are important determinants of individual behavior, and that the family has the greatest impact on these transactions. Pathological behavior is assumed to be both caused and maintained by family patterns of interaction. It further is assumed by family therapists that changes in these detrimental family patterns will result in the amelioration of pathological symptomatology.

THE THREE MODELS OF FAMILY THERAPY

The three major models of family therapy—psychoanalytic, behavioral, and systems—share the assumption that interpersonal variables affect individual behavior. They differ widely, however, in the extent to which they consider these variables necessary and sufficient for understanding and changing attitudes and/or behavior. Based on theoretical differences about which treatment variables will be stressed and which minimized, the models differ in therapeutic methods and goals. These three models will be examined in detail in later chapters as we examine how each model functions and contributes to family crisis intervention.

TREATMENT GOALS IN FAMILY THERAPY

The basic goal of family therapy is to restructure the modes of interaction among family members so that the family unit functions better. All models aim for changes in family interactions such that the pattern of mutual responding will be more mature (psychoanalytic), more positively reinforcing (behavioral), or more constructive and positively reinforcing (systems). Inherent in the goals of each of the three models is an implicit adherence to a tenet of "healthy" family functioning toward which the intervener should aim. The term healthy is used here expressly because of its vague quality, since the goals of healthy family functioning are not concretely defined by any of the three models. However, the emphasis of these models does vary along a continuum from broad, pervasive change (psychoanalytic) to a more molecular symptom orientation (behavioral), with the systems model coming in at some intermediary point.

TREATMENT METHODS IN FAMILY THERAPY

Treatment methods in family therapy consider the family as the locus of distress, rather than singling out one of its members as the patient/client. Treatment varies from conjoint family sessions in which all family members are seen together at the same time by the same therapist (Titchner, 1967; Wynne, 1971; Turner & Gross, 1976) to individual therapy with the identified patient, in which family members are seen occasionally to encourage their assistance and to urge them not to interfere with the patient's progress (Balint, 1966). Between the two extremes of conjoint family therapy and an individual focus lies a middle ground which encompasses such modes as collaborative family therapy, simultaneous individual therapy with the same therapist, and mixed membership therapy. In collaborative family therapy all family members may be seen together for diagnostic purposes. Then, based on individual need, they are assigned to different therapists who share information about treatment progress and goal planning. In simultaneous individual therapy with the same therapist, the family is never seen as a unit. Instead the therapist works with the members separately, and by viewing the parts of the whole, pieces together a picture of the family from which treatment goals are developed. In mixed membership therapy, the composition of the treatment group fluctuates based on the therapist's evaluation of need. Therapy sessions include individual treatment with one or more members of the family, meeting of various family subgroups on a conjoint basis, and conjoint sessions including all family members (Olson, 1976).

Treatment methods in family therapy, regardless of theoretical orientation, are primarily directed toward changing the current interaction of family members. While specific techniques of intervention differ according to the theoretical perspective of the therapist, a focus on here-and-now interaction is a common theme. Techniques of family therapy specific to adherents of particular theoretical approaches will be dealt with in later chapters.

CONSUMERS

Initially family therapy focused on the family with a schizophrenic member. The field has broadened considerably over the last two decades to encompass families in which members exhibit a wide variety of emotional disorders. Currently both the psychoanalytic and behavioral models focus primarily on families in which one member is exhibiting neurotic behavior, although both types do treat families with a psychotic member as well. The systems model has shifted its original focus on families with a psychotic member to include treatment of less dramatic behavioral problems. At this point in time, family therapists work with the entire range of emotional disorders, and there are no clear-cut boundaries concerning which problems are or are not amenable to family intervention.

Researchers in the family therapy area do not generally collect socioeconomic data related to their clients. However, a nationwide study of families seen at Family Service Agencies (Beck & Jones, 1973) indicated an increase over the last decade in the provision of family therapy services by these agencies to families from the lower socioeconomic group. While Beck and Jones (1973) report that a proportionately larger number of lower-class families are currently being seen, the usual social class of families receiving services from these agencies remains in the lower-middle- to middle-class range. Aside from this study, little can be concretely gathered from the literature with respect to the socioeconomic characteristics of those seen in family therapy. However, it is reasonable to conclude that if families are primarily seen by professionals in private practice (see the section on setting of intervention later in this chapter), then such families are likely to be in at least the middle-income level. Further, Minuchin and his colleagues (1967) report specifically on the applicability of family therapy techniques to lower-class families, suggesting that lower class families are more the exception than the rule in family therapy.

SETTING

In examining the field of family therapy, the Group for the Advancement of Psychiatry (1970) found that 90 percent of those family therapists who responded to their survey generally saw the family in their private offices.

However, more than 70 percent of these therapists visited the family at home on occasion. Interestingly, only 6 percent reported that they regularly did so, which suggests that the home is an infrequent family therapy setting.

Treatment settings other than the therapist's office vary widely, and include the clinic or agency (Beck & Jones, 1973), having family members join the patient at the hospital for designated sessions (Boszormenyi-Nagy & Framo, 1965), and having family members live at the hospital along with the designated patient for observation and treatment (Bowen, 1961; Nakhla, Folkart, & Webster, 1969). Sometimes, the family home is used as the primary treatment setting (Friedman, 1962; Levine, 1964; Speck, 1964).

POPULATION OF HELP GIVERS

Mental health professionals. A survey of family therapists conducted by the Group for the Advancement of Psychiatry (1970) indicated that of the 312 respondents, 40 percent were social workers and another 40 percent were psychiatrists and psychologists. As was mentioned earlier, the psychoanalytic model primarily employs psychiatrists extensively trained in psychoanalytic theory and procedures as help givers. Professional help givers in the behavioral model are primarily psychologists trained in learning theories and behavioral principles. The systems model makes use of the broadest range of mental health professionals, with no one discipline primarily responsible for service provision.

Paraprofessionals. Olson (1970) reports that there has been an increasing interest in the use of paraprofessionals as family therapists and in developing training programs for them. The systems model makes the most extensive use of paraprofessionals (Jackson, 1967; Haley, 1973), arguing that the para-professional's lack of exposure to traditional mental health training, with its individual orientation, is advantageous in adopting the transactional approach. No research has been done, however, comparing the effectiveness of paraprofes-sional and professional family therapists, and little can be said at this time about the efficacy of the use of paraprofessional interveners.

Adherents of the behavioral model do not report the use of paraprofession-als as direct interveners. However, their view that behavioral principles can easily be taught suggests that they would consider it appropriate to train paraprofessionals in behavioral family therapy. Conversely, the psychoanalytic model would not be amenable to the use of paraprofessionals because they believe that extensive training in psychoanalytic theory and procedure is required for effective intervention.

Natural help givers. Advocates of the behavioral approach also view themselves as trainers of family members, who in turn act as change agents. Natural help givers in the behavioral model have been trained primarily to act in this role only within their own family situation. However, several researchers (Ora & Wagner, 1970; Lindsley, 1966; Patterson, Cobb, & Ray, 1970) have pointed out that natural help givers can effectively teach other nonprofessionals to use these skills. The psychoanalytic model, which assumes that extensive training is required for effective family intervention would reject the use of natural help givers. The system model would permit the use of natural help givers but would require that they be given more extensive training than behavioral therapists deem necessary.

ROLE OF THE THERAPIST

The role of the therapist in family treatment is largely dependent on his theoretical perspective. Roles of therapeutic change agents in family therapy range from doctor/expert (psychoanalytic), to educator (behavioral), to engineer (systems). While the role of the therapist varies according to theoretical notions of treatment methodology, all share in common a significantly higher activity rate than is usually found in the individual therapies.

Roots of Family Crisis Intervention: Crisis Intervention

HISTORICAL DEVELOPMENT

Crisis intervention is both a theoretical framework and a method of preventive intervention. States of crisis are viewed as predictable, transitory and impactful. Successful crisis resolution may lead to reintegration of the personality at a higher level, while failure to resolve the crisis state may lead to regression and psychiatric symptomatology. Intervention is aimed at reducing crisis incidence and increasing successful crisis resolution.

The development of models of crisis process and intervention can best be understood as an outgrowth of specific historical factors in the last thirty years. The groundwork for crisis intervention was laid in the 1940s against the background of a world at war. At that time psychiatry was wedded in large part to psychoanalytic theory and its offshoots. In practice its goal was personality change through insight over an extended period of treatment.

The war era was characterized by the massive induction of young, healthy men into a situation containing a high risk of mutilation and/or death. For the military, a primary concern was to maintain the ability of such men to remain at the front line or to return to it as quickly as possible. Thus the rapid relief of battle-related psychiatric problems became a high priority. In response to the needs of the military, mental health practitioners developed an alternative model of intervention which had goals more limited than effecting major personality change, and which could be achieved in an abbreviated time span. Treatment facilities were located as far forward in combat zones as possible. The focus of intervention was on the immediate situational crisis and on an individual's feelings about what had happened to him. In addition, psychiatric intervention aimed at promoting group support, social manipulation, adequate rest, and rapid return to combat duties to maintain the individual's confidence in his ability to function (Glass, 1953). Studies indicated that providing supportive psychotherapeutic techniques as quickly and as near the front lines as possible, reduced regression and the development of more entrenched patterns of psychiatric disturbance (Glass, 1954; Hausman & Rioch, 1967; Menninger, 1948). These studies of individuals in distress laid the groundwork for both intervention at the secondary prevention level and for the individual model of crisis intervention.

The impact of the war at home also encouraged the development of the crisis intervention field. Massive induction of men into a high-death-risk situation heightened the general concern of the populace with death and related phenomena, and left few people in the United States untouched by the actual loss of a family member or close friend. The enormous increase in feelings of grief in response to war casualties in the forties supported the investigation of bereavement phenomena.

In fact, a study of bereavement reactions conducted during the war years (Lindemann, 1944) turned out to be of particular importance in the development of the crisis intervention field. In this study, Lindemann examined bereavement reactions among the survivors of those killed in the Coconut Grove Night Club fire in Boston. His classic paper on the symptomatology and management of acute grief reactions is based on observations of 101 individuals who lost a family member. Lindemann made four major points regarding the management of acute grief:

1. Acute grief is a definite syndrome with psychological and somatic symptomatology.
2. This syndrome may appear immediately after a crisis, it may be delayed, or it may be exaggerated or apparently absent.
3. In place of the typical syndrome, pathological patterns may occur, each representing one special aspect of the grief syndrome.
4. By use of appropriate techniques these pathological patterns can be successfully transformed into a normal grief reaction and resolution.

Lindemann's study is a classic not so much because he detailed the process of normal grieving, or even because of his descriptions of distorted and extended grief reactions, but because in so doing he laid a theoretical framework which can be used to examine crisis reactions in general. Referred to by Jacobson and his colleagues (1968) as the generic approach, this framework emphasizes the importance of defining characteristic behavior patterns which appear to develop in response to particular life crises. Treatment programs based on an understanding of these patterns tend to minimize the variation in individual personality and psychodynamics, and maximize the completion of tasks specific to the crisis stimulus.

Beginning in the 1950s, two major developments in mental health acted to further encourage the growth of the crisis intervention field. The first was in the area of community psychiatry, one of whose goals was to develop a range of intervention techniques that would provide an equitable distribution of mental health services to all social classes. Functionally this meant extending services to the lower classes, which had remained almost untouched by mental health practices up to that time (Hollingshead & Redlick, 1958). The provision of traditional therapy on such a massive scale would have required an unfeasible increase in the training of professionals and in the cost of providing service. Instead, advocates of community psychiatry encouraged consideration of alternatives to the traditional therapeutic situation, particularly the development of strategies for short-term intervention and the use of paraprofessionals on a major scale (Lieb, Lipsitch, & Slaby, 1973).

The second development to encourage crisis intervention was aimed at maintaining clients in their natural setting, or more specifically, outside a hospital setting. Much of this movement is based on studies which indicated the detrimental effects of long-term hospitalization (Stanton & Schwartz, 1954; Goffman, 1961; Wing, 1967). Additional motivation for the development of outpatient treatment alternatives resulted from the desire to decrease both the cost of inpatient care and the time commitment of mental health professionals. The movement toward treating clients in their natural setting led to a number of experimental alternatives to long-term hospitalization in the 1960s (Weisman, Feirstein, & Thomas, 1969; Langsley et al, 1968a).

While differences exist in the crisis intervention field at both conceptual and methodological levels, the rising demand for mental health services has led to a number of fairly unified and widely accepted principles of crisis intervention that distinguish it from traditional psychotherapeutic approaches (Aguilera, Messick, & Farrell, 1970; Jacobson, Strickler, & Morley, 1968; Lieb, Lipsitch, & Slaby, 1973; Thomas & Weisman, 1970). These principles include:

1. Active involvement of significant others in an individual client's life,
2. time-limited treatment contracts,
3. the liberal use of psychotropic agents for symptom relief,
4. focus on the current life situation,
5. the use of a team approach by interveners and the employment of multiple-therapy modalities as needed, and
6. a minimal goal of psychological resolution of the immediate crisis and restoration of the individual to at least the level of functioning that existed prior to the crisis period.

THEORETICAL FRAMEWORK FOR CRISIS INTERVENTION

Three major models of crisis intervention have been developed: individual, generic, and systems. These focus respectively on the individual's experience of the crisis, on the crisis stimulus itself, and on the interface between the individual in crisis and his social support system. While these models differ in focus, as well as in methods of intervention and their use of paraprofessionals, their differences are primarily of emphasis. All are grounded in a unified theory of crisis, which relies heavily on the early theoritical formulations of Erich Lindemann (1944) and subsequent elaborations by Gerald Caplan (1961, 1964, 1970).

As described earlier in the chapter, Caplan (1964) defines crisis as the confrontation of an individual by a problematic situation in which his typical problem-solving skills and usual supports are not sufficient for its resolution. To successfully resolve the crisis situation, usual patters of behavior must be transcended. Thus, crisis resolution may potentially lead to reorganizing of the personality at a higher level of functioning. Conversely, failure to resolve the crisis leads to increasing levels of anxiety and potentially to personality disorganization. This approach emphasizes the essential nature of the crisis as a vital point in one's life, one which could lead either to enhanced functioning or to increased vulnerability to mental disorder (Rapoport, 1962). This view of crisis differs from earlier theories in which stress was viewed only as a possible precipitator of mental disorder, and never as a potential growth factor.

Further, as described earlier, one of Caplan's (1964) main points is that, regardless of what the crisis stimulus is, all crises are dealt with in a predictable and patterned way. This process of crisis resolution proceeds through four typical phases, which were described earlier in the chapter.

It may be helpful to the reader to refer back to the six assumptions of crisis theory (Kalis, 1970). These can be summarized as: (1) the need of the human being to maintain homeostatis; (2) the need to try to restore homeostasis if it is disrupted; the fact that (3) certain kinds of disruption can by their characteristics be defined as crisis states; (4) individuals are more open to external influence during crisis; (5) the period of disruption is self-limited and will result in a new equilibrium or adaptation which may be better or worse than that which preceded the crisis; and finally, (6) equilibrium can be restored by changing the environment (stimulus), or by changing how one copes with it, or both.

It is important to note that no assumption is made regarding the cause of equilibrium disruption. In fact, no general agreement exists in the field of crisis intervention as to the primary cause(s) of crisis induction. This is the point at which the three models may be most clearly differentiated, with the individual model giving primacy to the precrisis personality, the generic model to the crisis stimulus, and the systems model to the interaction between the individual and his support systems at the time he perceives the stimulus.

MODELS OF CRISIS INTERVENTION

The three major models of crisis intervention (individual, generic, and systems) differ primarily in their assumptions about the major causes of crisis onset. They also differ to some extent in their description of intervention procedures. These three models parallel the psychoanalytic, behavioral, and systems approaches mentioned in relation to family therapy. In fact, the individual approach, in terms of how it conceptualizes human functioning, is primarily based on psychoanalytic theory. The generic approach focuses specifically on the problem or set of problems both provoking and maintaining the crisis, and therefore essentially derives from a behavioral approach to human functioning. Likewise, the systems approach focuses on the interactive behavior between the individual in crisis and the members of his environment, and is therefore a derivative of a systems theory of human functioning.

These three approaches will be discussed in more detail in Chapters 6, 7 and 8. It should be noted, however, that while theoretical differences exist in the crisis intervention approach, descriptions of actual crisis intervention programs frequently either leave the reader in some doubt as to which of the models is in use, or suggest that the models are being intermixed. Similarly, a review of evaluative research in the crisis intervention field reveals that such studies rarely discriminate between models.

TREATMENT GOALS IN CRISIS INTERVENTION

The minimal goal of crisis intervention is the restoration of the client to his precrisis level of functioning. This is sometimes called regaining equilibrium or returning to a homeostatic state. A more ambitious goal, again shared by all three approaches, is to have the client attain a level of functioning higher than that preceding the onset of the crisis situation.

TREATMENT METHODS IN CRISIS INTERVENTION

The various methods of crisis intervention fall within the framework of brief intervention strategies and are representative of attempts to provide mental health services to a larger population at a decreased cost in terms of personnel and facilities.

Numerous techniques are used in crisis intervention, and they vary with the orientation of the intervention and the role of the intervener. An admittedly partial list of specific techniques commonly used in crisis intervention is described below.

Time-limited contracts. Crisis intervention approaches are consistent in the use of time-limited contracts. Though such contracts vary somewhat in length (Weisman, Feirstein, & Thomas, 1969), the usual contract is probably for three to four weeks. The maximum length of crisis intervention contact tends to be about two to three months. A number of factors are relevant here. First, Caplan (1964) defines the crisis resolution process as one which is in itself time limited (four to six weeks). Equilibrium is restored in that period, either in a positive or negative direction. The fact that equilibrium is restored in four to six weeks would appear to limit the length of crisis contact to the same time period. This is consistent with reports of crisis centers, primarily those developed within the generic model, that clients consistently terminate contact after approximately four to six weeks. (Jacobson et al., 1965).

It is also worthy of note that this same time period is reported for premature termination (70 percent before the sixth session) in the traditional therapies (Lorr, Katz & Rubenstein, 1958; Brandt, 1956); furthermore, the majority of patients leaving psychotherapy prematurely come from the lowest socioeconomic class (Winder & Hersko, 1955; Frank, Gleidman, Imber, Stone, & Nash, 1959; Hollingshead & Redlich, 1958; Rubenstein & Lorr, 1956; Stern, Moore, & Gross, 1975). Since lower-class clients are orientated toward action, it is possible that they enter therapy for the purpose of seeking help with an immediate problem. Crisis intervention, then, with its relatively narrow focus on resolving the presenting problem, may provide a therapeutic approach more consistent with lower-class client expectations than does traditional therapy. Premature termination by lower-class clients may likewise reflect resolution of the crisis whose onset precipitated treatment.

Multiple-impace treatment. The concept of multiple-impact treatment (Weisman, Feirstein, & Thomas, 1969) involves the use of a team of interveners who work intensively with an individual, family, or social network over a brief period.

Use of medication. Liberal use of medication is a characteristic of all three models of crisis intervention (Koegler, 1966).

Provision of information and initiation of contact with appropriate referral agencies. Crisis workers generally provide basic information and sometimes assume the traditional social-worker/case-worker role in assisting the client to make contact with appropriate resources.

CONSUMERS

Three population bases are described in the literature as primary foci for crisis intervention: the lower socioeconomic segment of the population, populations at risk, and the general population of a geographical area. These are described below:

The lower socioeconomic segment of the population. As described earlier, crisis intervention developed in an atmosphere that encouraged the extension of mental health services to the lower socioeconomic segments of the population (Lieb, Lipsitch, & Slaby, 1973). Compared to the typical mental health clientele, this population is characterized by a lack of financial resources, a language style differing from standard English (Cohen, 1974; Stewart, 1964, 1968), and an orientation toward action rather than reflection (Bernstein, 1961). Requests for help are usually for an immediate problem, and expectations of long-term treatment are notably lacking. As a result of these differences in expectations, crisis intervention services have been geared to provide readily accessible emergency services, such as walk-in clinics, telephone crisis lines, and mobile response units for poor clients (Barten, 1971).

Populations at risk. A key concept, particularly of the generic model of crisis intervention, is the provision of crisis services to those at risk of being immobilized by crisis situations (Bloom, 1971). Examples of such populations include the mothers of premature infants (Kaplan & Mason, 1960), and surgical patients (Janis, 1958). In addition, populations at risk frequently lack family resources and are exposed to such frequent crises as housing relocation (Fried, 1963) and loss of employment (Koegler & Cannon, 1966; Normand, Fensterheim, & Schrenzel, 1967). Since populations with the greatest risk of crisis induction are frequently those with the least resources, they greatly overlap with the lower socioeconomic population already described.

General population of a geographical area. The provision of primary preventive intervention services for whole populations of a given area is another facet of crisis intervention, primarily within the generic model. This mode of crisis intervention takes the form of consultation and educational efforts aimed at reducing crisis incidence and/or impact (Bloom, 1971; Caplan, 1961). The populations selected for primary preventive intervention are those which face the greatest threat of a crisis such as having to move because of urban renewal, being hurt by a crime, and psychiatric disturbance. Again, such populations in large part overlap with the lower socioeconomic groups which, because they lack resources, are most crisis prone. In summary, the primary population served by crisis intervention programs appears to be the lower socioeconomic segment of the population.

SETTING OF INTERVENTION

Crisis intervention occurs in numerous settings: on the telephone (Litman, 1966), in walk-in clinics (Jacobson et al., 1965; Clark, 1965), in the natural setting through mobile response units and home visits (Gwaltney, 1974; McGee, 1974), in inpatient settings (Weisman, Feirstein, & Thomas, 1969), and in the hospital admitting office (Langsley et al., 1968). Although exceptions exist, one major rule of thumb appears to be that the less professional the crisis staff, the more mobile, in-home, and phone settings are utilized. The most common setting of crisis intervention services reported in the literature continues to be the walk-in clinic with an emergency phone line.

HELP GIVERS

There are four general classes of crisis interveners: mental health professionals, mental health paraprofessionals, volunteers, and natural help givers. There is much support in the crisis intervention literature for the training and use of paraprofessional and volunteer crisis workers. However, controversy continues to exist over the possible advantages (Michener & Walzer, 1970; McGee, 1974) and detrimental effects (McColsky, 1973) of utilizing anyone other than a highly trained professional in giving help. This issue will be explored more fully in the discussion on volunteers.

Mental health professionals. The term mental health professionals refers to psychiatrists, clinical and counseling psychologists with an M.A. or a Ph.D., clinical social workers, and psychiatric nurses. Such professionals are involved in all crisis intervention programs as supervisors or consultants. Major differences exist among programs in their utilization of professionals as direct crisis interveners. Two programs representative of the use of professionals in direct service are the Mobile Emergency Team in Ventura, California (Gwaltney, 1974) and the Crisis Counseling Program of the Escambia County Community Mental Health Center in Pensacola, Florida (McColsky, 1973). In the former, professionals provide direct service on a mobile basis in response to crisis calls from citizens and police. In the latter, professionals provide emergency phone response to citizens.

McColsky (1973) argues strongly for the exclusive use of professionals in crisis intervention, stating that:

> There is no logical justification for an emergency mental health service manned by unskilled workers. Logically, if professional training in one of the mental health disciplines is considered a requisite for management of psychological problems, then adjustmental crises or acute problems demand the utmost—not the least in expertise. Conceptually, the notion of using untrained persons to manage crisis reactions is as illogical and hazardous as attempting to stem a massive hemorrhage with a band-aid. (p. 53).

This argument is contrary to the findings of a number of studies (Wolff, 1969; Truax & Lister, 1970; Magoon & Golann, 1966) which indicate that lay therapists achieve therapeutic results at least equal to, and in some cases better than, those of professionals.

McColsky (1973) also argues that crisis intervention services provided by nonprofessionals, especially those concerned with suicide prevention, are redundant since their clientele has previously contacted, or is currently receiving some form of, professional help. At best this argument applies equally well to crisis intervention services provided by professional workers and stands more appropriately as a weak case against crisis intervention services per se. More pointedly, McColsky's findings may reflect the ineffectiveness of mental health services in general.

Mental health paraprofessionals. Paraprofessionals in mental health services include both individuals with subprofessional training (A.A. and B.A. degrees; Blau [1969] also includes M.A. degrees) in mental health fields, and individuals from the lower socioeconomic class who lack any formal training in mental health. Crisis workers from both groups are generally selected through screening procedures that focus on personal competence, potential abilities as a help giver, and life experience (Haley, 1973). They receive on-the-job training from professional staff personnel. Blau supports the use of subprofessionals to meet manpower needs, but cautions that there is a need for effective quality control. In this regard he suggests that it is the responsibility of mental health professionals both to set standards for the quality of care provided by subprofessionals and to monitor and evaluate their functioning.

Berman and Haug (1973), and Grosser (1966) focus on the trend in numerous crisis intervention programs to hire indigenous residents of lower socioeconomic communities. Indigenous crisis workers are often viewed as mediators of cultural differences between middle-class professionals and lower-class clients. Indigenous workers are seen as "bridges" "because they are more familiar with the life-styles and problems encountered in the community" (Berman & Haug, 1973, p. 49). No evidence, however, is presented to support the notion that indigenous workers as a group are more effective help givers for lower-class clients than other classes of service providers.

Volunteers. McGee (1974) believes that suicide prevention and crisis intervention systems have been able to grow and develop across the country only because nonprofessional volunteers are used and accepted. Indeed, Dublin (1969) argues that the "lay volunteer was the single most important discovery in the fifty year history of the [suicide prevention] movement. Nothing else of any significance happened until he came into the picture". Michener and Walzer (1970) claim that volunteers not only accelerate the treatment process, but also are able to interpret mental health objectives and mobilize community support because they have community ties and a lay viewpoint. In counterpoint, McColsky (1973) has argued that nonprofessionals are ineffective, if not detrimental, agents of change. Unfortunately, minimal data is available to support either assertion.

In a recent article, Durlak (1973a, 1973b) reports his conclusions about the effectiveness of nonprofessional interveners based on an earlier review (1971) of the research literature. Noting that much has been written both in favor of and in opposition to the use of nonprofessionals, he concluded that most of these articles are polemic and not tied to evaluative outcome studies. In reviewing over 300 references relevant to the selection, training, and therapeutic functioning of nonprofessonal mental health personnel, Durlak (1971) found that studies specifically examining individual client changes in response to therapy by nonprofessionals showed a very small percentage of overall negative clinical changes (3 out of 151 clients in a composite analysis of three studies). Furthermore, in half the studies comparing the therapeutic effectiveness of nonprofessional and professional interveners, nonprofessionals achieved significantly better therapeutic results; in other studies, results of the two groups were comparable. "In no study have lay persons been found to be significantly inferior to professional workers" stated Durlak (1973b, p. 4). Considering Durlak's findings, it seems reasonable to presume that nonprofessional interveners, while not a panacea, are a viable source of additional manpower in the mental health field.

Throughout the literature on volunteers, serious concern is shown about their selection, training, and supervision. The literature is consistent in describing extensive selection procedures designed to eliminate applicants not suitable for crisis intervention. For example, McGee (1974) describes the procedures an applicant must follow at the Crisis Intervention Center in Gainesville, Florida: fill out an application form, have an initial interview followed by psychological testing (California Personality Inventory, The Philosophy of Human Nature Scale, and the Myers-Briggs Type Indicator), and enroll in a training program. This is a self-screening procedure in which 48

percent of the original pool of volunteers withdrew themselves from consideration. Only after the volunteer actually begins to intervene does staff screening
of volunteer effectiveness occur. What is lacking both in the description of this
program and in the literature on selection in general is a statement clearly
defining volunteer selection criteria other than perseverance and self-selection.

Training of volunteers appears to take place, with some regularity, both
prior to assignment to direct service work and on an in-service basis. Trainers
are either experienced volunteers or professionals. Kinds of training vary from
the extreme of an essentially experiential model (Berman, 1973) to that of an
essentially didactic model (Berman & McCarthy, 1971), with many variations
in between (McGee, 1974). The literature suggests, however, that a greater
emphasis is placed on experiential rather than didactic training.

Supervision of volunteers varies from the monitoring of calls (Burhenne,
1974), to case conferences (Michener & Walzer, 1970), to the pairing of
experienced crisis workers with new volunteers (McGee, 1974). Again, though
supervision is discussed with consistency, the literature lacks detailed criteria of
adequate volunteer performance.

Natural help givers. The fourth group of crisis interveners is the natural
help givers (Levy, 1973). Natural help givers are those who, either because of
their work or because of their relationship to the individual in crisis, are
naturally present in that person's environment and are viewed as sources of help
by the individual. These natural help givers have no attachment to the mental
health system and "do not generally conceive of their role as primarily related
to a mental health function" (Levy, 1973, p. 19). Examples of natural help
givers include members of the extended family, the police (Newman, 1968;
Bard & Berkowitz, 1967, 1969), teachers and parents (Ulrich, Stachnik, &
Mabry, 1970), and ministers, physicians, and lawyers (Levy, 1973). Mental
health professionals operating within the generic model of crisis intervention
have tended to identify such resources and to develop liaisons and consultative
relationships with them.

Implied in this consulting role is the concept that community organization
is an integral part of mental health work. Levy and Rowitz (1971) found that
well-organized, tightly-knit communities in which individuals feel that they
have some control over their lives tend to produce fewer psychiatric casualties.
The literature suggests that efforts to increase the effectiveness of the
community's natural help givers is part of this community organization effort,
and that it will lead to both an increase in successful crisis resolution and a
decrease in the number of psychiatric casualties. No data are presented,
however, to support this claim.

Role of the intervener. Crisis interveners appear to play two kinds of
roles: the traditional expert-doctor, and the advocate-mediator. The traditional
expert-doctor role emphasizes the intervener as both diagnostician and healer
(Normand, Fensterheim, & Schrenzel, 1967). Interveners who work within
this role generally view crisis from a medical model viewpoint, describing the

individual in crisis as a patient in need of psychiatric treatment. Defining the "real" or "underlying" problem and determining appropriate treatment goals reflect traditional therapeutic processes. Though the focus in crisis intervention is narrowed and the intervention is of shorter duration, there are major parallels between the expert-doctor role in crisis intervention and the role of the therapist in traditional individual therapy. The expert-doctor is most closely associated with the individual model.

In the advocate-mediator role, the crisis worker views crisis from an educational and interactional framework. The individual in crisis is not viewed as sick or incapable, but is assumed to be "stuck" in formerly successful behavior patterns which are no longer sufficient to meet the crisis situation. Interveners who work within the advocate-mediator role may act as agents of the individual in crisis in dealing directly with environmental and community resources and making referrals for job placement and housing. Likewise the cirsis worker actively takes the role of mediator between the individual and the larger social network of which he is a part. Frequently this social network is the family (Kaplan, 1968; Weakland, Fisch, Watzlawick, & Bodin, 1974), but it may also encompass work groups and other affiliations. Interveners in both the generic and systems models employ the advocate-mediator role.

Comparison of Family Therapy and Crisis Intervention Frameworks

As has been pointed out, family crisis intervention is based on a synthesis of strategies developed in family therapy and crisis intervention. For this reason we will now focus our discussion on a comparison of these two "parent" approaches in order to examine the roots of family crisis intervention.

DIFFERENCES

The fields of family therapy and crisis intervention differ in terms of goals, assumptions about treatment, feelings about the role of symptomatology, and the populations receiving treatment..

Goals. The minimal goal of crisis intervention is the prevention of deterioration and the return of the client(s) to precrisis levels of functioning. A broader goal is to provide the client(s) with an increased ability to deal effectively with future crisis situations.

At first glance, the most frequently stated goal of family therapy, to alleviate symptoms, appears to parallel that of crisis intervention: to return the client to a precrisis level of functioning. However, even though symptom alleviation is frequently used as a convenient success criterion, almost without exception family therapists view symptom alleviation within the broader context of a positive change in family interaction patterns. For family therapists, symptom alleviation functions essentially as an indirect measure of their success in manipulating a broader and more basic aspect of the transactional style in the family. These differences in the statement of outcome goals are more a matter of shading than of stark dissimilarity, and reflect differential assumptions regarding what constitutes the essence of the problems and how treatment should proceed.

Assumptions about treatment. Crisis interveners focus treatment on returning the client to a precrisis functioning level based on the following assumptions. First, the precrisis functioning of the client(s) is presumed to have been adequate, and therefore does not constitute a treatment concern. Second, it is the client's response to the introduction of a novel and problematic situation that has provoked his distress or symptom; therefore treatment should specifically focus on resolution of the crisis. Third, the longer the crisis remains unresolved, the more symptomatology and regressions will occur; therefore intervention should occur as quickly as possible following crisis onset, and proceed as intensively as possible to provide rapid closure. Based on these assumptions, crisis intervention procedures are designed to maximize the speed and intensity of a narrowly focused treatment approach.

On the other hand, family therapists focus on changing basic family interaction patterns based on a different set of assumptions. First, the presenting problem (crisis, pathological symptomatology) is itself presumed to be an indicator of an entrenched pathological family equilibrium; therefore treatment should stress the transactional patterns of the family while giving less importance to the presenting problem. Moreover, this assumption minimizes the need to provide service while the problem is "hot." Also, it is assumed that producing basic changes in family patterns will yield symptom alleviation as a by-product. This again reinforces a treatment plan which focuses more on family patterns than on either the presenting problem or the distress of an individual family member. Based on these assumptions, family therapy procedures are designed to emphasize the observation and manipulation of family interaction. The need for rapid service provision and an intensified treatment schedule are deemphasized in the family therapy approach. Once again, these differences are more a matter of degree than of kind and will be emphasized or deemphasized depending on the particular model of family therapy or crisis intervention under consideration.

Population. Crisis intervention has primarily provided service to two overlapping populations. The first consists of clients in acute emotional distress from various economic backgrounds. Members of the second group are from a lower socioeconomic stratum, and use the crisis facility much as they do the hospital emergency room, in lieu of other mental health services. In contrast, family therapy has generally provided services to members of the middle socioeconomic class on a prearranged appointment basis. This model has tended to view treatment from a tertiary prevention framework, rather than the secondary prevention framework utilized in crisis intervention. Some convergence between the two fields is evident in this area. Specifically, a number of family therapy programs have begun to focus both on earlier treatment to prevent symptom stabilization and on applying family therapy techniques to clients from the lower socioeconomic class (Minuchin et al., 1967)

   Role of symptomatology. In family therapy, symptomatology is given two functional roles in the family. First, symptoms serve to maintain an existing family equilibrium, the notion being that the symptom bearer begins displaying pathological behaviors in an effort to "save" the family from additional stress and crisis. Secondly, symptoms essentially are a vehicle of communication within the family and are chosen for their message value within that group. The major point of difference between the two frameworks lies in the fact that family therapy emphasizes the functional value of symptomatology, while crisis theory does not treat conceptualized symptoms in this manner. At issue here is not a divergence of opinion between the two frameworks, but an area in which one framework conceptualizes a process not addressed by the other.

SUMMARY

   Four major differences between family therapy and crisis intervention have been discussed. First, family therapy has a broad goal—to change basic family functioning patterns—while crisis intervention aims at resolving the immediate problem and returning the client(s) to his precrisis level of functioning. Secondly, based on differing assumptions about the treatment process, family therapy emphasizes manipulation of family transactions by the therapist and minimizes the need for rapid and intense treatment of symptomatology. In contrast, crisis intervention stresses rapid and intense treatment in a narrowly focused approach. Third, the two approaches attract different client populations. Middle class clients are more frequently involved in family therapy, and those from the lower socioeconomic class, in crisis intervention. Finally, family therapists emphasize the adaptive, communicational aspects of symptomatology, while crisis interveners do not address this issue.

SIMILARITIES

   The fields of family therapy and crisis intervention share a number of perspectives. Both stress the social/environmental context, partially share a population base, share an intervention process, emphasize behavioral change, and are moving toward a more prevention-oriented model of therapy.

   Emphasis on the social/environmental context. Both crisis intervention and family therapy emphasize the importance of the interpersonal aspects of individual functioning in understanding individual distress and symptomatology. Further, both frameworks emphasize the need to enlist significant others in the treatment process, and both minimize intrapsychic variables.

   Overlap in population. Crisis intervention and family therapy sometimes serve the same population, families in crisis. Since the goal of this synthesis, family crisis intervention, also deals with this population, it will be examined in some detail. As shown in Figure 1-2, families experiencing a crisis may be treated by interveners from a crisis, family crisis, or family therapy framework. Based on their respective orientations each will assess the problem somewhat differently, emphasizing and deemphasizing certain variables. For example, a family in crisis may be seen by a crisis intervener who would emphasize the crisis situation and minimize concern over precrisis dysfunction. Furthermore, the crisis intervener would be likely to assess that the crisis belongs to one family member (client). The family might be included in treatment for its supportive function, but would not be regarded either as the primary locus of the problem or as the primary unit of treatment.

If the same family were to be seen by an intervener from a family crisis perspective, emphasis would likewise be placed on the immediate crisis situation. In contrast to the crisis intervention approach, however, the family crisis intervener would be more likely to view the crisis as belonging to the family unit rather than to an individual member, and family crisis treatment would follow.

As a third possibility, a family in crisis might be seen by a family therapist. An adherent of this approach would minimize the crisis situation, viewing it as a sign of longer-standing dysfunction within the family unit. While differing from the two previous approaches in this respect, family therapy, like family crisis intervention, would view the problem as belonging to the family unit and would proceed with family treatment. Although the three approaches vary in their assessment of the crucial elements presented by a family crisis, it is clear that they share in large measure a similar population base.

Shared process. One way to view family therapy and crisis intervention

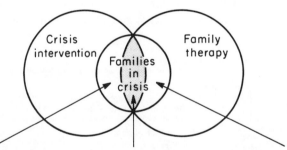

Crisis continues to be seen as belonging to an individual; the family is involved in treatment	The family is seen as in crisis; family treatment is undertaken to resolve that crisis	Family crisis seen as a symptom of long-standing dysfunctional family patterns
Crisis Intervention with a Family	**Family Crisis Intervention**	**Family Therapy with a Family Experiencing a Crisis**

Figure 1-2.
Overlap in Population.

with families is by considering them as interventions at different temporal points in crisis management. Crisis intervention is designed to increase effectiveness by intervening while the crisis is current and the system is in flux or disequilibrium. As shown in Figure 1-3, intervention is aimed at outcome 1; that is, a successful crisis resolution yielding a reequilibrium of the system at a level equal to, or higher than, that prior to the onset of the crisis. Intervention procedures are specifically designed to give help during the period of disruption through the use of 24-hour walk-in clinics, mobile units, and crisis phones. Emphasis is placed on reaching the client(s) at this point, when brief, focused intervention can presumably increase the likelihood of outcome 1 and prevent outcome 2 (unresolved crisis resulting in the stabilization of pathological patterns of behavior). Thus crisis intervention and family crisis intervention constitute secondary prevention approaches to treatment.

While in some cases family therapists may intervene at the same point (A), it is more likely that initial contact will be made (B) when the family has stabilized in a dysfunctional pattern (2). In part this appears to be a result of the methods generally employed by family therapists in making contact with families (i.e, prearranged appointments, waiting lists). These methods delay getting help to the family for a significant period of time.

Both Turner and Gross (1976) and Minuchin and Barcai (1969) describe the process of family therapy in terms which support the notion that a shared process of treatment exists between the crisis intervention and family therapy approaches. They argue that families in treatment typically demonstrate an entrenched pathological interaction pattern. Therefore they suggest that a major aspect of family therapy is the induction of a family crisis (C) by the therapist, followed by intervention aimed at positive crisis resolution (D). The induction of a therapeutic family crisis is viewed as a method of upsetting the

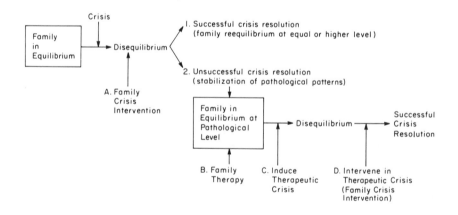

Figure 1-3.
Points of Intervention in Family Crisis.

entrenched pathological equilibrium in order to provide an atmosphere in which change is possible.

By this reasoning the process involved in family therapy parallels the process of crisis induction and crisis intervention. There is a difference, however. In the crisis model, crisis induction is a natural, uncontrolled phenomenon; while in family therapy the crisis is consciously and purposefully imposed by the therapist. Further, the family therapist's intervention in the induced therapeutic family crisis (D) appears to parallel that of the family crisis intervener in the original family crisis (A) (Turner & Gross, 1976).

Emphasis on behavioral change. In general it can be said that in evaluating treatment outcome, both family therapy and crisis intervention emphasize behavioral rather than attitudinal change. It is evident that the theoretical models within each field vary in the degree to which attitudinal change is advocated, with the psychoanalytically based models (psychoanalytic family therapy and individual crisis intervention) at the upper extreme. Yet in general both intervention frameworks would fall more toward the behavioral end of the spectrum than toward the attitudinal one.

Prevention orientation. An orientation toward preventive intervention is particularly evident in the crisis field. Here intervention is primarily defined in terms of preserving mental health and preventing dysfunction; in other words, as secondary prevention. In addition, crisis intervention has focused on primary preventive intervention to decrease the incidence and impact of crisis situations. In family therapy there is not only a movement toward early treatment to prevent symptom entrenchment, but a recognition of the adaptive, functional nature of symptoms themselves. Treatment acknowledges the communicational aspects of symptoms. While family therapy primarily retains a tertiary prevention stance, the field is broadening to include a secondary prevention focus as well.

SUMMARY

The fields of crisis intervention and family therapy have been shown to share a number of similarities, including an emphasis on interpersonal context, an overlapping population base, a shared intervention process, an emphasis on behavioral change, and a movement toward a preventive concept of mental health intervention. While sharing a population—namely, families in crisis—each field views the problem from a particular perspective, emphasizing certain variables and minimizing others.Then, too, although both fields share a common process of intervention, differences in approach do exist. These differences have been discussed in terms of the point in the crisis management process at which intervention occurs.

2

Psychoanalytic Model
of Family Crisis
Intervention

Among psychoanalytic theorists and practitioners there does not exist one psychoanalytic model for family crisis intervention. There are, however, psychoanalytic theorists and practitioners who share a similar outlook in understanding family crisis and developing strategies for intervention. In this book the authors will utilize the term "psychoanalytic family crisis intervention model" to describe those proponents who believe the influence of the organism to be the key variable in understanding family crisis.

The psychoanalytic model perceives the personality of individual family members and of the family as a whole to be the main causative agent in the production and maintenance of family crisis. While crisis itself is viewed as a stress agent that induces a state of disequilibrium, the intensity an breadth of this disorganization is considered a function of the general level of ability of the family and its members to cope with life situations, as well as a function of their previous level of coping. In other words, the psychoanalytic family crisis model assumes that for the most part, crisis exists only if the family or a subsystem of the family lacks the coping mechanisms adequate to deal with it. The critical variable is the personality of individual family members and of the family as a whole. Thus the first crucial task for an adherent of this model is to assist a family in determining its present coping level abilities by assessing the personality strengths and weaknesses of the individual members and of the group as a whole.

Once this is accomplished, the matter becomes one of assisting the family to reestablish its family coping mechanisms at its previous effective functioning level. The model assumes that families in crisis lack these mechanisms for two major reasons.

First, the family and/or its individual members have a low stress tolerance, so that confrontation with a stress stimulus produces a breakdown of usual (functional) defenses. Second, both individually and as a group the family may be fixated at an earlier stage of development, thereby lacking the individualization necessary to cope with the situation at hand. Therefore, proponents of this model aid in reestablishing family coping mechanisms by supplying encouragement, support, and, when necessary, assistance in working through past family developmental issues that directly effect the current family situation.

In general the psychoanalytic family crisis intervener conceptualizes family crisis resolution within a medical or health/sickness orientation. From the psychoanalytic perspective, the presence of a family crisis presents the dangers of symptom onset and regression. Family crisis represents a crucial turning point for the family. The possibilities for change include the turning toward psychological health and the restoration to the previous effective level of functioning, or the turning toward psychological sickness and the "solidifying of regressive patterns."[1]

ASSUMPTIONS OF THE PSYCHOANALYTIC MODEL

1. The personality of the family as a whole and of its individual members is the major variable to be examined in psychoanalytic oriented family crisis intervention. This includes such facets of family functioning as adaptability, flexibility, competence, and coping ability.

2. Psychological health is developed within the individual and can be maintained only within the context of a psychologically healthy family (Ackerman, 1966, p. 46).

3. The interpersonal realtionships between family members, and the personalities of family members, are perceived as causative factors in the crisis process.

4. Family crisis is primarily a stressful event which creates disequilibrium and may result in regression induction rather than in family and individual psychological health.

5. During the immediate disequilibrium resulting from family crisis, rapid intervention is essential to halt the solidification of regressive patterns and symptomatology.

6. The psychoanalytic treatment strategies utilized to assist individuals in crisis are applicable and effective in family crisis intervention when the unit of analysis is the family.

7. Family crisis can be resolved by (a) reconstituting family coping mechanisms and by (b) gaining insight to previous traumatic events which are directly affecting current family life situations.

8. Intervention focuses on (a) the accurate assessment of family strengths and weaknesses, (b) the rapid provision of support and encouragement, and (c) the working through of whatever issues from the past (e.g. from families of origin) are related to the current situation.

9. Interveners must be highly skilled, with an extensive background in psychoanalytically-oriented theoretical constructs, methodology of intervention, and outcome goals.

GOALS OF PSYCHOANALYTIC FAMILY CRISIS INTERVENTION

The major goal of psychoanalytic family crisis intervention is to restore the family to its previous equilibrium. Psychoanalytic family crisis intervention places the greatest stress upon attaining insight into past experiences that directly inhibit the family's ability to cope with the current situation. This type of intervention is not greatly concerned with insight that would foster major personality changes. These major changes in family interactional patterns or family roles are viewed as necessitating the long-term depth-oriented process associated with psychoanalytic family therapy. The basic goal of the psychoanalytically-oriented family crisis model is to rebuild the formerly functional defenses of the family. The broader goal is to strengthen these defenses for the purpose of increasing the family's tolerance to future stressful events.

ASSESSMENT METHODS

An accurate assessment of the strengths and weaknesses of the family and of its individual members in response to a stressful life situation is deemed essential in determining the degree of family disequilibrium. Since the accuracy of this assessment is believed to be directly related to the duration of time between the therapist's observation of the family's response and the event itself, the psychoanalytic family crisis model would provide assessmemt services to the family in crisis as soon after crisis onset as possible. Thus the utilization of mobile response units, crisis phones, and walk-in clinics would be expected.

Psychoanalytic family crisis assessment would involve meetings with the family and its subgroups. These sessions would focus upon both the responses of the family and its members to the current situatpon and upon the developmental history of the family and its individual members. The latter would be explored to the extent that it aided in gaining a clearer understanding of the current crisis.

A major part of the assessment process would be the observation of the verbal and nonverbal reactions of the family and its members to questioning by the therapist. The psychoanalytic family crisis therapist questions family members individually, while at the same time observing the other family members' verbal and nonverbal reactions to the responses being given and to the questioning itself. The verbal and nonverbal reactions between and among the family members provide data the psychoanalytic therapist can use in assessing the types of family coping mechanisms employed and the extent of other impairment or damage. Once the assessment is completed, thz therapist has a basis for developing the particular type of intervention strategy necessary for reconstituting these defenses. Although there are no specific questions used by most psychoanalytic family crisis interveners, it would be expected that early childhood experiences and previous strategies of coping would be explored.

TREATMENT

Following the assessment, intervention focuses on three strategic aspects of the family crisis. Its first goal is to halt regression, thereby short-circuiting the development of additional symptomatology. This would involve the use of such techniques as the provision of support and encouragement by the intervener and the liberal use of psychotropic drugs to reduce anxiety. Once the process of regression is halted, the intervener focuses on "working through" relevant past experiences, either within the developmental history of the family or from the marital partners' respective families of origin. As these experiences are explored, the intervener stresses the achievement of insight by the family, so that it can bridge the connections between the present crisis and the past experiences under discussion. As previously suggested, the utilization of the process strategies of working through conflictual material and attaining insight is narrowed in both scope and depth to those areas directly relevant to the current crisis situation. As the family achieves an understanding of the causes of its present disequilibrium, formerly functional defenses and coping mechanisms would be expected to reassert themselves, and in turn the family would regain a functional equilibrium. In addition, the possibility of these reasserted defense mechanisms being strengthened would make it possible that the family would be more capable of tolerating future stressful events.

In terms of duration and frequency, the psychoanalytic family crisis model of treatment can be described best by comparing it with the psychoanalytic family therapy model of treatment. Family crisis intervention would diverge from the once or twice weekly appointment mode used in psychoanalytic family therapy. Sessions most likely would last longer and occur more frequently. The duration of treatment would range from a minimum of one session to a maximum of three months, with sessions more frequent at first and decreasing in frequency over time. In summary, termination occurs at a point in time when the family defenses are operating at the precrisis level and the family appears to have gained the resiliency necessary to withstand future stressful events.

THERAPISTS

Background and Training. Both because this model is strongly dependent upon an accurate assessment and because of the delicacy required in reconstructing the defense mechanisms of the family and its members, the psychoanalytic family crisis model demands the utilization of only highly skilled psychoanalytically trained professionals as therapists, most of whom are psychoanalytically trained psychiatrists. However, because such therapists are in great demand and, since training is so expensive, psychologists with Ph.D.s, and social workers with M.S.W. degrees, who have been similarly trained and are often supervised by psychoanalytically trained psychiatrists, are being used increasingly.

The training experience of the psychoanalytically-oriented family crisis intervener can best be characterized by its intense in-depth quality. Training involves a thorough study of psychoanalytic theory and its application to analytically based assessment and treatment methods. Training also involves a personal analysis with a recognized psychoanalytially trained psychiatrist who specializes in training psychoanalytic therapists. The psychoanalytic family crisis therapist in training undergoes this personal analysis in conjunction with didactic studies and practicum experiences with both individuals and families.

In general the psychoanalytically-trained family crisis therapist essentially functions within the medical model in the role of the doctor-expert. The individual family member exhibiting the acute symptomatology is present during the assessment intervention and treatment intervention phases. The family assessment appraisal as well as the determination of treatment direction is the sole responsibility of the therapist, based on his assessment of the family members' ego strength and of their ability to handle conflictual materials.

Role. The psychoanalytically-oriented family crisis therapist perceives himself as providing an emotionally nurturing, knowledgeable, parental figure to the family and its individual members. He sees himself as a controller of danger and a time-limited source of emotional support and satisfaction. He supplies those elements the family presently needs but lacks (Ackerman, 1966). In order to lessen the family's fear of further regression (family movement toward emotional illness) and to facilitate the delicate process of defense mechanism regeneration (family movement toward emotional health), he encourages the family's dependency upon him. In encouraging this dependency, the therapist attempts to change the family's perception of him as an "outsider" to one of seeing him as a valuable personal instrument for reality testing.

Throughout the assessment and treatment phases of therapy, the psychoanalytically-oriented family crisis therapist is calmly and authoritatively active and directive in his interventions. He assumes primary responsibility for creating an empathetic, trusting, hopeful atmosphere by arousing and enhancing a meaningful emotional interchange between family members and himself. He intervenes as quickly as possible at the point of crisis (an individual family member exhibiting acute symtomatology) and assumes sole responsibility for consistently and discriminately limiting the depth of the family's coping mechanisms. As the family's defense mechanisms regain strength, the therapist supplies additional encouragement and support by gradually returning the parenting responsibility to the appropriate family members. In so doing, the psychoanalytically-oriented family crisis therapist further ensures that the family feels hopeful and confident in its ability to successfully handle future stressful life situations.

It is difficult to be more specific about therapists' activities, as their major intervention strategy involves insight and support, both of which are process variables that are difficult to operationalize.

SETTING

The psychoanalytic family crisis intervention model's concern with the speed of intervention greatly influences the employment setting of the psychoanalytic family crisis therapist. Most such therapists operate from such facilities that strongly encourage first- and second-level intervention strategies as community health centers and family crisis centers. Psychoanalytically-oriented family crisis therapists are used increasingly in emergency rooms of both mental and general hospitals for the purpose of determining the need for institutionalization of specific family members exhibiting acute symptomalogy. Also, because they are scarce and often in great demand, psychoanalytic family-crisis-oriented psychiatrists tend to function in various settings simultaneously. They practice mainly at teaching-treatment facilities, engaging in training, consultation, supervision, and psychotherapy, though most are in private practice.

CONSUMER

In general the psychoanalytic family crisis model is designed to be effective in situations where the family is in crisis or in a state of disequilibrium. Specifically this model would be most appropriate when the family crisis involved the acute emotional distress of a family member. These situations would be termed psychiatric emergencies and would include such patterns as suicidal threats, acute anxiety states, and the sudden onset of bizarre behavior. Thus chronic dysfunctional patterns of family interaction—such as family crises in which there is no identified patient (e.g. marital discord)—would be viewed as less appropriate for psychoanalytic family crisis intervention. According to this model, such stabilized symtomatology as marital discord would demand basic changes in the family interaction patterns, and would therefore require long-term family therapy.

A further constraint upon the usage of the psychoanalytic family crisis model lies within the area of client expectations and possible corresponding cultural and class differences. The psychoanalytic model requires a willingness and ability on the part of family members to examine and share feelings as well as to reflect upon past events. Cohen (1974) suggests that lower socioeconomic clients are more oriented toward action than reflection, and that their verbal style differs from that of middle- and upper-class clients. Since the psychoanalytic model relies heavily on verbal communication between clients and therapists and emphasizes reflection, these differences may limit the utility of this model for lower-class families.

In sum, the psychoanalytic model of family crisis intervention appears to be best suited for more reflective, verbal families. Most of the time this will mean middle- and upper-class families in crisis, in which one member is feeling acute emotional distress and in which there is not a past history of chronic psychiatric symptomatology.

Notes

1. "Solidifying of regressive patterns" refers to a process of dealing with stress whereby the personality of the individual becomes less differentiated and is frequently described in terms of regression to earlier stages of development. Loss of differentiation is pervasive; that is, it affects all spheres of functioning (e.g., cognitive, emotional). For example, loss of differentiation in the cognitive sphere would result in the individual responding more globally and in a less articulated manner. Regression is considered by psychoanalysts as both pervasive and resistant to change. On this basis it is assumed that when regression has occurred, treatment must focus not on symptom removal but on broad personality change through in-depth long-term treatment.

The assumption that symptom removal represents only surface change and will be followed by symptom substitution has been challenged by adherents of the behavioral approach. Data reported by behavioral therapists on the question of symptom substitution do not support analytic assumptions.

3

Problem-Oriented Model of Family Crisis Intervention

Like the psychoanalytic model, there is no approach specifically labeled the behavioral or problem-oriented model of family crisis intervention. The terms "behavioral approach" and "problem-oriented model" serve as generic labels for the numerous approaches that share a basic learning or stimulus-response framework for understanding family crises and for developing strategies of intervention (see London, 1972 for a detailed paper on the issue of theory versus technique in behavioral approaches; also see Lazarus, 1976).

We will use the term problem-oriented model to refer to approaches to family crisis intervention that emphasize the importance of the crisis stimulus. This model assumes that for each type of crisis there is a characteristic response pattern, and furthermore that there is a specifiable sequence of tasks that families must follow in order to successfully resolve the crisis. Therefore, the critical function of the problem-oriented family crisis therapist is to help the family learn the specific tasks that will aid them in resolving their current crisis. Adherents of the problem-oriented model view crisis as a situation in which specific behaviors (tasks) related to the crisis stimulus must be learned (mastered) in order to successfully resolve a crisis. Crisis resolution is viewed primarily within a learning or educational framework. A review of the literature suggests three factors that differentiate a crisis from a noncrisis state: a stressful precipitating event recognized by at least one member of the family; a significant and rapid deterioration of the family's usual coping mechanisms; affective and cognitive disruption for longer than one week.

Most of the information accumulated during the past three decades categorizes crises as either developmental or situational. Developmental crises are assumed to occur at normal transition points in family life cycles (Havighurst, 1953; Erikson, 1959; Sheeney, 1976). These crises are presumed to be predictable and therefore amenable to preplanned intervention. Intervention guides the family through the critical period of readjustment and serves as a primary prevention measure during the time that the family is vulnerable

(Neuhaus & Neuhaus, 1974). For example, the adjustment necessary for the husband and wife when their children enter kindergarten, while conceptualized as normal but emotionally hazardous, is characterized by tension-induced behaviors conducive to temporary family disequilibrium. At this time, situational events that would not typically precipitate a crisis become unmanageable and require secondary prevention. Thus a visit by the in-laws during this period may be perceived as a crisis, while in the past the visit was viewed as a manageable, perhaps even welcome, event.

One implication of this classification system is that developmental crises can be treated by giving the family an opportunity to develop its solution to this normal but unsettling event. Treatment here is analogous to the psychoanalytic concepts of catharsis and insight. In contrast, the situational crises are construed as events that are not predictable and over which the family has no control; accidents, natural disasters, crimes, unexpected deaths, and so on. Typically, situational crises handicap the family's coping mechanisms and lead to a more intense sense of helplessness and disorganization of behavior than occurs with developmental crises. Treatment is presumed to require more active intervention in order to effect a positive resolution of the crisis. In addition, it is more typical in situational than in developmental crises for one person, rather than the whole family, to be identified as having the greatest need for assistance. In developmental crises, it is more usual for all family members to perceive themselves as needing assistance.

The problem-oriented model conceptualizes the family as an interlocking network of reciprocal behaviors. A family crisis represents a situation in which the family either lacks appropriate behaviors to produce resolution and/or maintains reciprocal behaviors inconsistent with resolution. Thus the behavior of the family in crisis is inconsistent (randomized trial-and-error) and/or dysfunctional (maladaptive, habitual) in its attempts to cope with the crisis stimulus. A crisis represents a point at which the family can make choices. These choices include the potential for incorporating new problem-solving skills and more gratifying reinforcement patterns, as well as the possibility of eliminating less advantageous patterns of interaction.

ASSUMPTIONS OF THE PROBLEM-ORIENTED MODEL

1. The family is the major source of reinforcement for an individual and it is in a position to influence aspects of the environment that can serve to increase or decrease specific behaviors of the person.

2. The crisis stimulus is the major variable to be examined in problem-oriented family crisis intervention, including consideration of its suddenness, magnitude, duration, intensity, and proximity (Kalis, 1970).

3. Family members can be taught to use behavioral principles to produce behavioral change.

4. Behavioral principles used to change individual behavior are equally applicable to and effective with interactive behavior among individuals.

5. Family crises can be resolved by either altering the nature of events (e.g., modifying contact with school or social agencies) and/or altering the methods of dealing with the events—that is, changing the behavior of family members).

6. It is possible to specify in behavioral terms what family members must do to achieve mastery of a crisis situation (Kaplan, 1970).

7. Intervention focuses on provision of practical alternatives and support, rather than on dynamic or genetic insight, understanding, or interpretation (Schneidmen, 1973).

8. Interveners do not need extensive training in traditional personality assessment or treatment, but must be trained in principles of behavior management.

GOALS OF PROBLEM-ORIENTED FAMILY CRISIS INTERVENTION

1. The basic goal of the problem-oriented family crisis model is that the family learn the skills necessary to resolve the immediate crisis.

2. Problem-oriented family crisis intervention focuses basically on changing behavior in relation to the crisis stimulus, and minimizes concern with insight and attitudinal change.

3. The major goal of problem-oriented family crisis intervention is to achieve resolution of the crisis so that the family can return to normal functioning.

4. A broader goal would include the generalized learning of problem-solving skills such that the family will be able to successfully resolve future crises without outside intervention.

ASSESSMENT METHODS

The first step of problem-oriented family crisis intervention involves a careful assessment of the factors precipitating the crisis and the specification of tasks that the family members need to engage in to resolve that crisis. Included in this process would be the observation and recording of relevant current behaviors of family members. This process is likely to include the charting by family members of the occurrence of various disturbing behaviors. Both family and therapist participate in an "objective" recording of the current maladaptive behaviors, as well as of the family's antecedent and consequent behaviors to the crisis stimulus and/or to the current stimuli that are maintaining the crisis. The intervener utilizes this data to determine what behaviors are lacking and/or inconsistent with achievement of the desired outcome.

For example, Gottman, Notarius, Gonso, and Markman (1976, pp. 178–181) suggest that couples use a "Problem Inventory" as an aid in selecting an issue that both partners want to work on (See Table 2-1). The "Problem Inventory" lists areas of disagreement experienced by many couples. Each partner is instructed to indicate the severity of the problem by placing a number from 0 to 100 in the first column, with zero indicating that the problem is not

Table 2-1
Problem Inventory

How severe?   How long?

1. Money

2. Communication

3. In-Laws

4. Sex

5. Religion

6. Recreation

7. Friends

8. Alcohol & Drugs

9. Children

10. Jealousy

Please feel free to write down any other problem area(s) which you may feel is (are) relevant.

11.

12.

Adapted from J. Gottman, C. Notarius, J. Gonso & H. Markman. *A Couple's Guide to Communication.* ©1976, pg. 180. Reprinted by permission of Research Press, Champaign, Illinois.)

severe, and 100 indicating that it is very severe. Each partner also is asked to write how long (years, months, or days) this area has been a problem. After each partner fills out a separate inventory, both can compare their responses and select an issue for discussion.

Once the problem has been noted, it is broken down (Carkhuff, 1973). This means obtaining a clear, specific definition of it so that goals may be stated in behavioral language. Problems should be defined in observable and measurable units of human behavior. For example, "dissatisfaction with sex" can be defined in terms of infrequent sexual intercourse and even less frequent orgasms. The clearer the problem is to the therapist and client, the clearer the goals—and, it is believed, the more effective the intervention strategy will be.

Once the problem is defined in terms of specific behaviors that the client would like terminated, decreased, increased, modified, or perhaps developed, the next step is to keep a record of the behaviors (see Table 2-2). Early records serve as a baseline to which later records can be compared and changes in behavior assessed. Clients are often given blank charts to record the frequency of various behaviors for some period between three days and three weeks (Gottman, et al., 1976; Knox, 1971; Stuart, 1973).

In addition, Knox (1971, pp. 12–13) supplies his clients with observation tables on which they can record samples of their interaction at home (see Table 2-3).

Table 2-2

Behavioral Record

Week of ———————————

Behavior being observed ————————————————————

Observed by ————————————————————

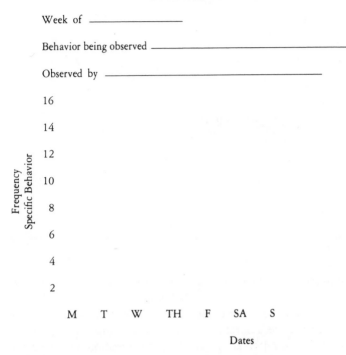

(Adapted from D. Knox, *Marriage Happiness: A behavioral approach to counseling.* ©1971, pg. 12. Reprinted by permission of Research Press, Champaign, Illinois.)

TREATMENT

When assessment is completed, intervention proceeds in one of two ways. The intervener may directly manipulate the relevant behaviors of the family members by using behavioral techniques (e.g., shaping, giving instructions, and modeling behaviors not in the family's repertoire, and giving negative reinforcement or teaching deceleration techniques for inconsistent behavior). Or the intervener instructs one or more family members in the use of specific behavioral principles in order to manipulate the behavior of other family members. In either case the problem-oriented family crisis intervener also functions as a provider of support and encouragement (as a reinforcer) to the family. Feedback and data collection are used to adjust reinforcement schedules as needed and also to assess the effectiveness of the intervention.

In working with four couples experiencing marital discord, Stuart (1973) instructed the individuals in the use of a token system to modify their partner's behavior. Each wife had requested that her husband "converse with her more fully." The level of intensity of the conversation that each wife considered

Table 2-3
Observation Table

Wife records her response to specific
desirable and undesirable behaviors
of her husband   Wife's Observations

Day_____ Date_____

Husband's Desirable Behavior	Husband's Undesirable Behavior	Your Response to Behavior

(Adopted from D. Knox, *Marriage Happiness: A behavioral approach to counseling.* ©1971, p. 13. Reprinted by permission of Research Press, Champaign, Illinois.)

positively reinforcing was made clear and was rehearsed during treatment sessions.

As soon as her husband came home, the wife set a timer. The husband received one token when the bell rang after each hour in which he conversed at the criterion level. If the husband did not meet the criterion level within the first half hour of the time limit, the wife was to tell her husband how he could improve. The timer could then be reset if the husband so desired. If the wife neglected to give her husband hints as to how he could redeem himself, she would have to give him a token regardless of his behavior level. The criterion level for conversation was negotiable between the couple.

The husband could redeem the tokens for physical affection as previously negotiated. Each couple had desired to have sex more frequently. The husband was charged a lesser number of tokens for kissing, and a higher number for intercourse.

The behavior checklist was used to provide graphic data of interactional behavior and to record tokens earned and spent. In addition, each spouse was asked to complete a short inventory assessing personal satisfaction in and commitment to the marriage and his perception of how his spouse would respond. This inventory was completed at the start of treatment, at the conclusion of regular scheduled interviews, and at follow-up.

By the end of therapy, and at the follow-up point, the rates of conversation and sex increased sharply for all four couples. In addition there was an increase in reported satisfaction.

The method outlined here focuses primarily on changing the family's response to the crisis stimulus. The problem-oriented model, however, also may become involved in changing the crisis stimulus itself, by actively intervening with systems external to the family (i.e., school, relevant social agencies) in order to change the stimulus value of the crisis for the family.

For example, a behavioral consultant may directly intervene in the classroom by placing a "work box" or signaling apparatus near the target child. If so programmed, the "work box" can provide immediate feedback to the child for appropriate as well as inappropriate behaviors. Back-up reinforcers for points registered on the "work box" may be individual, or may be group rewards delivered to the entire class. Following is a case study involving direct intervention in a classroom as reviewed by Whaley and Malott (1971):

> Earl was a hyperactive child whose parents and grandparents had been extremely brutal and cruel to him. His skull had been fractured before he was one year old; as a result he suffered brain damage. When he was three years old, Earl was adopted by parents who were much kinder; however, he still had adjustment problems. When he was nine, he had not progressed beyond the second grade and was almost always misbehaving in the classroom. He was easily distracted and worked only short periods of time. Earl's hyperactivity took the form of talking, pushing, hitting, pinching, looking around the room and out the window, leaving his desk, tapping, squirming and fiddling with objects. In addition he was aggressive, pinched other children, and threw himself into groups of children, disrupting their work or play. One extreme behavior he occasionally engaged in was shoving his desk around the classroom, pushing aside all children and desks in his way. Because Earl was an aggressive nine-year-old in a classroom of seven-year-olds, the other children consciously avoided him (pp. 28–29).

A behavioral consultant (Patterson, 1965) observed Earl in his classroom and found that he received a lot of attention that reinforced his misbehavior. It was decided that strong positive reinforcers such as M&M's and pennies would be used to condition more appropriate behavior. A "work box" with a light bulb and counter inside it was placed on Earl's desk. At the end of each ten-second interval, if Earl properly attended to his school work the light would flash and the counter would add a number. At the end of each lesson, which lasted from five to thirty minutes, Earl received a penny or an M&M for each count or number.

The other students were told that some of the "goodies" earned by Earl were to be shared with them. They were encouraged to help Earl by not distracting him. These other students also provided Earl with added reinforcement by applauding his lesson scores after each session.

After ten days of such conditioning, Earl's disruptive/inattentive responses decreased from 25 percent of the time to 5 percent of the time, about an average percentage for the normal child. At follow-up, Earl's behavior on the playground had also improved to the point where he actually played with other children. In addition, other children were coming to Earl's home to play for the first time.

Direct intervention by a behavioral consultant has the advantage of reducing the amount of teacher time required to alter high-rate deviant behavior (Conway & Bucher, 1976). Once changes have been initiated and the deviant behavior decreased, control of the "work box" may be transferred to the teacher, who can continue to reinforce the child's appropriate behavior until the "work box" can be faded out.

In summary, the goal of problem-oriented family crisis intervention is to produce change either in the crisis stimulus itself or in the family's methods of dealing with the crisis stimulus. Thus the focus of the problem-oriented model on crisis-related task mastery is based on the assumption that the critical treatment variable is the crisis stimulus, and that organismic variables (individual differences) are peripheral.

THERAPISTS

Background and Training   There are two general types of therapists within the problem-oriented model: mental health professionals and natural help givers. Most of the former are psychologists. It is probable that the problem-oriented psychologist has earned a doctorate in a behaviorally-oriented clinical and/or counseling psychology program. In general these training programs emphasize the link between practitioner and researcher, stressing the need for constant data-based monitoring of intervention strategies and encouraging practitioners to evaluate the short- and long-term effectiveness of their interventions.

There are two other kinds of mental health professionals: psychiatrists and social workers. Their training typically would include learning various behavioral techniques, rather than having an emphasis on research and evaluation, as is the case with psychologists. In practice there is probably minimal difference in therapeutic effectiveness among experienced problem-oriented family crisis therapists, regardless of their professional affiliation. For the most part the mental health professional functions in one of two roles, either as a direct intervener in family crisis or as a consultant-trainer for natural help givers.

The term "natural help givers" includes family members as well as individuals whose job will bring them into contact with families in crisis (e.g., policemen, teachers, clergymen, etc.). In the role of consultant-trainer to natural help givers, psychologists (frequently) have served as educators for police (Newman, 1968; Bard & Berkowitz, 1967, 1969); suicide prevention volunteers (Schneidman, 1973); and teachers (Ulrich, Stachnik & Mabry, 1970). Though other professionals are involved in training natural help givers, the major impetus for developing and implementing training programs has come from psychologists (Patterson, Ray & Shaw, 1968; Knox, 1971).

Most often the natural help giver is taught how to provide immediate aid to the family. It is expected that if additional contact is needed by the family, the natural giver will refer it to appropriate facilities within the community. However, it should be noted that many families in crisis do not require more than one or two meetings with a help giver, and therefore the natural help giver serves for these families as the major, if not only, source of outside aid.

Role. The problem-oriented therapist perceives his role as that of a neutral but sensitive information seeker who wants to know what family behaviors are maintaining the crisis. His goal is to provide the family members with corrective behavioral prescriptions that they learn and apply. It is critical to the therapist that he be able to evaluate the effectiveness of his intervention by assessing specific behavioral objectives. The therapist presents himself to the family as a sensitive, concerned scientist. This role enhances his ability to obtain information that is painful for the family to share by minimizing the emotional reactions of family members both to him and to his probing as well as toward each other. This is because the family issue becomes a matter of learning or education rather than focusing on who is "sick," "bad," or to blame for the current crisis.

The role of the problem-oriented therapist as scientist-practitioner by no means precludes the necessity of establishing rapport and developing an atmosphere of trust and hope (Lazarus, 1976). However, the therapist's utilization of such apparatus as charts and other forms of objective data collection encourages family members to perceive him as a sensitive scientist-educator who is able to provide the family with the information necessary to resolve their current crisis. This image of the therapist leads family members to expect that once he has collected the necessary data, he will be able to aid the family in coping with the crisis. An important aspect of the therapist functioning as data collector is to convey hope to the family that the problem is both manageable and solvable.

SETTING

Many problem-oriented family crisis therapists are likely to work in settings that are either within or affiliated with a university. This choice of setting is probably a function of the therapist's interest in research, which in turn is an activity that is rewarded more within university settings than in most mental health facilities. However, in light of recent litigations and legislation that mandate evaluation of psychiatric services, it is probable that problem-oriented family crisis interveners will increasingly function in traditional mental health agencies.

CONSUMER

The problem-oriented family crisis model appears to be most appropriate for dealing with families who are in crisis due to a lack of the approprite skills or behaviors needed to resolve a specific situation. These problems tend to arise from one of two sources: normal life crises or externally caused crises. Such situations require the family to deal with external systems which then often require that the family reorganize internally. The problem-oriented therapist helps the family learn the specific behaviors necessary to effectively negotiate with those external systems. The therapist emphasizes direct behavior change and encourages active involvement by all family members. Although the approach requires that individuals be both able and willing to maintain behavioral records, it appears to be more suited to individuals who are more action oriented than to those who value a more verbal, attitudinal approach.

The problem-oriented model is well suited for families who are extensively involved with external agencies (e.g., social welfare agencies). Thus the model is suited for lower- and lower-middle-class families who have an action orientation, families with a delinquent or criminal member, and families where there is a specific disturbing behavioral pattern (e.g., suicide attempts). In situations where the acute emotional distress of a family member is not related to a specific crisis stimulus or where there are existential concerns, this model would not be appropriate.

4

Systems Model of Family Crisis Intervention

Currently, there is no approach specifically labeled the systems model of family crisis intervention. The term systems model will be used here to refer to approaches to family crisis intervention that emphasize the importance of current systems interactions in crisis resolution. The systems approach defines any crisis as a social system crisis (i.e., a problem of triadic interactions in a system with a history and a future). Most often the social system is the family. Therefore it is suggested that the term "systems family crisis intervention" is a more appropriate label than systems crisis intervention. (see Chapter 8).

This section will simply highlight the major notions of systems family crisis intervention. The reader is referred to Chapters 8 and 11 for a more detailed discussion. The systems model stresses the importance of social context in the production and maintenance of family crises. It suggests that the crisis frequently may be induced by the family's current system of interaction. Further, the family crisis must be currently receiving reinforcement by the system in order to continue to exist.

The system of interaction is defined as a set of triadic or three-party transactions. That is, we act not simply in response to an other, but in the *context* of others. Thus, behavior can not simply be explained in terms of dyadic or two-person interactions. Triadic transactions are viewed as the primary locus of the crisis, and their change becomes the major focus of treatment. Since individual distress or symptomatology is viewed as a sign of system conflict or disequilibrium, intervention does not focus directly on symptom alleviation, but views this as a by-product of system change.

ASSUMPTIONS OF THE SYSTEMS MODEL

1. Family crisis and/or symptomatic behavior is functional and necessary for the continued functioning of a particular family system.

2. Family crisis and/or symptomatic behavior is a product of triadic transactions.

53

3. Individuals relate to one another through patterned behavior or redundancies called rules (Jackson, 1967; Turner & Gross, 1976).

4. Symptomatic behavior is currently being reinforced or it would cease to exist.

5. Family crisis can be resolved by correcting ineffective or detrimental patterns of relating within the family system.

6. Insight and awareness are not causal in producing change in triadic transactions.

GOALS OF SYSTEMS FAMILY CRISIS INTERVENTION

The goal of systems family crisis intervention is the alleviation of self-reinforcing and mutually destructive patterns of interaction (Jackson & Weakland, 1961). Essentially systems family crisis intervention aims to produce change in those sequences of behavior within the family that are maintaining the crisis. Although the crisis frequently is presented by the family as belonging to one family member, the alleviation of his distress is seen as a by-product of the change in the triadic system by the systems intervener. The minimal goal of the systems model is the return of the family to a level of functioning which existed prior to the crisis and which therefore represented a more functional balance. However, systems interveners also have the broader goal of developing transactional patterns in the family which will provide more mutual support and decrease the need for outside assistance.

ASSESSMENT METHODS

Assessment in systems family crisis intervention aims to clarify the current transactional patterns which have produced and are actively maintaining the family crisis. This assessment is primarily a clinical evalution by the intervener in the context of treatment, and does not constitute a separate stage of intervention.

TREATMENT

Intervention generally consists of joint meetings with the family as a unit. Its primary focus is the manipulation or change of current patterns of interaction on the assumption that it is precisely these patterns that are impeding crisis resolution. Systems family crisis intervention is aimed at influencing the alteration of self-reinforcing and mutually destructive interaction patterns. In focusing on current transactional patterns the intervener attempts to have the family members interact with each other and acts to direct and refocus their interaction. As with all system models, the specific methods used to influence change include relabeling the symptom, modeling clear communication, prescribing symptoms and giving paradoxical instructions (see Chapter 11 for details). These intervention strategies are designed to upset the current dysfunctional pattern of family interaction and to provide a basis for more effective communication. The importance of attitude change, insight, and understanding of the historical causes of the current crisis are minimized by systems interveners. Systems interveners play an active role in manipulating and prescribing changes in interaction patterns. Ths first goal of the systems intervener is to gain control of the family system in order to impose change in the patterns maintaining the famiy crisis.

THERAPISTS

Background and training. It is assumed that help givers in the systems model of family crisis intervention need to be highly skilled both in assessing transactional patterns and in using methods for effecting change in systems. Training in systems intervention skills most frequently takes place in practical and institute settings, rather than in academic programs. The systems model therefore encourages the use of individuals not normally a part of the mental health service delivery system as interveners. Since a major commitment to ongoing training is required, the systems model encourages the use of paraprofessionals rather than volunteers or natural help givers. Traditional training in individually-oriented assessment and treatment skills is considered neither essential nor helpful in effective systems intervention. Therefore mental health professionals are viewed as no more qualified or skilled than paraprofessionals, and they are expected to complete the same specialized training programs.

Role. Therapists using the systems approach view their role as intrusive, active, and manipulative. They view their goal as gaining control of, and then imposing that on, the current dysfunctional family system in order to produce change. Intervention techniques are viewed as strategic moves designed to accomplish this goal. Therapists see their role as one of forcing the family to move from a perception of the crisis as an individual problem of one family member to a realization that the crisis is a function of how the family unit operates and which, in order to be resolved, necessitates change in the entire family system.

SETTING

Systems approaches to family crisis intervention will be most typically located in facilities that offer twenty four-hour emergency service (such as community mental health centers or admitting offices of psychiatric inpatient facilities). They also may be found as adjunct services (e.g., at a children's hospital) or as mobile units operating out of mental health facilities, and responsive to calls from police and community members.

CONSUMERS

Adherents of the systems approach argue that the only necessary requirement for this approach is that the family currently be in crisis or disequilibrium. Like the psychoanalytic model, the systems model of family crisis intervention would be appropriate in cases in which the family crisis revolved around the acute emotional distress of one or more family members. The systems model differs from the psychoanalytic, however, in assuming that systems family crisis intervention also is appropriate in cases where this acute emotional distress is a flare-up of chronic symptomatology. Systems adherents also would view this model of family crisis intervention as appropriate in cases of family crisis in which no one family member was the identified patient because of psychiatric distress, but where the presenting problem was interpersonal (e.g., a marital argument or a parent-child conflict).

Although the systems model indicates that relevant systems are the focus of intervention, in practice, systems adherents typically focus on the nuclear family. Thus the systems model might be less appropriate for family crises which are externally caused and for which resolution of conflict between the family and the external system would be most effective (e.g., housing relocation). This type of issue would probably be more appropriately treated by the problem-oriented model.

5

Crisis
Intervention

Overview

Crisis marks a period of upheaval in one's life. Former, trusted methods of problem solving prove inadequate, with anxiety, frustration and confusion as typical and frequently overwhelming side effects. According to Caplan (1974), crisis refers to a short period of psychological distress which occurs from time to time when a person must deal with problems temporarily beyond his capacity.

TYPES OF CRISIS

Crisis stimuli can be categorized according to their source as either *maturational* or *external*.

Maturational crises also are known as internal (Burgess & Lazare, 1976), normative (Lazarus, 1976), developmental, or endogenous (Caplan, 1974). Maturational crises are described by Burgess and Lazare (1976) as *"expected events occurring normally to most individuals"* (p. 61; our emphasis) in the course of living. These events might include adolescence, marriage, parenthood, and old age. Since such crises are normative and predictable, they provide us with the opportunity to plan for them.

There are periods of life in which the occurrence of maturational crises is more common. Such periods correlate with transitional periods in biological and psychological development (Lazarus, 1976). Caplan (1974) defines maturational crises as those which are the product either of inevitable transitional stages between successive developmental ones or of complicated biopsychological imbalances (e.g., adolescence).

Maturational crises most often are described as reflecting periods of transition from one level of functioning to another. Erikson (1963) has conceptualized periods of transition between one stable developmental phase of human functioning and the next. These transitional times are described as periods of flux in which behavior becomes more disorganized. Erikson lists eight developmental crises in terms of the problems that must be resolved in each phase:

1. basic trust versus mistrust
2. autonomy versus shame and doubt
3. initiative versus guilt
4. industry versus inferiority
5. identity versus role confusion
6. intimacy versus isolation
7. generativity versus stagnation
8. ego integrity versus despair.

Burgess and Lazare (1976) indicate that mastery of maturational crisis largely determines the ego strength of the individual.[1] Negative resolution of the crisis is presumed to result in fixation at that stage, thereby hampering future growth and development. Notman and Nadelson (1976) say further that even in cases where the crisis is the result of an externally imposed event, the clinician should take note of the current developmental phase of the individual since the interaction of the developmental phase with the crisis event may influence the crisis response.

External crises also are called exogenous, environmental, situational (Caplan, 1974), or adaptive (Lazarus, 1976). External crises are those which may occur to anyone at any time as the result of outside events. Caplan (1974) suggests three reasons for the occurrence of an external crisis: (1) the loss of a source or sources for satisfying basic needs. Examples might include the death or departure of a significant other, a crippling illness, and loss of bodily integrity; (2) the possibility of such a loss; (3) a challenge which overtaxes one's capacities; for example, a job promotion for which one is not prepared (p. 201).

Burgess and Lazare (1976) suggest a slightly different categorization of external crises:

Unanticipated life events refer to incidents that are unpredictable from the point of view of the individual experiencing them (e.g., hospitalization, the birth of a handicapped child).

Victim crises include involvement in an "overwhelming, hazardous situation . . . in which the individual may be physically or psychologically injured, traumatized, destroyed or sacrificed. Such an event involves a physically aggressive and forced act identified by another person, a group of persons, or by an environment" (pp. 64–65). Examples include war, riots, racial persecution, rape and assault.

Anticipated life events concern predictable changes in the life cycle that involve a certain degree of participation by the individual. Examples include the birth or adoption of a sibling, the divorce or separation of one's parents, breaking up with a lover, or an outstanding personal achievement. Anticipated life events appear to overlap to some extent with Caplan's notion of a challenge that overtaxes one's capacities.

Underlying all of these categories of crises is the notion that *any* life change is stressful. The degree of stress interacts with the individual's coping ability and with the social setting to provide the potential for crisis. The premise that all life-change events involve stress and are potentially crisis-provoking leads to an additive notion of crisis induction. Thus for a particular individual a stressful event (e.g., retirement) might be manageable. The same individual also might be able to handle the death of a close friend or a divorce, if these were to occur singly. But if all three events took place in rapid succession, the individual would be likely to experience crisis. This notion is frequently borne out in therapeutic contact with suicidal people and in postsuicide investigations. In such cases a review of recent events in the subject's life frequently indicates the occurrence of multiple crisis stimuli.

Studies of the effects of various life change events are currently being made. Rahe, McKean, and Arthur (1967) had 394 people rate the amount of social readjustment required for each of 43 life events. The events were those listed most frequently by Rahe's patients. The Life Change Units (LCUs) are shown in Table 5-1. For each life change a mean value or calculated weight is shown. This weight indicates on a 100 point scale the amount of social readjustment necessary to adapt to this event. Alkov (1975) found that people experiencing a number of life changes concurrently were more susceptible to injury and illness. For example, of persons with LCUs over 300, 79 percent reported physical injuries and/or illness. Preliminary findings by Alkov (1975) suggest that the simultaneous occurrence of a number of life change events, each of which individually is not particularly undesirable, frequently leads to infection, allergy or accidental injury, and the total impact predisposes the individual to a lowered ability to cope with illness or subsequent stress (p. 20).

EFFECTS OF INDIVIDUAL DIFFERENCES

Tom Jones and Marvin Smith each are faced with bankruptcy proceedings. Mr. Smith collects his friends, buys them a round of drinks, and leads them in a lively wake. He comments, "Like the proverbial phoenix, I shall rise again." Four years later he has sizable holdings in several corporations.

Mr. Jones collects his belongings and gives them to his friends, saying, "I won't be needing this any more," or, "You've always admired this; I want to be sure you have it." Two months later he is found hanged in his basement.

A major source of differences among people in responding to crisis stimuli appears to be a result of individual variation. Intrapersonal variables frequently mentioned as affecting crisis performance are frustration tolerance, prior crisis experiences, and ego strength. For example, Torrance (1965) states that parental overprotection is correlated with poor crisis response, since the individual has been deprived of experience in coping with frustration and failure.

Ego strength will be used here to illustrate the role of individual differences in crisis response. Ego strength refers to the logical, problem-solving, or "executive" ability of the individual to manage feelings and tensions. Figure 5-1 suggests that in low-stress conditions, individuals with varying degrees of ego strength function similarly. In the three cases illustrated, performance follows a sine curve indicating adequate functioning with normal fluctuations.

Table 5-1
Holmes-Ray Stress Adjustment Chart
Life Change Units

Family Constellation	Mean Value
Death of spouse	100
Divorce	73
Separation	65
Death of close family member	63
Marriage	50
Marital reconciliation	45
Change in family member's health	44
Pregnancy	40
New member added to family	39
Sexual difficulties	39
Arguments with spouse	35
Children leaving home	29
Trouble with in-laws	29
Change in living conditions	25
Move or change in residence	20
Change in schools, recreation, church activities,	20
and social activities	19
Change in sleeping habits	16
Change in number of family get-togethers	15
Change in eating habits	15
Vacation	13
Holidays	12
Individual Changes	
Jail term	63
Personal injury or illness	53
Death of a close friend	37
Outstanding personal achievement	28
Revision of personal habits	24
Minor violation of the law	11
Employment and/or School	
Fired from job	47
Retirement	45
Business readjustment	39
Change in job	36
Change in work responsibility (promotion or demotion)	29
Spouse begins or stops work	26
Begin or end school	26
Trouble with boss	23
Financial	
Change in financial status	38
Mortgage or loan over $10,000	31
Foreclosure	30
Mortgage or loan under $10,000	17

(Adapted from Ann Wolbert Burgess and Aaron Lazare, *Community Mental Health: Target Populations* © 1976, pg. 59. Reprinted by permission of Prentice-Hall, Inc., Englewood Cliffs, New Jersey).

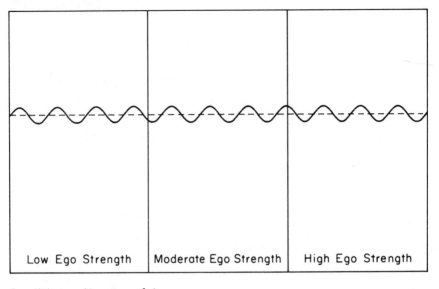

Low Ego Strength | Moderate Ego Strength | High Ego Strength

Conditions: Nonstressful
Ego Strength: Varying

Figure 5-1
Performance in Low Stress Condition

Graph indicates theoretical performance and shows low variability

(Adapted from E. Paul Torrance, *Constructive Behavior*, Wadsworth Publishing Co., Belmont, California, © 1965, p. 30. Reprinted by permission of the author.)

In Figure 5-2, individuals of varying ego strength are confronted with a high-stress situation.

Variability of response to the crisis stimulus is evident. Subjects with low ego strength are presumed to be incapable of managing internal tensions provoked by the high-stress condition, and immediately experience a crisis in terms of their functioning ability. High- and moderate-ego-strength subjects are spurred to increased efforts to resolve the crisis. The illustrated differences in response of moderate- and high-ego-strength subjects suggest that the amount of ego strength required to meet a crisis stimulus is directly related to the intensity of the crisis stimulus.

Figures 5-3 and 5-4 graphically represent the effects, respectively, of successful crisis resolution and of failure to resolve the crisis. They indicate that ability to function is affected by one's capacity for effectively resolving crisis stimuli. As Figure 5-4 indicates, failure to resolve the stimulus condition results in the individual's functioning at a reduced coping level. One may extrapolate from such information that the ability to respond to future crisis stimuli is affected by one's previous success or failure.

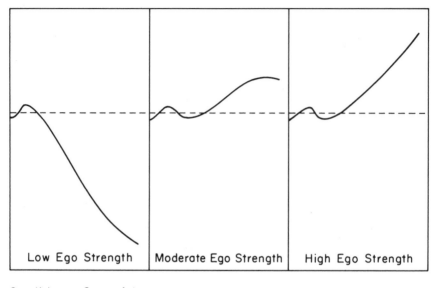

| Low Ego Strength | Moderate Ego Strength | High Ego Strength |

Conditions: Stressful
Ego Strength: Varying

Figure 5-2
Performance in High Stress Condition

Graph indicates theoretical performance and shows high variability

(Adapted from E. Paul Torrance, *Constructive Behavior*, Wadsworth Publishing Co., Belmont, California, © 1965, p. 31. Reprinted by permission of the author.)

CRISIS RESPONSE

People cope with crisis in a multitude of ways. Coping refers to "what a person does to handle stressful or emotionally charged demands" (Lazarus, 1976, p. 74). Coping may be *direct*—that is, aimed at altering one's relationship to the environment—or *palliative*—that is, directed at reducing, eliminating, or tolerating distressing bodily, motor, or affective distress once it has been aroused. Coping mechanisms include combinations of such actions as cognitive strategies (i.e., thinking and planning), physical actions, verbal strategies, and defense mechanisms (Burgess & Lazare, 1976).

It is assumed that all individuals when subjected to a sudden crisis frequently exhibit a set of similar behaviors. Such behaviors may be described as normative immediate responses to crisis. They range from being preoccupied with the crisis stimulus to relying on people not normally considered part of the natural support system. Hansell (1976) identifies eight observable and typical changes in behavior as signposts of crisis response (see Table 5-2). These include changes in attention, affectional attachments, identity, role performance,

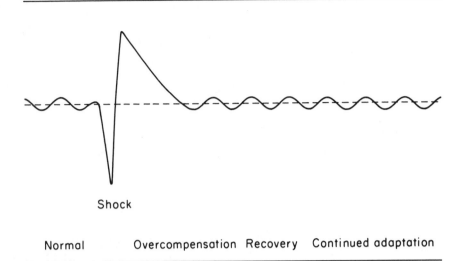

Shock

Normal   Overcompensation Recovery   Continued adaptation

Figure 5-3
Performance Under Stress With Resolution

Graph indicates theoretical performance under stress and in which stress is mastered.

(Adapted from E. Paul Torrance, *Constructive Behavior*, Wadsworth Publishing Co., Belmont, California, © 1965, p. 22. Reprinted by permission of the author.)

network attitude (the perceptions of significant others), memory, decision making, and signaling.

Attention. A crisis-involved individual is typically preoccupied with his own situation. When confronted with a set of stimuli unrelated to the crisis, he is likely to demonstrate frequent randomized shifts of attention. Such a person is likely to express disinterest in current interactions unless they pertain to the crisis. One might also expect such a person to keep focusing his attention and therefore the topic of conversation on the crisis at hand (Hansell calls this the topic-of-choice phenomenon).

Affectional attachments. When confronted by crisis the individual tends to drop out of his ordinary patterns of social interaction. This appears to occur largely because usual social interactions are bound by interpersonal rules limiting intimacy and affection. Also, typical involvement with groups or projects requires that a set of expectations about giving attention and performing a role be fulfilled. For a person in crisis both of these limitations may make

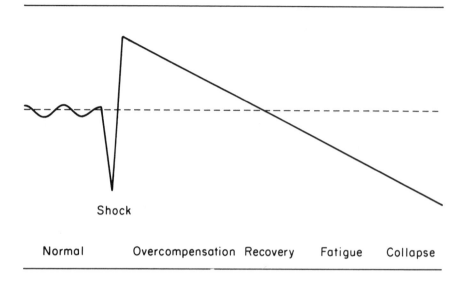

Shock

| Normal | Overcompensation | Recovery | Fatigue | Collapse |

Figure 5-4
Performance Under Stress Without Resolution

Graph indicates theoretical performance under stress which continues over time and is not mastered (collapse).

(Adapted from E. Paul Torrance, *Constructive Behavior*, Wadsworth Publishing Co., Belmont, California, © 1965, p. 23. Reprinted by permission of the author.)

such interactions unsatisfying. Individuals in crisis often complain of feeling alone, isolated, and distant.

At the same time people in crisis exhibit a number of behaviors suggesting their desire to be close (e.g., standing nearer to someone than is generally considered appropriate, using intimate language, offering uncensored information, and touching or making prolonged eye contact with relative strangers). In a sense people in crisis frequently want to grab hold of anyone immediately present, especially if such a person is offering or is in a position to help resolve the crisis. Hansell (1976) notes:

> It often appears that, coincident with the decline in older, regular attachments, the individual develops a random, migratory "search and attach" pattern. The person feels, acts and signals as if in readiness to "latch on and hold." People who work in clinical settings that receive many individuals-in-distress have abundant experience with this urgent, diffuse attachment behavior. Clinicians experienced in reception work often report a "clutchy," "clingy," "demanding"

Table 5-2
Characteristic Behavior of Persons at Crisis

Aspect of Behavior	Usual Appearance in Crisis
Attention	Migratory, narrowed, fixed Focuses on crisis
Affectional attachments	Loosened, widened, acquisitive
Identity	Diffuse, vague, convertible
Role performance	Decayed, unreliable, convertible
Network attitude	Fragmenting, malleable Readiness to embrace or extrude
Memory	Random access, reduced certitude Flowing "whir and blur"
Decision activity	Halting, meandering Strikingly improved with outside input
Signaling	Distress situation is present Direct and indirect requests for protection

(Adapted from Norris Hansell IV, *The Person-In-Distress: On the biosocial dynamics of adaptation*, © 1976, p. 29. Reprinted by permission of Human Sciences Press, New York, New York.)

component regularly present in the behavior of people in profound trouble. (pp. 16–17)

Hansell warns clinicians that they are not singled out because they are necessarily attractive persons, but rather simply because they are frequently present during critical crisis periods.

The heightened need for social attachments in crisis can have such negative consequences for the individual as being taken advantage of. This is especially true for the individual who prior to crisis onset functioned adequately but was somewhat of a recluse or was socially isolated. Such a person in crisis may be viewed by others only in the context of his current (crisis-responsive) behavior and is therefore vulnerable to being negatively labeled (e.g., being viewed as crazy rather than being seen as not himself). Certainly such labeling may take longer in the case of individuals exhibiting similar behaviors, but against a backdrop of extensive, long-term friendships and social networks.

Identity.   During times of normal functioning most people are able to make fairly definite statements about who they are, what they do well, what they like and dislike. In crisis, however, an individual frequently seems to have lost confidence that what he believed to be true is actually true. The individual's experience of his own identity becomes "diffused, vague and volatile" (Hansell, 1976, p. 18).

While losing the security of a clear concept of self, the individual also demonstrates an increased sensitivity to the perceptions and judgments of others.

> Persons-in-trouble quite often seem to play out a drama which can last for years, using identities and roles taken up quickly at crisis. When a person does not know who he is, those who appear to tell him acquire a capacity to create an identity for him, to select one out of ambiguity. *During crisis, an individual's identity lies substantially in the social surround.* (Hansell, 1976, p. 19).

The precrisis or "normal" behavior of those individuals with strong established social networks is emphasized and rewarded in the context of their crisis behavior. Thus the social network serves a stabilizing function, encouraging the individual to define himself as he has in the past.[2]

Again, the isolated individual is exposed to the greatest risk. Since behavior in time of crisis is less functional and more randomized, feedback from a social network with no historical (precrisis) recollection of the individual may provide him with information leading to a much more negative self-assessment and identity. In this way temporary actions in crisis may become a more permanent stabilized action agenda.

For a clinician the identity diffusion of the individual in crisis presents an extremely important consideration. To the extent that our training leads us to view people more in terms of their symptoms than their strengths, we risk contributing to the creation of chronic dysfunction.

Role performance. People's lives are generally governed by the ordered and predictable completion of specified sets of tasks. When an individual is confronted with a crisis, his behavior, including the performance of his expected roles, becomes more random and unpatterned. Hansell (1976) points out that in crisis, biochemical and physiological changes occur, providing the individual with the characteristics described in the literature as "general adaption syndrome." For instance, higher concentrates of epinephrine and nor-epinephrine are present.

While the individual in crisis is not performing his usual roles effectively, he is extremely open to "putting on" new roles, especially those suggested by people in the crisis environment. On the positive side, the individual's shedding of old roles and willingness to try new ones affirms Caplan's (1974) notion that crisis is an opportunity for growth and expansion. On the negative side, new roles may be more restrictive and dysfunctional (e.g., being a patient or casualty; Hansell, 1976).

Network attitude. We have already mentioned the effects of the attitudes and behaviors of significant others (including those given places of significance because they are available in a crisis) on the individual's identity and role performance. Significant others' perceptions of the individual in crisis greatly influence the outcome of the crisis episode. These people may discount crisis behavior and reinforce previous effective role behavior. For example:

"Martin is having a bad day."
"He's O.K., he's just upset by his wife's death."
"Hey, just forget it, he didn't mean what he said. You know him better than that . . ."
"He's under a lot of stress. Leave him be, he'll snap out of it."

On the other hand, loss of role performance or distancing from the group can be threatening to members of the social network, leading them to disqualify the individual. Examples include:

"If he's going to act like that, he better not come around here . . ."
"He can't even shine his shoes."

The longer the individual in crisis exhibits similar behavior, the more the network will view such behavior as signs of a general (permanent) loss of competence.

"I don't know about Martin. I can't trust him anymore."
"The way he's acting, he'd better check himself in to the loony bin."

In such instances the network is likely to withdraw from the individual.

Memory. In crisis, the individual's memory, like his attention, becomes more random. Forgotten past experiences suddenly come clearly to the fore. Experiences normally within one's purview suddenly become confused or recede into the background, causing one to feel perplexed and uncertain. If one describes these occurrences to significant others, they generally consider them annoying or bizarre. Hansell (1976) argues that the tendency to have more random memories can be an asset in crisis resolution when it is combined with the problem-solving (focusing) skills of a person who is not in crisis.

Decision making. The individual in crisis is engaged in a more random trial-and-error method of dealing with events than is normal for him. Because it is a task requiring a systematic assessment of and commitment to a course of action, decision making is largely outside the realm of the individual in crisis. Such an individual is willing to consider a large number of potential solutions (frequently more than someone not experiencing a crisis), but is unable to sort and select among them. Thus the individual in crisis presents himself as ready for change, but is unable to select the necessary course of action. Significant others (family, associates, therapists) are likely to a large extent to influence the course eventually selected.

Signaling. The individual in crisis notifies other people in the social network of his distress through verbal and nonverbal behavior. Hansell points out that such signaling is a characteristic of many species, and that a typical response to distress signaling is a "helping" activity. "The general activities called forth in such attitudes are clustering, assessing, embracing, or helping if possible; and extrusion of the signaler, or flight, if no satisfactory response can be developed quickly" (Hansell, 1976, p. 28). Attitudes toward individuals in crisis, as described earlier in the chapter, support Hansell's notion that social networks have characteristic patterns of buffering and protecting, as well as of disowning, them.

MODELS OF CRISIS INTERVENTION

In the preceding sections information has been presented regarding the effects of individual differences on crisis response, the typical behaviors and blocks to problem solving generally true of persons in crisis, and the effects of significant others on the crisis behavior of individuals.

The three models of crisis intervention which will be described in the succeeding chapters vary primarily in the amount of emphasis they place on each of these factors. The *individual* model focuses on the issue of individual differences, contemplating such questions as:

Why is this crisis stimulus overwhelming to this particular individual, and not to others?

What prior experiences has the individual had with crisis stimuli?

How were previous crises handled/avoided?

The *generic* model focuses on the pervasive "normative" crisis response behavior and the problem-solving tasks elicited by the crisis stimulus. This model raises such questions as:

What problem-solving skills does this person have/not have relevant to resolving the situation brought on by the crisis stimulus?

What has the person's response to the crisis stimulus been so far?

What crisis tasks has the person completed/not completed?

Has he expressed the feelings, thoughts, actions normally predicted for this situation?

Has he taken actions generally indicative of success or of failure in resolving this crisis?

The third perspective, focusing on the social network, is represented by the *systems* model. This model emphasizes such issues as:

What has been the response of significant others to the individual in crisis?

Is he being encouraged to resolve crisis stimuli? To take on the role of patient?

Does the social system need this person in this role to protect other members from chaos?

Notes

1. Note that in the next section ego strength will be used as an example of a variable correlated with ability to effectively deal with crisis. Thus a circular relationship is indicated, in which previous success in resolving crisis defines ability to resolve crises.

2. Of course, if the social network's view of the person is a constricting one, its reinforcement may tend to retard the individual's growth and personality expansion. In sum, the network tends to encourage one to remain one's old, predictable self, for good or ill.

6

Individual Crisis Intervention

The individual model of crisis intervention views crisis basically as a stress agent that induces disequilibrium in an individual. The intensity and breadth of this disorganization depend upon the individual's previous level of functioning and his general ability to cope with life situations. Therefore, according to this conceptualization of crisis, the key variable to be examined is the individual's personality. Thus the individual model focuses primarily on organismic factors, rather than on the precipitating event or the situational factors related to the particular crisis.

Generally it is considered that the individual model utilizes a method of secondary prevention. Its adherents use psychoanalytic theory as the primary theoretical framework for understanding individual responses to crisis situations. The model emphasizes early diagnosis and prompt treatment. The most effective time to intervene is assumed to be at the first sign of problem onset, which is characterized by emotional turmoil, an increase in random behavior, and an openness to the helping process (Parad, 1965). Immediate treatment is encouraged on the assumption that prompt intervention can effectively prevent regression patterns from solidifying. The model assumes that a person can benefit from brief, focused treatment which allows him to reintegrate his mechanisms of defense so that they are back to their precrisis level. Unresolved crises of long duration (months or more) call for a longer, more depth-oriented treatment process because of increased resistance and the secondary gains associated with symptomatology. For example, an individual who has a difficult time asking others to care for him directly, during crisis will find himself being cared for without needing to ask. This comfort serves as secondary gain for the client and can function to maintain the individual's dysfunctional behaviors.

ASSUMPTIONS OF THE INDIVIDUAL MODEL

The basic assumptions of the individual model are grounded in stress research and psychoanalytic theories of ego functioning (Kalis, 1970).

1. Individual personality is the key variable to be examined in crisis intervention, including such facets as adaptability, flexibility, personal competence, and coping ability.

2. Crisis is primarily an event which may result in regression induction rather than in personality growth.

3. Accurate assessment of individual personality strengths and weaknesses is essential to effective intervention.

4. The successful resolution of a crisis depends on working through issues from the individual's past history that are related to the current situation.

5. Regression and disequilibrium must be halted by providing the individual with support and encouragement and by working through previous traumatic events.

GOAL OF TREATMENT

The minimal goal of treatment in the individual model is a return of the individual to his precrisis level of functioning. Treatment is specifically aimed at halting regression and providing support in order that the individual survive the crisis situation while maintaining his usual functioning ability. Ideally treatment also increases the individual's resistance to similar stress agents through his gaining greater insight into personality processes and the effects of early learning. Major personality (or behavior) change, however, is seen as outside the realm of crisis intervention because of the model views such change as a long, slow process involving numerous regressive episodes.

ASSESSMENT METHODS

The individual model emphasizes assessment of the intrapsychic processes of the person experiencing a crisis. Interpersonal relationships are viewed as potentially helpful in the reequilibrium process, but are not considered causative in the crisis process and are not a major focus of assessment. In general the individual model differs from traditional psychotherapeutic practices in its emphasis on the more immediate causes of the client's current state of disequilibrium. Little concern is expressed for the developmental history of the client, except insofar as it is revelant to a clearer understanding of the crisis situation.

TREATMENT

While family members and others significant in the client's life may be involved in the treatment process, such involvement is ancillary to the main work of returning the client to a precrisis level of functioning through insight-oriented treatment (Langsley et al., 1968a). The crisis intervener, following his more circumscribed intervention strategy utilizes a great deal of supportive intervention as well, making liberal use of psychotropic drugs in order to reduce anxiety and prevent regression. While processes similar to those used in psychoanalytically-oriented psychotherapy are employed, they are differentiated by their more limited focus, the more active involvement of the intervener, and a consistent limit on the depth of the self-exploration process. Essentially, differences between psychoanalytically-oriented individual therapy and psychoanalytically-oriented crisis therapy are a matter of degree rather than of kind, and the assumptions underlying treatment are similar.

Two approaches are subsumed within the individual model of crisis intervention; these are the recompensation approach and the brief- or limited-therapy approach. These two methods differ in terms of their emphasis on past experience (Langsley et al., 1968a).

The recompensation approach. This views the client as currently "falling apart" as a result of the crisis situation. Treatment is seen as a matter of "putting him back together." Minimal attention is given to life history, and no attempt is made to explain why the client is unable to cope at this time, and with this situation. The intervener takes at face value the client's regression or decompensation, and aims at halting the process and having him regain his equilibrium.

One example is the military treatment method developed in response to war-induced stress (Glass, 1953). Treatment occurs near the front lines, and consists primarily of providing a time out from stress stimuli combined with support in the form of encouragement and ego enhancement. A second example is the traumatic neurosis method (Semrad & Zaslow, 1964), which is becoming a frequent part of general hospital and other crisis treatment facilities' emergency services (Burhenne, 1974). Individuals in crisis are provided with short-term care (generally not exceeding twenty four hours) in the form of overnight lodging, food, and supportive counseling. These services give the individual a period of brief recompensation and rest.

The assumption of these methods of recompensation is that the individual's personality has been overwhelmed by the stressful situation, and that a time period in a "safe" environment will allow the individual to regain equilibrium. He then is assumed to be able to meet the stress situation more effectively. Inherent in this approach is the assumption that the individual has the ability to meet the crisis effectively, but temporarily has been overwhelmed by its intensity.

The recompensation approach has the same perspective as the psychoanalytic model—that crisis primarily functions as a stress agent, presenting the individual with the risk of disorganization and regression. This approach similarly views rapid intervention as essential in reducing the threat of personality disorganization. It diverges from the traditional model of psychoanalytic intervention, however, in its assumption that a brief period of rest in a non-stressful environment is sufficient to allow the individual to "pull himself together" to meet the crisis. Thus the recompensation approach does not view insight and working through of past but related conflicts as essential to crisis resolution. Essentially the recompensation approach is a descendent of the older analytic view of abreaction, and the even older view of moral therapy, in which the provision of peace and quiet in a friendly atmosphere was considered curative.

The brief-therapy approach. In the brief-therapy approach, crisis is viewed as the repetition of earlier traumatic situations. Like the recompensation approach, it views the client as "falling apart." However, unlike the former, the etiology of the falling apart is attributed to the reactivation of old complaints. "What is most characteristic in the reaction to a trauma is that associative connections are immediately established between the trauma and the infantile conflicts that become activated . . . The trauma may be experienced as a repetition of older traumata of childhood" (Fenichel, 1945).

Essentially the goal of brief therapy, as in more traditional forms of psychoanalytically-oriented psychotherapy, is for the client to achieve insight. But in the case for brief therapy the range of that insight is severely limited, for the client is assisted in achieving insight only within the specific area of the crisis. As Coleman (1960) describes it, the goal of brief therapy is "a minimal restructuring of a key conflictual area in an acutely decompensated personality [to] bring the patient back to his previous level of functioning or halt further decompensation."

Thus, the intervener focuses on past history only as it relates to the immediate situation. Insight into the causal links between this situation and developmental conflicts is assumed to be a requisite of behavior change or crisis resolution.

THERAPISTS

Background and training. Adherents of individual crisis intervention emphasize traditional clinical assessment and the use of analytically-based treatment methods. For these reasons interveners are restricted to mental health professionals who are highly skilled in personality assessment and extensively trained in psychoanalytically-oriented intervention techniques. Advocates of this model reject the use of interveners with limited training. Most of them are psychoanalytically-oriented psychiatrists.

Role. Interveners who utilize the individual approach to crisis intervention tend to function in the role of expert-doctor, which emphasizes the intervener in his capacity as a diagnostician and healer (Normand, Fensterheim, & Schrenzel, 1967). Such interveners generally view crisis from a medical model viewpoint, describing the individual in crisis as a patient in need of psychiatric treatment. Definition of the "real" or "underlying" problem and determination of appropriate treatment goals reflect traditional analytic processes and are within the domain of the therapist, not the client.

SETTING

Therapists using the individual crisis model tend to provide services at walk-in clinics, which often are open on a twenty four-hour basis (e.g., Jacobson, Wilner, Morley, Schneider, Strickler, & Sommer, 1965; Clark,

1965). These clinics are usually found in community mental health agencies or hospitals involved with the training and teaching of psychiatric residents.

CONSUMERS

Adherents of this approach describe it as appropriate for individuals dealing with a recent crisis, since rapid intervention provides the greatest opportunity for halting regressive behavior patterns. Clients with longer-standing crises are not considered appropriate for this approach since it is predicted that some regression and stabilization of symptoms have occurred. In addition, clients for whom the current crisis is a recurrence of previous crises or an exacerbation of chronic complaints are not deemed appropriate for this mode of intervention. In such crises a more intrusive and long-term therapeutic modality such as psychoanalytically-oriented family therapy is recommended.

7

Behavioral Crisis Intervention

Currently no approach has been labeled a behavioral model of crisis intervention per se. The generic model of crisis intervention, which focuses on the specific stress agent or crisis stimulus (Langsley et al., 1968a), conceptually and pragmatically can be classified as a behaviorally-oriented intervention strategy. Our discussion of the generic model's assumptions and goals will clarify the rationale for our classification decision. We will consider the generic and behavioral models of crisis intervention as synonymous.

The generic model emphasizes the characteristic, "normative" course of particular crises. Crisis intervention from this perspective is based on five principles which describe crisis reactions (acute stress disorders, according to Kaplan):

1. Crisis reactions are typically acute, with a specifiable onset and relatively brief period of duration, whether outcome is adaptive or maladaptive.
2. These reactions follow a limited number of adaptive and maladaptive courses.
3. These courses of response are clinically identifiable and predictive of outcome.
4. The observable symptoms of stress response are not always indicative of chronic mental illness, but such symptoms are often *transitory* aspects of the struggle to master the stress situation.
5. The essence of the struggle for stress mastery can be specified by characteristic psychological tasks that each stress situation poses for the individual. It is possible to specify clearly what the individual must do, psychologically and behaviorally, to achieve mastery of each stress problem (Kaplan, 1970, pp. 278–279).

From this perspective, crisis is caused by the introduction of a novel stimulus for which one's usual coping methods are not sufficient. Adherents of the generic model view this as a situation in which tasks related to the specific crisis must be mastered in order to achieve successful crisis resolution. Crisis resolution is primarily viewed within an educational (task-mastery) framework, in contrast to the individual model's use of a medical or pathology-oriented framework.

ASSUMPTIONS OF THE BEHAVIORAL MODEL

Basic assumptions of the behavioral model are grounded in disaster research (Kalis, 1970), and in the writings of Caplan (1961, 1964) and Lindemann (1944).

1. The crisis stimulus is the key variable to be examined in crisis intervention, and includes such facets as suddenness, magnitude, duration, intensity, and proximity (Kalis, 1970).

2. Hazardous events may be prevented or mitigated by a) altering the nature of events, or b) providing the person in crisis with support in the community.

3. Successful resolution of a crisis depends on finding an effective solution to the specific dilemma presented by the crisis stimulus.

4. Intervention is aimed at members of a target group at risk or the population at large, not specifically at individuals.

5. It is possible to specify clearly what individuals must do to achieve mastery of each stress problem (Caplan, 1970).

6. Intervention should focus on providing practical support and alternatives, rather than on insight or interpretation (Schneidman, 1973).

7. Interveners need not be skilled in traditional assessment and treatment techniques but may be individuals from a variety of backgrounds who have mastered the specific techniques necessary to aid in crisis resolution (Specter and Clairborn, 1973).

GOAL OF TREATMENT

The goal of intervention in the behavioral model is to return the individual to his precrisis level of functioning. The behavioral model views this goal from the perspective of mastering a series of tasks related to the crisis situation. Intervention aims to assist the individual in mastering specific tasks in order to decrease the likelihood of failure and possible personality disorganization. Successful crisis resolution is seen as a possible growth factor in that the successful completion of specific tasks related to this crisis may lead to an increased ability to deal with novel stimuli and to successfully complete novel tasks.

ASSESSMENT METHODS

The behavioral model assesses the type, duration, and magnitude of the major stimulus that determined the crisis. Its emphasis is on analyzing the crisis stimulus and the behavioral tasks needed to resolve it. Assessing characteristics of the individual is not a major focus. Once the crisis stimulus has been identified and analyzed, a specific series of crisis resolution tasks will be defined. Any individual exposed to that stimulus must perform them to effect resolution. Crisis intervention consists of teaching the individual how to complete the required tasks. It should be emphasized that in behavioral crisis intervention, the assessment of the crisis stimulus determines the specific types of tasks that the individual needs to master, and is thus an integral part of treatment.

TREATMENT

Intervention can occur either following crisis (secondary prevention) or prior to crisis (primary prevention).

Secondary prevention Intervention at the secondary prevention level is specifically directed at assisting in a satisfactory resolution of the current crisis situation. Such intervention is intended to be effective for any member of a given group (e.g., mothers of premature infants). While individual differences are important in terms of task mastery, they are minimized; for treatment focuses on accomplishing crisis-related tasks. Intervention involves assessing the nature of the major crisis inducing stimulus, delineating the tasks to be successfully completed, and providing practical support and assistance in accomplishing these tasks (Schneidman, 1973). This last sometimes involves the intervener as an active participant in crisis resolution. The intervener acts as a mediator between the individual and significant elements in his environment (e.g., school, family, social services, employment).

Numerous studies have examined specific crisis stimuli in order to delineate the specific tasks involved in their successful resolution (Lindemann, 1944; Kaplan & Mason, 1960; Janis, 1958). In general, such studies have noted that completion of these tasks is related to successful crisis resolution, and that failure to complete them leads predictably to a serious emotional reaction and to pathological symptomatology.

For example, Kaplan (1970), in a follow-up study of the reaction of mothers to premature birth (Kaplan & Mason, 1960), found that the completing of specific tasks (e.g., preparation for the possible loss of the child, acknowledgement of feelings of failure, resumption of the process of relating to the child, understanding and preparing for the special needs of the child, viewing these special needs as temporary) was positively correlated with experimenters' ratings of the mother's early relationship with the child. Additional studies have focused on the management of acute grief (Lindemann, 1944), reactions to anticipated surgery (Janis, 1958), reactions of individuals and groups to natural disasters, migrations, and retirement (Tyhurst, 1957), wartime separation and social and economic difficulties (Koos, 1946), entering college (Silber et al., 1961a, 1961b), children's developmental crises (Murphy, 1956), feelings of stress among nursing students (Rosenberg & Fuller, 1955), crises in pregnancy (Caplan, 1961; Bibring et al., 1961), and vulnerable subphases of marriage (Rapoport, 1963).

Each of these studies delineates which tasks must be mastered in order to resolve a given crisis. It is important to note that in each study the same generalized process of crisis resolution is involved. Successful crisis mastery in this framework involves the following tasks:

1. Making a correct cognitive perception of the situation, furthered by seeking new knowledge and by remaining aware of the problem;
2. Managing affect by being aware of feelings and appropriately verbalizing them, which leads to tension discharge and crisis mastery;
3. Developing patterns of seeking and using help from others with actual tasks and feelings through use of interpersonal and institutional resources (Rapoport, 1962).

Primary prevention. This is aimed at warding off the occurrence of the crisis stimulus, or at lessening its impact on individuals. Primary prevention programs either focus broadly on the entire population of a geographical area or more specifically on groups at risk (Bloom, 1971). Groups at risk are composed of those individuals most likely to be faced with the crisis situation (e.g., the aged, children of one-parent families, the handicapped).

Primary prevention emphasizes two intervention techniques: anticipatory guidance and consultation. Anticipatory guidance generally takes the form of a group meeting with individuals likely to face a particular type of crisis (e.g., engaged couples, new parents). In such meetings discussion focuses on potential problem areas and the tasks necessary for their successful resolution. Consultation provides guidance and feedback by a mental health professional to individuals in a position to minister to the mental health needs of a segment of the population (e.g., school teachers, clergymen, public health nurses). Such people are viewed as natural links between the populace and the mental health profession because of their social roles (Levy, 1973).

THERAPISTS

Background and training. The belief that extensive professional training is not a prerequisite for effective behavioral crisis intervention has led mental health professionals to function primarily as supervisors and consultants both to direct service workers, most often paraprofessionals, and to natural help givers in the community.

Adherents of the behavioral model perceive training in traditional diagnostic and therapeutic techniques as unnecessary, since successful crisis resolution requires the completion of specific tasks characteristic of the crisis stimulus and not tied to the personality of the individual. Not only does the model deemphasize personality as a critical variable in treatment, but it also argues that personality characteristics of the help giver are not critical to effective interaction. The literature does suggest that many crisis programs function on the assumption that to be an effective intervener all one needs is the desire to help (McGee, 1974).

Role. The therapist functions more as an educator-trainer than as a doctor-expert. The therapist perceives himself as a provider of information about what the person needs to do in order to cope with a difficult situation. The kind of relationship advocated between the therapist and the person in crisis, and its relative importance for intervention success, is not explored in the literature, except that it is noted that the relationship should facilitate the educational process. One might hypothesize that a good crisis intervener would need skills in quickly developing rapport, a knowledge of tasks related to specific crisis stimuli, and the ability to teach problem-solving skills. Since the literature does not provide any description of a program for training people to become practitioners within this model (except to say what the training does *not* consist of), our hypothesis about which skills are needed can be thought of as suggesting the kinds of training required.

8

Systems
Crisis
Intervention

The systems model of crisis intervention emphasizes the social context in which the individual and the crisis stimulus come together. It is based on two assumptions. First, an individual's perception of stressful events depends on the social context in which they occur. If this context is viewed as nonsupportive or if help is unavailable to the individual when the stressful event occurs, the individual is more likely to perceive it as a crisis.

Secondly, an individual's ability to successfully resolve crises is viewed as dependent on the availability of a supportive social context. Langsley and his colleagues (1968a) suggest that the social system within which the individual decompensates, reactivates an old conflict, or has to deal with a new crisis, has a major effect on the outcome. The social system may be the individual's family, work group, or another subgroup.

Systems adherents argue that the investigation of such individual variables as personality traits, coping ability, and problem-solving ability, as well as of such crisis stimulus variables as intensity, and duration, are in and of themselves insufficient to predict the outcome of a crisis. Systems therapists contend that both psychodynamic and problem-oriented approaches to crisis intervention do not give enough weight to the role of social context in successful problem resolution.

Systems adherents view the social system as the major factor in both the production of the crisis situation and in its resolution. Stanton and Schwartz's study (1954) exemplifies the system's role in both induction and resolution of crises. They observed both staff and patient behavior on the ward of a psychiatric hospital and found that staff conflicts were correlated with increases in patients' disturbed behavior. For example, when staff conflicts over coworker relationships and patient treatment goals remained unresolved, patients' disturbed behavior, including outbreaks of violence, increased. The occurrence of the disturbed behavior was of such proportion that a crisis was produced in the management of ward behavior. Further, when staff conflicts were resolved (taking the form of negotiated role definitions and mutually agreeable treatment plans), patients' behaviors returned to their precrisis level, including in several cases the disappearance of overt psychotic symptomatology. Thus disequilibrium in the social system (staff conflict) was found to be directly correlated to the production of a crisis situation; and the reequilibrium of the system (staff conflict resolution) was correlated to the resolution of the crisis in ward management.

In a similar vein, the symptoms of a family member are seen by adherents of this model as an expression of family conflict or disequilibrium (Ackerman, 1958; Bateson, et al., 1956; Boszormenyi-Nagi, 1962; Lidz & Fleck, 1960; Turner & Gross, 1976). Langsley and his colleagues (1968a) provide three related, but alternative, explanations of symptoms within the context of the family system. First, by being in a state of crisis, the individual may be acting as the spokesperson for the family's distress. Second, the individual may be in a crisis state in order to protect the family from further disorganization and conflict (scapegoating phenomena). Third, adequate individual functioning may be dependent on a minimal level of family stability; an individual's crisis state would indicate that this stability is lacking.

The systems model "maintains that there is a direct relationship between the individual state of mental health and the degree of conflict or equilibrium in the family" (Langlsey et al., 1968a, p. 10). While this model is directly applicable to the study of the family, it applies equally well to such other systems as institutions and work groups (Flomenhaft & Kaplan, 1968; Meyer, Jones, & Borgatta, 1956; Young, 1954; Cohen, Gross & Turner, 1976).

ASSUMPTIONS OF THE SYSTEMS MODEL

Basic assumptions of the systems model are grounded in systems theory and ecological research (Haley, 1971; Jackson, 1967).

1. The key variable is whether an effective support system is provided to the individual (or group) experiencing the crisis situation.

2. Interaction between the personality of the individual in crisis and the crisis stimulus occurs in a social context (Kalis, 1970).

3. Return of the individual to a homeostatic state may involve correcting ineffective or detrimental patterns of relating within his social system.

4. The focus of intervention should be on changing those current patterns of interaction that are maintaining the crisis.

5. Assessment of etiology is not relevant to crisis resolution.

6. Insight and awareness are not causal in producing change in current patterns of interaction.

GOALS

The systems model shares the minimum goal of all crisis intervention approaches; that is, of returning the individual to a level of functioning equal to that existing prior to the crisis. Thus symptom alleviation can be viewed as one criterion of success. However, a greater goal of systems intervention is to provide individuals within the system with a means for dealing more effectively with future crisis situations. Systems intervention focuses on developing patterns of interaction within the system that provide more mutual support and decrease the need for further outside intervention. Thus the major goal of systems crisis intervention can be defined as developing a supportive social context so that future stressful events can be handled more effectively.

ASSESSMENT METHODS

Traditional assessment and diagnostic techniques are played down by adherents of the systems model. This is in large part because, rather than seeing the difficulty as either individual (individual model) or environmental (generic model), the crisis is viewed as a problem in the relationships of individuals within their social system. Assessment aims at clarifying the current transactional patterns which have produced or are actively maintaining the crisis state in the individual or group (Weakland et al., 1974). This assessment is primarily made through clinical evaluation by the intervener rather than through the use of assessment instruments like symptom checklists. Furthermore, such an assessment most often occurs in the context of treatment and does not constitute a separate stage of intervention.

One assessment tool of the systems model is the Genogram developed by Guerin and Pendagast (1976). A Genogram is used to show the relationships between, and the positions of, all family members. It acts as a "roadmap" of the family relationship system. It uses a diagram to pictorially record names and ages of family members; dates of marriages, deaths, divorces, and births; physical locations of family members; frequency and types of contacts; emotional cutoffs; toxic issues; nodal events; and which relationships are open and which are closed. This initial evaluation allows important information concerning membership and boundaries of the system, and its surrounding emotional processes, to be learned right away. After this evaluation, the therapist is prepared to present to the family what he has learned about it. He can then start to chart a general course of action for therapy.

Another assessment approach is the Family Choreography developed by Papp (1976). Family members are asked to dramatically demonstrate the way they experience the problem. The intention of this technique is to transcend the barrier of language games and to allow the underlying emotional tracks of the family to emerge. In order to elicit systematic pictures from the family members, the therapist asks systematic questions which are aimed at illuminating the family's transactional patterns (e.g., alliances, triangles, shifting emotional currents). The identification of the processes of the family system during evaluation sets the stage for the development of therapy goals, which include the ways in which the family system should and could be realigned.

TREATMENT

Treatment generally consists of conjoint meetings with the individual in crisis and the members of the social system. Intervention aims to assist the group in renegotiating current patterns of interaction on the assumption that it is precisely these patterns which are impeding crisis resolution. Based on this assumption, historical data per se are seen as irrelevant to the main focus of changing current relationship patterns. Likewise, this focus suggests that insight and understanding of cause are not of major interest. Indeed, the gaining of (intrapsychic) insight is not considered necessary for change by advocates of this model.

As in systems family therapy, the systems crisis intervener aims to gain control of the system in order to impose change in interaction patterns which serve to maintain the crisis. Common techniques include relabeling the symptom, prescribing symptoms, and using paradoxical instructions (see Chapter 11 for further details). One intervention technique often used during the initial session(s) is to redefine the crisis as an interpersonal rather than an individual problem. This serves as a specific example of relabeling, and as a basic example of changing the ongoing system.

Turner and Gross (1976) argue that couples need to learn a problem-solving process that will allow them to monitor and modify their rules of interaction. To accomplish this, they teach family members a six-stage problem-solving process. First they focus on members' feelings about themselves and others in regard to specific behaviors. For example, Turner and Gross would encourage a depressed, suicidal individual to share his feelings about himself and his spouse when the latter says, "You can't expect much from him; he's always been sickly." They argue that the first step in change is to recognize what you are feeling about yourself and others so that you have an option in terms of how to behave rather than thinking that you do things without choosing to. Although there are similarities between Turner and Gross's problem-solving model and such techniques as relabeling, the role of the therapist is quite different in the former, in which the therapist must be able to recognize his own feelings about himself and his clients, while in the latter, the role of the therapist's feelings is minor. A more detailed discussion of the role of the therapist will be presented in the family therapy section and later this chapter.

THERAPISTS

Background and training.   Systems crisis intervention requires a high level of training, though this need not necessarily involve a traditional academic background. At the same time that systems adherents, like advocates of the psychodynamic models, consider training essential to effective crisis intervention, they differ in their view of what constitutes such training. Traditional training in individual assessment and therapy techniques is seen as irrelevant to systems intervention. Rather, training focuses on assessment of transactional patterns and development of effective methods (e.g., paradoxical intention, role reversal) for enacting change in such patterns. For these reasons, crisis interveners using the systems model are generally professionals and paraprofessinals from mental health and related fields.

The focus on nontraditional training content has led to minimal use of formal academic settings as training sites (Stanton, 1975). Training most frequently occurs on site and at such special training centers as the Behavior Research Institute (Weakland et al., 1974). It generally consists of direct observation of interventions by trainers and immediate feedback to the trainee. Videotape is commonly used as a feedback mechanism. The high level of training advocated, with its need for intensive supervision, has led to minimal use of volunteers as crisis interveners within this model.

Role. The role of the intervener is an active one, focusing on the manipulation and prescription of changes in interaction patterns. Essentially the intervener attempts to gain control of the system in order to impose change in patterns that are maintaining the crisis.

Turner and Gross (1976), for example, perceive the therapist's role as active, directive, and involving extensive disclosure about how the therapist feels about himself and specific family members in regard to their interaction. For instance, a family may come to a crisis unit with their daughter who has made six suicidal attempts and report that they are willing to do anything, but don't know what to do. If the therapist can focus on how helpless he feels when he sees the husband dismiss the wife's suggestions, the wife dismiss the husband's ideas, both dismissing the daughter, and everyone telling the therapist yes, but . . . and if the therapist can stress how angry he gets at each individual—in fact, so angry and frustrated that he would like to swallow a bunch of pills and then have them have to take care of him, vomit and all—then he can help the family members recognize what they are feeling—dismissed, unimportant, and angry—and he can then begin to focus on what changes they need to make. The therapist must be able to recognize feelings such as helplessness and anger and also must be able to use his feelings as a guide to diagnosis and intervention (a more detailed description will be presented in the family therapy section). This approach, termed the affective rule-altering model, differs from other system models in its focus on affect.

SETTING

Systems crisis intervention is most typically located in mental health facilities that offer twenty four-hour service and do not require appointments or maintain waiting lists. Such settings frequently include special units of community mental health centers and admitting offices of psychiatric hospitals. Home visits are more common after the initial contact (Langsley, et al., 1968a).

CONSUMER

Like followers of other crisis approaches, adherents of the systems approach perceive their model as appropriate for both maturational and environmental crises. In practice and in theory, there is no crisis for which the systems approach is not presumed to be a viable treatment modality. The one exception may be the true social isolate or recluse, for whom social system involvement is impractical. The major difference for consumers between the systems approach and models that are psychoanalytically- or behaviorally-oriented is that the systems therapist is more likely to desire the involvement of members of the social network in the treatment process.

9

Psychoanalytic Model of Family Therapy

Psychoanalytic family therapy is based on psychoanalytic principles, which are applied to family development and functioning.

Psychoanalysis, in particular, despite a period during which innate causes of libidinal fixation were emphasized, has directed attention to maternal nurturant behavior, the parental attitudes toward feeding, bowel training, and childhood sexuality, sibling rivalries, and internalization of parental attributes of ego and superego formation, etc., and Freud's discovery of the oedipal configuration opened the way for study of the family dynamics. (Lidz, 1963, p. 7)

Perhaps the first, and most historically significant, departure from the individually-oriented psychoanalytic ideology can be credited to Nathan Ackerman, whose 1937 paper, "The family as a social and emotional unit," focused on the interrelatedness of the family in the form of intimate networks among and between members. According to writers such as Guerin (1976), Ackerman's ideas, with their emphasis on family functioning, were not acceptable to practitioners of psychiatry until many years later. By the 1960s family therapy had become an acceptable though by no means welcomed (Guerin, 1976) mode of treatment, and until the late 1960s family therapy studies predominantly reflected the psychoanalytic viewpoint (Zuk & Rubenstein, 1965). As late as 1967, in an overview of the family therapy field, Zuk was able to conclude: "for the most part writers on technique have essentially adhered to the view that to promote beneficial change in patients the therapist must formulate and communicate insights and work through unconscious resistances" (1967, p. 71). Psychoanalytic family therapy functions within the traditional rules of individual psychoanalysis; for example, it safeguards the privacy of the doctor/patient relationship and prevents any intrusion into the process of transference. The controversial issue of transference can serve as a differentiating variable for two popular forms of psychoanalytic family therapy (see the section on treatment).

Despite various theoretical differences, psychoanalytic family therapists appear to have reached consensus in defining a family in developmental terms. To account for the communication style the family may adapt to express emotionality, Titchner (1967) proposes a phase of ego development that can be delineated according to Erickson's series of epigenetic crises. Titchner defines the capacity of a child to respond to at least two others simultaneously in a triadic communication system as the beginning of the family experience for a child (Titchner & Golden, 1963). Prior to the acquisition of this triadic ability, the child experiences an essentially dyadic level corresponding to the first stage of Erikson's framework, "basic trust versus basic mistrust." In such families, Titchner contends that the children will lack the ability to deal with ambivalence and change. Treatment would focus on helping "individuals overcome fundamental jealousies and rivalries from which the basic insecurity of each family member emerges" (Titchner, 1967, p. 101). This is the most individually-oriented of the family therapy approaches, according to Titchner, as the family has not yet reached the triadic level at which genuine family interaction is present.

The next three stages of family organization are parallel to Erikson's individual stages of development and focus on the issues of autonomy versus shame and doubt, initiative versus inferiority, and identity versus identity diffusion. According to Titchner, the second stage, autonomy versus shame and doubt, is the primary stage at which families bring in offspring for psychiatric help. Goals and methods of treatment for this and the two succeeding phases of family functioning would differ according to the basic conflict involved. While Titchner does not elaborate further on the process of choosing appropriate goals and methods, he implies that they follow deductively from an analysis of the family's developmental stage.

There is some confusion in the psychoanalytic family therapy literature regarding the dyadic-triadic levels of family interaction. While Titchner posits dyadic interaction as a process of the earliest stage of family functioning which should be superceded by triadic functioning, most writing in the psychoanalytic family tradition focuses on dyadic relationships (Boszormenyi-Nagy, 1967).[1] This suggests three possibilities, first, that treatment focuses on this initial stage; or second, that dyadic interaction is a factor in family functioning throughout the family's development. This issue of what the primary unit of focus ought to be is not addressed in the literature and appears to reflect a difference of opinion in the psychoanalytic field. A third explanation may be inferred from the psychoanalytic model's focus on the dyadic unit. For example, Titchner's (1967) notion of family developmental stages may be construed as dyadic functioning; a conflict-free marital relationship (one dyad) appears to be a prerequisite to a successful resolution of psychosocial attitudes related to the child's libidinal and maturational processes. This approach suggests that the child's sex and role identification (second dyad) are with one parent, not both. Helm Stierlin (1959) is explicit on this issue, conceptualizing family disturbances as "transactional modes" (dyadic) occurring throughout the individuation and separation process. His model emphasizes the parent-child relationship from a multigenerational perspective, the assumption being that either or both parents may psychologically exploit the offspring in their attempt to resolve their own parent-child conflicts. Transactional modes are classified as follows: (1) binder-bindee, or "id-binding" of the child if it occurs on the dependency level, and "ego-binding" if the child's cognitive level is involved; (2) the delegator-delegate mode, which involves the parent's unrealized "ego-ideals" and their imposition on the child's development, (3) the expeller-expellee, representing premature parent-child separation (Stierlin, 1971, 1972, 1974, 1977). Treatment would focus on one or more bonds (dyads), with a heavy emphasis on the parents' relationship with the family of origin.

Lidz (1963) noted that although psychoanalytic theory has emphasized the parent-child relationship, in practice analytically-oriented psychotherapists have focused on the marital relationship. Lidz contends that the basic dynamic framework of the family depends upon the marital pair's "ability to form a coalition, maintain boundaries between the generations, and adhere to their appropriate sex-linked roles" (Lidz, 1963, p. 9).

Thus Titchner, Stierlin, and Lidz all emphasize two points: that (a) dyadic functioning is implicitly or explicitly expressed in psychoanalytic theory, and (b) psychoanalytic family therapists share a definition of mature family functioning in which differentiation of members parallels intrapsychic differentiation. Failure of the family system to deal with individuation and eventual separation may be equated to the individually-oriented psychoanalytic concept of fixation. From this perspective, the basic assumptions and general modus operandi that constitute the psychoanalytic family therapy approach will become more meaningful.

ASSUMPTIONS AND GOALS OF PSYCHOANALYTIC FAMILY THERAPY

The same assumptions Freud made regarding the conflict between an individual's inner needs and the demands of the external environment form the base on which the psychoanalytic family therapy paradigm rests. Assumptions about change and the kinds of therapeutic activities which produce it (e.g., interpretation, transference) remained virtually intact when the concept of family dysfunction superceded the notion of individual pathological symptomatology. For example, marital dysfunction is assumed to be the result of unconscious needs transferred from the family of origin to the marital relationship. The underlying assumption is that one or both partners may be fixated and that the activities of the psychosexual stage involved are being manifested in the relationship. Further, various kinds of family dysfunction can be identified based on the developmental stage, involving types of bonds and rivalries, at which the family is functioning. What this assumption implies is that certain members of the family exploit others in order to satisfy their unconscious needs, usually in a dyadic configuration. Third, family dysfunction involves the mutual interaction of attempts to fill unconscious needs by two or more family members. In other words, a vicious circle is established. In an effort to satisfy these needs, all the members become bound to the forced reality that the parents originally created and in which the offspring's psychosexual stages must be traversed and interpreted.

The fourth assumption of psychoanalytic family therapy is that treatment must focus on making family members aware of the dysfunctional interaction patterns of the family and their antecedent causes. That is to say, each family member must achieve consistency of id, ego, and superego in the process of family living. From this premise one can conclude that symptom alleviation is not a sufficient criterion for success in psychoanalytic family therapy. Friedman and his colleagues (1965) note that understanding and support are often adequate to relieve immediate, acute family stress, but that this is not a sufficient level of change to be considered therapeutic success. Rather, more significant and basic change in family image and patterns is to be achieved through intensive (in-depth) processes of working through and restructuring of the family system. Insight is a necessary condition for such change and must be followed by the working through of conflictual areas to achieve mature family patterns that encourage individualization. (Despite Bowen's (1966) contention that his model can be best classified as a systems approach, the authors perceive his model as functionally closer to the psychoanalytic model of family therapy with emphasis on individuation and the need to work through earlier conflicts with members of one's family of origin.) Mature family patterns are defined as those motivated by current stimuli rather than by unconscious needs from members' families of origin.

This notion parallels that of personality change in individual therapy. However, its components are tied neither to specific overt behavior changes nor to specific observable behavioral patterns. Since the family is not in a position to evaluate the presence or absence of unconscious material, the assessment of whether therapy has been successful remains a matter of subjective assessment by the therapist. The lack of an objectively specified outcome criterion suggests the possibility of wide variation among practitioners in determining treatment outcome.

ASSESSMENT METHODS

Assessment in psychoanalytic family therapy focuses on collecting current and historical data regarding both the individual personalities of family members and the functioning of the family as a group. Titchner (1966) emphasizes the importance of initially making individual diagnostic evaluations of marital couples. These evaluations focus on each spouse's configuration of relations with his or her family of origin. According to Titchner, these pictures of the couple's respective families of origin are essential to the therapeutic process because patterns congruent with these configurations are embedded in the current marital interaction (p. 325).

Ackerman (1958) sanctions both an individually-oriented and a family-interaction focus in assessment. Evaluation of the individual is similar to a traditional, analytically-oriented diagnostic assessment. The family member designated as the primary patient is seen by the psychoanalytic family therapist for initial exploratory interviews and to take his history. This process is supplemented by taking a history from other family members. This is frequently done by other members of the clinical team. Ackerman does not specify the major variables around which this assessment process is to focus. While this process parallels the assessment procedure used in individual treatment, Ackerman emphasizes the need to interrelate these histories and clarify discrepancies in order to obtain a family diagnostic picture.

The second focus indicated by Ackerman is the direct observation of family interaction. He contends that observation of the family should occur both in the context of office interviews and through the use of an extended home visit. Again, Ackerman does not specify the variables to be considered in this procedure, but suggests that the therapist can gain valuable clinical information regarding both individual personalities of family members and their patterns of interaction.

Like Ackerman, Titchner does not specify the major variables to be assessed, but both argue that diagnosis in psychoanalytic family therapy combines traditional clinical assessment of current and historical data regarding individual personalities with a composite picture of past and present family functioning.

TREATMENT

Wide differences exist among psychoanalytic family therapists in the composition of the therapeutic group. Therapy varies from conjoint family sessions in which all family members are seen together at the same time by the same therapist (Titchner, 1967; Wynne, 1971), to individual therapy with the identified patient, in which family members are seen occasionally to encourage their assistance and to urge them not to interfere with the patient's progress (Balint, 1966). Balint suggests that conjoint therapy has an advantage over other methods in that insights gained in the session can be tested immediately since other family members are present. Thus he suggests the possibility of immediate change in family interaction patterns.

Between the two extreme types of family therapy lies a large middle ground which encompasses such modes as collaborative family therapy, simultaneous individual therapy with the same therapist, and mixed membership therapy. In collaborative family therapy, all family members may be seen together for diagnostic purposes, and later assigned on an individual need basis to different therapists who share information about treatment progress and goal planning. In simultaneous individual therapy with the same therapist, the family is not seen as a unit. Instead the therapist works with each member separately, and by viewing the parts of the whole, pieces together a picture of the family from which treatment goals are developed. In mixed membership therapy, the composition of the treatment group fluctuates based on the therapist's evaluation of need. Therapy sessions include individual treatment with one or more members of the family, meetings of various family subgroups on a conjoint basis, and conjoint family sessions.

All of these methods are viewed as family therapy vehicles within the psychoanalytic framework. As mentioned previously, psychoanalytic family writers do not specify the conditions under which one method is more appropriate than another. In most cases, selection of a specific method of psychoanalytic treatment appears to reflect the biases and preferences of the therapist involved as well as an attempt to utilize and observe the process of transference either between individual members of the family and the therapist and/or between family members.

Treatment appears to progress through a number of phases. The initial phase is the assessment, which Kaffman (1963) indicates may include about four sessions, and encompasses the gathering of data as previously described. Next the therapist's goal is to clarify the communication system among family members. Kaffman describes this as a period in which the family presents initial resistances designed both a) to exclude the therapist from the family process, and b) to block the awareness of treatment and emotional participation in it, by one or more family members. Through the use of questions and interpretations, the therapist aims to break down the family members' initial distortions of the treatment process in order to bring hidden communication channels to the surface. Essentially this appears to be a continuation of the initial assessment phase, with the addition of the therapist's tentative speculations and interpretations of the family's ongoing functions and their antecedent causes. These processes of breaking down initial distortions, bringing unconscious material to the surface through interpretation, and working through resistances suggest that psychoanalytic family therapists share the basic assumptions of traditional psychoanalysts as to what constitutes the conditions necessary and sufficient to produce behavior change.

The therapist makes consistent interpretation of current interactional patterns in light of their historical significance. The aim of these interpretations and their subsequent working through for the family system is defined by Titchner (1966) as an increasing neutralization of pathological patterns of relating, and by Stierlin (1977) as "unbinding." This working through is accomplished by bringing from the unconscious to the conscious level aggressive and libidinous needs of family members which have been carried over from their families of origin. As these needs are articulated, the family members become able to consciously monitor them, and they thereby lose their controlling and pathological characteristics. By this defnition, a mature/healthy family functions such that its interactions are predicated on current stimuli, rather than on unfulfilled past needs. It is assumed that a considerable period of therapy will be necessary to overcome individual and interactional defenses to the therapist's interpretations. Thus the therapeutic process is described as taking a year or more.

ROLE OF THERAPIST

The role of the psychoanalytic family therapist is described by Mitchell (1961) as that of a social parent able to introduce order, aid in establishing improved communication patterns, and reduce feelings of helplessness. Since the family members are unconscious of the pathological patterns to be changed, the therapist ultimately defines (diagnoses) the underlying problem and therapy goals, and implements the treatment plan. Thus the therapist functions primarily in the role of doctor-expert, viewing himself, rather than the family, as the judge of treatment progress.

Friedman and his colleagues (1965) note that a major therapeutic factor is the awareness of the therapist of his own patterns of interaction based on his family background. In fact, since psychoanalysts are required to undergo psychoanalysis as part of their training, it has been recommended that aspiring psychoanalytic family therapists undergo family treatment (Boszormenyi-Nagy, 1966).

Many psychoanalytically-oriented writers in the family field urge the use of two therapists (Whitaker, Malone, & Warkentin, 1956); Loeffler & Weinstein, 1954; Mintz, 1963), and usually specify a heterosexual cotherapy team in family treatment (Demarest & Leider, 1954; Sonne & Lincoln, 1965, 1966; Markowitz & Kadis, 1968). Carl Whitaker has written of the need for two therapists (1966) as follows: "The psychiatrist who elects to treat the psychopath or the family by himself is either heroic or foolish. I see no excuse for such heroics" (p.398).

Markowitz and Kadis (1968) describe the role of the heterosexual cotherapy team as a screen on which family members project intrapsychic mechanisms. The team members function as parental prototypes, providing the opportunity for perceptual change and movement toward maturation among family members. Markowitz and Kadis's description of the cotherapy relationship suggests the notion of the therapist a blank screen used in individual psychoanalysis. However some significant differences exist between the two. First, the cotherapists in the family session are significantly more active than the term "blank screen" would suggest. Secondly, it appears that the cotherapists are engaged in modeling a heterosexual relationship in which processes of mutual support and effective decision making can be demonstrated.

Sonne and Lincoln (1966) not only emphasize the therapists' mutual need for protection from the pathological family system, for mutual validation, for giving clear reinforcement of gender identification, and for maintaining unity in a healthy marriage; they also stress that cotherapists can provide a model of a healthy marriage to all the family members. In using this heterosexual team approach, psychoanalytic family therapists accentuate the traditional social roles associated with gender. For example, Sonne and Lincoln report that in the early phases of treatment it is important "for the female cotherapist to support the male therapist's aggressiveness," and in the latter stages, ' 'for the male therapist to particularly support the female therapist's femininity" (p.200). This would suggest that the psychoanalytic family therapy paradigm assumes that social roles or temperaments are sex-specific and that mature family functioning must reflect these social roles. Lidz (1963) believes that the family's major function is to enculturate new members, that is children, by providing each child with a source of stability by specifying his status, incentives, and roles both within the family and in the larger social system.

SETTING

The setting facilitates and reinforces the family's perception of the therapist(s) in the role of doctor-expert, for it tends to be within a traditional mental health environment, such as a hospital. An exception is reported by Friedman and his colleagues (1965), who suggest home treatment as the most effective intervention plan for families with a schizophrenic member.

CONSUMERS

The suitability of a family for psychoanalytic family therapy is suggested by Wynne (1971), who reports that conjoint family therapy is indicated "for the clarification and resolution of any structural intrafamilial relationship difficulty" (p. 97). He further indicates that the assessment of existing reciprocal interactional difficulties of a family system is accomplished primarily through the unfolding of family patterns in conjoint treatment sessions. By suggesting that the assessment of the family's suitability for psychoanalytic family therapy be made after the members are engaged in such treatment, Wynne is arguing in a somewhat circular fashion and implying that psychoanalytic family therapists lack clear boundaries as to where their approach is and is not effective, and that at least one session is needed to determine by some unspecified process which families and problems are appropriate for psychoanalytic family therapy.

Grunebaum, Christ, and Neiberg (1969) suggest that couples should be seen conjointly when both are committed to the marriage and the presenting problems seems acute, ego alien, and mostly marriage-related. The couple should be seen separately by the same therapist when the couple is committed to the marriage, able to communicate with each other, and problems exist both inside and outside the marriage. Couples should be seen separately by different therapists when they are not committed to working on their marriage, or when marital problems seem to be secondary to immaturity or severe pathology.

Kaffman (1963) reports four signs contraindicating short-term analytically-oriented family therapy: 1) long-standing psychosis, 2) sociopathic personality or a need for institutional care, 3) established neurological damage and/or mental deficiency as the established clinical problem, and 4) chronic severe psychopathology in which symptoms are highly structured and have been present and unchanged for several years. Significantly, these four signs parallel contraindications generally invoked for both individual and group treatment within an analytic framework. Thus Kaffman seems to suggest that neuroses and situational disorders, symptom clusters within the bailiwick of traditional analytic treatment, also are appropriate for family therapy. The issue of what kinds of symptom patterns are amenable to psychoanalytic treatment remains open to investigation. At present, relevant empirical data have not been reported in the literature.

There appears to be considerable variability among psychoanalytic family therapists in defining when family therapy is the treatment of choice. Specifically Grunebaum and his colleagues (1969) suggest that conjoint family therapy is the preferred treatment mode only when individual symptomatology is minimal and the major complaint is marital discord. In contrast, Kaffman (1963) suggests that psychoanalytic family therapy is appropriate when the presenting problem involves neurotic or situational disturbances of an individual family member. Wynne (1971), on the other hand, reports that psychoanalytic family therapy is appropriate whenever the presenting problem appears to involve ineffective or destructive interactions among family members. There appears to be no generally agreed upon criterion for selecting family therapy as the treatment of choice within the psychoanalytic model. Selection criteria remain subjective and therefore permit wide variability among practitioners in selection procedures.

As mentioned at the outset, it appears to the authors that there are some methodological and theoretical constraints that restrict the effectiveness and suitability of psychoanalytic family therapy for certain populations. First, as Cohen (1974) suggests (and as we suggested in an earlier chapter), clients from the lower socioeconomic class are oriented more toward action than reflection, and have a different verbal style from middle- and upper-class clients. These differences seem to limit the utility of the psychoanalytic model for lower-class families.

Second, practitioners within the model tend to provide services in private clinics or individual practices. Further, since therapy extends over a relatively long period of time, its cost is generally high and therefore limited to middle- and upper-class families. Finally, the psychoanalytic approach's emphasis on traditional social roles associated with gender suggests that it may not be suitable for nontraditional families.

SUMMARY

The psychoanalytic model of family therapy appears to be largely an extension of traditional, individually-oriented psychoanalytic theories and procedures to include interpersonal dynamics. Thus current family dyfunction is viewed as a result of unconscious needs carried over from each spouse's experiences in his or her family of origin. Clinical assessment therefore focuses on a) individual personalities and their historical significance and b) the current interactional patterns of the family. Treatment is considered in-depth therapy on the surface-depth continuum and aims to have family members achieve insight into formerly unconscious processes.

The therapist functions within a doctor-expert role, interpreting resistances and attempting to break down pathological defenses. Therapists within the psychoanalytic family model are primarily middle-class psychiatrists who have had extensive training in psychoanalytic theory and practice.

Treatment is limited primarily to the diagnostic category of the neuroses, although the model has been used with schizophrenic families (Friedman, et al., 1965). Successful therapeutic intervention is viewed as an in-depth, long-term process, with the reorganization of family functioning at a higher developmental level as its goal.

Notes

1. Use of the term "dyadic relationship" is not meant to imply an exclusive focus on the marital relationship. Boszormenyi-Nagy (1967) discusses dyadic relationships in terms of "the relating self and the other to whom the self is related" (p. 58), and applies this definition to the interaction of any two family members.

10

Behavioral Model
of Family
Therapy

The behavioral model of family therapy applies behavioral principles to family systems. The basic tenets of the behavioral approach were not developed specifically in relation to family and marital problems, but are assumed to be directly applicable to them.

Behavior modification is a process for dealing with the socially relevant problems of human beings. Several assumptions underlie this process, the most definitive one being that deviant behavior is subject to the same laws governing all human behavior; therefore, the procedures useful in changing any behavior can be applied to modifying deviant behavior.

The primary datum of behavior modification is observable and objectively defined behavior in relation to the environment. More specifically, behavior is affected by events that precede it and follow it, and, therefore, cannot be meaningfully considered in isolation from these events; the most important of these antecedent and consequent stimuli affecting any person's behavior are the behaviors of other people (LeBow, 1972, p. 347).

Since antecedents, consequents, and environmental factors are considered the critical determinants of behavior, behavioral intervention focuses on producing change in current interpersonal patterns of behavior. Thus the behavioral model differs significantly from the psychoanalytic model on two theoretical dimensions. First, unlike the psychoanalytic model, the behavioral model minimizes the importance of historical data (e.g., childhood experience, relationships to family of origin) and stresses the importance of current patterns of behavior. Second, the behavioral model emphasizes producing change in behavioral sequences and minimizes the need for "deep" client insight and a dynamic understanding of these sequences or their antecedent causes. However, the role of insight and understanding has become more and more important as behavioral practitioners have increasingly taken into account concepts about the individual that, earlier, were considered unimportant. For example, the cognitive-affective components of attitudes, motivations, interactive person perception, and the like, now are seen as directly affecting the facilitation and permanence of behavior changes (Greene, 1970; Rotter and Tinkleman, 1970; Lazarus, 1970, 1971). Lazarus (1958) appears to be one of the most outspoken among behavioral therapists in terms of recognizing the limitations imposed by a strict adherence to the operant paradigm: "Where necessary, the behaviorist or objective psychotherapist employs all the usual psychotherapeutic techniques, such as support, guidance, insight, catharsis, interpretation, environmental manipulation, etc., but in addition . . . the behavior therapist applies objective techniques which are designed to inhibit specific neurotic patterns." This paradigm shift is threatening the uniqueness claimed by proponents of behavior therapy, and shrinking the gap between the behavioral approach and other therapeutic orientations to family therapy.

The behavioral model views the family as a system of interlocking reciprocal behaviors. Therapy is based on the premise that the people in a position to most affect an individual's behavior are members of his family. The goal of behavioral family therapy is to change the family's usual provision of consequences of behavior or contingencies of reinforcement (Liberman, 1970). The behavioral approach to families primarily has been within an operant conditioning rather than a classical conditioning paradigm and has focused on changing dyadic patterns in the family system. While more than two family members may be engaged in conjoint family treatment, the behavioral literature suggests that the behavioral family therapist most often aims to manipulate the interlocking behavior patterns of family members in dyadic units (parent-child, spouse-spouse). Thus behavioral family therapy appears to focus either on producing change in one dyad or in a number of dyads concurrently. This dyadic focus is one of the major functions that distinguishes the behavioral from the systems approach.

The behavioral therapist focuses on four major aspects of the dyadic structure: (1) status (power), (2) roles (expected behavior), (3) norms (accepted and expected behaviors), and (4) communication patterns (how, when, and to whom two people communicate). Based on information derived from an analysis of these components, the therapist plans a course of treatment that may differ from dyad to dyad. The type and degree of contingencies of reinforcement may vary depending on whether the dyadic unit is the marital pair, parent-child, or siblings. A major factor that probably accounts for the behaviorists' emphasis on dyadic units is that the therapist's ability to control and manipulate the environment decreases dramatically once he is dealing with units larger than a dyad (Kanfer & Saslow, 1969; Madsen & Madsen, 1972; Patterson & Reid, 1970; Reid & Hendriks, 1973; Lederer & Jackson, 1968; Patterson, 1976). Since the bulk of experimental data deals with behaviors between two individuals, therapists are at a disadvantage in formulating acceptable criteria to determine manipulation, control, and quantifiable data collection beyond the optimal family group size of two or at most three (Mitchell, 1963).

The focus on dyadic units is disputed by some behaviorists. Liberman (1970) states that "the behavioral approach does not simplistically reduce the family system and family interaction to individualistic or dyadic mechanisms or reinforcement" (p. 116). As an example, Liberman reports on an eruption of fighting between parents as changes in child-parent dyads occurred. Liberman does not present this case example in enough detail to clarify the treatment process used or for the reader to be able to determine whether a dyadic or broader focus was employed. While some adherents of the behavioral model may employ a broader (triadic) focus, the typical unit of treatment within the behavioral model does appear to be dyadic. (For a recent review of behavioral marital therapy see Jacobson & Martin, 1976).

Previously, when behavior therapy was applied to the family, it focused on the child as the unit whose behavior was targeted for change, thereby limiting the family's involvement to providing a context in which subsequent modification of the child's behavior would be facilitated, as the term "parent training" implies.

Recently, however, the definition of the "client" and the focus of treatment has shifted away from a particular family member exhibiting a problem behavior and toward the whole family, which is conceptualized as a social unit of interlocking behaviors. This shift in therapeutic focus has necessitated the development of additional therapeutic techniques. Reward systems have been supplemented by formal contracts for regulating the exchange of rewards (DeRisi & Butz, 1975). Implementation of social-ecological engineering and strategies of self-control have become part of the therapist's repertoire (Feallock & Miller, 1976), suggesting that the typical conditioning and learning principles that developed in the laboratory have proved insufficient for managing a complex family system involving reciprocal influences. Along with a decreased emphasis on models designed for a unit of one, great stress is placed on techniques developed for dyadic units within the family system. Consequently, four family sub-units have been singled out in therapeutic processes, taking into account the children's influence on the parents: (1) the marital pair, (2) the parent-child pair, (3) the sibling pair, and (4) the relationship of parents to their parents.

ASSUMPTIONS

Regardless of a behavioral family therapist's orientation toward the inclusion of cognitive and affective variables in treatment, most behavioral therapists share four basic assumptions:

1. Behavior, including deviant behavior, is a function of its consequences and antecedents.
2. Behavior can be changed by manipulating its antecedent and consequent stimuli, particularly the behavior of other family members.

3. The family provides a major portion of the reinforcement available to an individual and is in a position to modify environmental contingencies.

4. Interactive behavior among family members is interlocking, so that a change in the behavior of one member of a dyad affects a change in the behavioral contingencies experienced by the other, thereby changing his behavior as well.

In addition, Stuart (1969) defines three assumptions underlying the operant approach to marital therapy. First, the pattern of interaction between the spouses at any point in time is the most rewarding of all available alternatives between them. By this he means that interaction between the members of this dyad is never accidental and represents the best possible balance between individual and mutual rewards and costs (Thibaut & Kelley, 1959). Stuart does not seem to be implying that a marital relationship is by definition the most rewarding relationship available to each spouse, nor does he specify the limitations or qualifiers of the interaction between the two that defines its reward properties. He does seem to be suggesting that at any given point in time the relationship between a marital pair is as rewarding as it can be considering the effects of all relevant variables. Thus Stuart would define a "discordant relationship" (unhappy marriage) as one in which one or both spouses perceived the individual costs required to maintain the current marital interaction to exceed mutual rewards. It follows that the goal of therapy would be to reverse the relationship of these contingencies.

Stuart's second assumption is that there is an expectation of reciprocity between marital partners. Essentially reciprocity implies that each spouse is expected to dispense social reinforcement at an equitable rate (Patterson & Reid, 1970). This would appear to be analogous to the quid pro quo, or "something for something," agreement in marriage described by Jackson (1965). A number of empirical studies (Bachrach, Candland, & Gibson, 1961; Brewer & Brewer, 1968; Komorita, Sheposh, & Braver, 1968; Stuart, 1969) point to the development of reciprocity as a consequence of a history of positive reinforcement. In disordered marriages, each partner is found to reinforce the other at a low rate, and therefore is relatively unreinforced by the other. "Reciprocity counseling," a therapeutic approach designed to increase mutual reinforcement, is reported by Azrin, Naster & Jones (1973), and reviewed by Jacobson & Martin (1976).

The third assumption Stuart (1969) discusses is that modification of marital interaction requires the development of the power of each partner to mediate rewards for the other. Stuart differentiates successful from unsuccessful marriages on the basis of reinforcement strategy. In successful marriages, the level of mutual rewards is high, while individual costs are low. "Each partner controls sufficient rewards to compensate the other for rewards expected and received from him" (p. 676). In unsuccessful marriages, positive reinforcement is replaced by negative reinforcement (cessation of an aversive (noxious) stimulus following the expected response). Operant marital therapy aims to increase the frequency and intensity of mutual positive reinforcement. Janis and Gilmore (1965) report that the effect of positive reinforcement is an increase in positively "biased scanning," or in searching for assets rather than liabilities in the spouse. It is assumed that "positive scanning will replace negatively biased attitudes, making positive responding more likely. Positive responses, in turn, are intended to augment the range and importance of social reinforcement mediated by each spouse for the other, leading to reestablishment of successful interaction patterns" (Stuart, 1969, p. 676).

While the assumptions put forth by Stuart and other behaviorists focus on interaction between spouses, they are assumed to be applicable to family and parent-child interaction as well, even though, as in the psychoanalytic approach, the major focus is on dyadic interaction, with the strongest emphasis on the marital pair.

Assumptions about marital interaction vary among behavioral researchers. For example, Weiss, Hops, and Patterson (1973) define three basic categories of dyadic functioning: the exchange of affectional behaviors, problem-solving activities, and attempts to change the behavior of the other. Of these they assume the last to be the primary cause of marital discord. Specifically, spouses are assumed to try to increase or decrease behaviors in their partners primarily through the use of aversive techniques such as nagging and threatening. It is assumed that over time these techniques are strengthened through a simple negative reinforcement paradigm:

> Sharon nags Bill. Bill learns that doing what Sharon wants terminates her nagging. At the same time Sharon learns that nagging is an "effective" behavior-change technique, and is more likely to use it again.

It is not clear whether Weiss and his colleagues intended three orthogonal categories of dyadic functioning. What does seem certain, however, is that emphasis on *behavior-change attempts* indicates an emphasis on treating "process" rather than outcome. Examination of Weiss's treatment process supports this notion in its primary emphasis on teaching couples more effective communication skills. Weiss and his colleagues suggest that a couple's success in learning communication skills is a prerequisite for (predictor of) success in behavior change.

Azrin, Naster, and Jones (1973) share Stuart's (1969) assumption that marital happiness reflects the situation in which reinforcement within the marriage exceeds reinforcement received from other sources. Azrin and his colleagues, however, go on to indicate the following areas of potential marital discord.

1. Receiving too little reinforcement from the marriage.
2. Too few needs are given marital reinforcement.

3. Marital reinforcement no longer provides satisfaction.

4. New behaviors are not reinforced.

5. One spouse gives more reinforcement than (s)he receives.

6. Marriage interferes with extramarital sources of satisfaction (e.g., career, affair).

7. Communications about potential sources of. satisfaction are not adequate.

8. Aversive control predominates over positive reinforcement.

Thus Azrin and his colleagues assume that marital discord may reflect multivariate causes, while Stuart and Weiss et al. suggest that marital conflict reflects a skewed set of interaction strategies in which aversive control predominates (Azrin's eighth causative agent).

GOAL OF TREATMENT

The minimal goal of treatment generally espoused by behavioral family therapists (Azrin et al., 1973) is to eliminate the undesirable behavior or behavior pattern, or to increase the positive behavior desired by the family. "For many families, a major goal of intervention should be to increase positive responsiveness of some or all family members to . . . appropriate social stimuli and the agents dispensing them" (LeBow, 1972, p. 353). As this quote suggests, the operant family therapist does not passively accept the stated goals of the family. Instead, one intermediate goal of operant family therapy involves changing the family's view of the problem. Typically a family enters therapy requesting that the therapist help them reduce and eliminate a negative behavior. The therapist redefines the goal as increasing positive and incompatible behaviors. A second intermediate goal is the redefinition of the problem as one that is interpersonal in nature (belonging to one or more dyads) rather than belonging to an individual family member. Thus while operant family therapists primarily discuss behavior change, there is a significant element of attitude change involved.

More recent studies (Harrell & Guerney, 1976; Weiss, Hops, & Patterson, 1973) indicate some interest among behavioral family therapists in teaching families conflict resolution skills. This focus seems to be based on Sprey's (1969) suggestion that conflict management skills are an integral part of marital satisfaction, since distressed and satisfied couples appear to differ in their abilities to handle conflict, rather than in the actual types of problems experienced.

A higher-level goal espoused by some behavioral family therapists (Weiss, Hops, & Patterson, 1973) is not only the elimination of undesirable behavior or an increase in positive behavior, but a changed pattern of interaction in which new, undesirable behaviors could be modified without outside intervention. Thus many operant family therapists appear to aim for the generalized learning of behavioral principles within the family so that new problems can be handled internally.

The issue of generalization of treatment effects across behaviors and situations has been problematic for behavioral family therapists in their efforts to measure the efficiency of applied techniques (Conway & Bucher, 1976). The assumption that behavior is situation-specific implies that transference of behavior change to other situations cannot be effectuated unless "comparability" across situations is established. The definition of "comparability" is circular, and analogous to the behaviorist's definition of reinforcement, which leaves the behavioral family therapist to his own devices in trying to establish comparability.

Review of the writings of family therapists and researchers within the behavioral framework indicates that there has been a progression in conceptualization of treatment goals, from changing a specific individual behavior (e.g., tantrums), to changing a specific dyadic behavior, to changing the process of interaction of the dyad (e.g., reinforcement strategy, communication skills, conflict management techniques).

ASSESSMENT METHODS

Behavioral assessment consists of defining, observing, and recording the frequency of the behavior that is to be changed, and the events that precede and follow it. The clear definition of behaviors to be observed and recorded is considered essential to effective assessment (O'Leary, O'Leary, & Becher, 1967). Behavioral definitions must be both specific (at least two separate observers must agree that the event occurred) and reliable to be useful in treatment planning (LeBow, 1972; Bijou, Peterson, & Ault, 1968). Both specificity and reliability are reduced significantly if inferences about motives or feeling are recorded. Primarily, behavioral assessment aims to record the behavior of each member (what is said and done) and the temporal relationships between antecedent and consequent stimulus events for each behavior under study (Knox, 1971).

Various methods have been employed for assessing behavior problems. Basically they fall into three major categories: interview, observation, and baseline data (LeBow, 1972).

Interview. The initial interview with the family or a subgroup of its members is used by the therapist to gain information including the family's definition of problems, potential reinforcers, and to develop a specific intervention strategy.

Observation. Initial observations of family or parent-child interaction are used to define important events and to establish criteria for behavioral recording. Bijou, Peterson, and Ault (1968) suggest recording all behavioral events in a limited time period as a first step in observation. They also emphasize the importance of temporal relationships in the form of antecedent events, responses, and subsequent events.

The specification of antecendent-response-consequence may be viewed simplistically as a linear sequence. This is only possible in behavioral family therapy when the problem is defined as a particular behavior of one family member (i.e., tantrums, depression). When, however, the focus of behavioral family therapy is on reciprocal behavior change, the specification of antecedent-response-consequence is not as simple, since one spouse's response may act as the antecedent behavior for the other spouse. The second spouse's behavior then may be viewed from one perspective as the consequence, and from another perspective as a response which will be followed by yet another consequent behavior in spiral fashion. Thus the pattern of interlocking behaviors may be viewed not in a linear construction but in a mutually reciprocal framework. As a result the definitions of terms such as reinforcers and consequents become circular in nature, and must be viewed as dependent on the perspective of the observer rather than as objective phenomena.

Gathering baseline data.   Prior to the initiation of treatment, data are gathered regarding the frequency of occurrence of the behaviors to be modified. This procedure usually involves recording behaviors at specific intervals over given periods of time (Schaefer & Martin, 1969). Baseline data can be recorded either by the therapist (Patterson & Reid, 1970) or by one or more family members (Knox, 1971).

TREATMENT

Knox (1971) outlines three major aspects of treatment using the behavioral family approach. These are the specifications of the behaviors to be manipulated, recording of baseline frequencies, and the actual manipulation of stimulus variables. The first two have just been discussed. This section will therefore focus on methods and procedures for the manipulation of stimulus variables.

Behavioral family therapists either attempt to directly establish control of environmental contingencies using the techniques described below, or attempt to teach their clients to manipulate these contingencies in order to influence each other's behavior. The latter approach tends to increase generalization of behavior change. According to a number of researchers in the field (Patterson, Ray, & Shaw, 1968; Patterson, Cobb, & Ray, 1970) the most likely way to produce durable behavior change is to alter the environment maintaining the deviant behavior. "This involves altering a family's reinforcement practices and providing them with techniques for maintaining behavior change as well as remediating new problems as they arise" (LeBow, 1972, p. 360). Techniques used to increase the likelihood of generalizing behavior change include moving toward the use of intermittent positive reinforcement schedules (Patterson, McNeal, Hawkins, & Phelps, 1967), the fading of material reinforcements and the shaping of social ones (Allen & Harris, 1966; Wetzel, Baker, Roney, & Martin, 1966; Wahler, 1968), and the use of self-control procedures (Goldiamond, 1965; Nolan, 1968).

One method of increasing generalizability of behavior change in behavioral family therapy involves teaching parents to act as behavior modifiers for their children (Patterson & Brodsky, 1966; Patterson et al., 1967; Patterson, Cobb, & Ray, 1970; Dardig & Heward, 1976). Both a group approach (several sets of parents meeting together with a therapist; Rose, 1961) and an individual family approach (therapist meets with only one set of parents; Wagner, 1968) to parental training have been used. The group approach relies heavily on lectures, readings, and homework assignments. Modeling of techniques also has been employed (Walder et al., 1969), as have home practice sessions (Salzinger, Feldman, & Portnoy, 1970) and feedback sessions (Walder et al., 1969). The individual family approach utilizes similar methods and is employed by itself or as an adjunct to the group methods. In both approaches training generally occurs without the child being present.

BEHAVIORAL CHANGE TECHNIQUES

Acceleration Techniques. Acceleration techniques involve the contingent application of positive and negative reinforcement. Positive reinforcement of desired behavior is the technique most frequently used to strengthen desired behavior patterns. An often-used paradigm (Premack principle) is having the opportunity to emit a high probability behavior serve as a reinforcer for emitting a low probability behavior (LeBow, 1972). Both material and social reinforcements have been employed (Wahler, 1969). Contingent positive reinforcement is used both to strengthen low-frequency behaviors (Patterson et al., 1967) and to develop ways of behaving which are not currently in the person's repertoire (Wolf, Risley, & Mees, 1964). Negative reinforcement consists of either terminating an aversive stimulus in response to the desired behavior or postponing the onset of such a stimulus (Lovibond, 1963). Techniques based on negative reinforcement principles have been used in family treatment, though not extensively.

Deceleration Techniques. Deceleration techniques involve the contingent application of two types of punishment (presentation of aversive stimuli and withdrawal of a positive stimulus) and extinction. "Response-contingent aversive stimulation describes a punishment procedure in which a painful or unpleasant event . . . is presented contingent on the emission of a behavior" (LeBow, 1972, p. 356). Very little use of this technique has been made in family therapy, although it has been used with children (Jacobson & Martin, 1976). The withdrawal of a positive stimulus involves the removal of the individual from the opportunity to receive positive reinforcement or termination of a reinforcing event contingent on the emission of an undesirable behavior. The most common techniques in this area consist of time outs—withdrawal from a reinforcing situation (Reese, 1966; Zeilberger, Sampen, & Sloane, 1968; Steeves, Martin, & Pear, 1970), and response cost—subtracting positive reinforcers from the individual's pool of available reinforcers contingent on the emission of undesirable behavior (Holland, 1969; Engeln et al., 1968). The latter technique has not been used extensively in behavioral family therapy.

Extinction procedures discontinue the reinforcement that is maintaining an undesirable behavior. The result is a decrease in such a behavior to its operant (or pre-reinforcement) level of occurrence. Behaviors maintained by positive reinforcement have primarily been extinguished through ignoring them (Allen & Harris, 1966; Safer, 1966). Extinction of negatively reinforced behavior has not been used extensively in either the parent-child or the marital area.

Decelerating undesirable behavior often is accompanied by techniques which accelerate or strengthen a behavior that is incompatible with the dysfunctional behavior. Thus acceleration and deceleration techniques are freqently used together to enhance intervention effectiveness (Ayllon & Michael, 1959; Lovaas, Freitag, Gold, & Kassorla, 1965; Holland, 1969).

As can be seen from this presentation of acceleration and deceleration techniques, only positive reinforcement is consistently and widely used in operant family therapy. Negative reinforcement and deceleration techniques are used infrequently, and usually only in conjunction with positive reinforcement techniques. Stuart (1969) acknowledges the primary commitment of operant family therapists to the use of positive reinforcement techniques, arguing that "the difficulty with attempting to decelerate behavior is that its attainment would require the use of aversive stimuli or extinction paradigms and the typically unhappy couple already is disproportionately committed to these negative strategies" (p. 678).

Stuart seems to be suggesting that families seeking therapy make predominant use of negative reinforcement and deceleration techniques, and implies that this reinforcement strategy is the root of their problem. Thus the operant family therapist's predominant use of positive reinforcement techniques may function to restore the family's ability to make a balanced use of various modes of reinforcement. Stuart's comments may reflect both the basic commitment of behavior therapists to positive reinforcement strategies and the much more equivocal nature of outcome literature, which focuses on the effectiveness of negative reinforcement and deceleration techniques compared to positive reinforcement strategies.

Behavioral family therapists who aim to increase positive reinforcement between spouses seek to teach couples to negotiate noninterlocking contracts.[1] Such therapists (Weiss, Hops, & Patterson, 1973; Stuart, 1969, 1975; Azrin, Naster, & Jones, 1973) emphasize that a "good" contract specifies an independent agreement for desired behaviors by husband and wife (Y and X, respectively). Separate, noninterlocking rewards are specified for each X and Y, so that failure to emit behavior X produces no reward for the wife, but does not affect the husband's ability to perform Y and be rewarded.

Sample Contracts:

If Mary has dinner ready at 6:00 each week night, Bill will take her out to dinner on Saturday.

If Bill spends half an hour playing with the children each weeknight, Mary will not object to his having one night "out with the boys."

A second characteristic of "positive reinforcement" contracting is that behaviors X and Y should be specified in accelerated rather than decelerated terms.

Not: If Mary doesn't burn dinner more than twice . . .

Instead: If Mary has dinner cooked properly at least three times . . .

The assumption held by such therapists is that couples in marital conflict too often develop implicit interlocking contracts: "If you do X, I'll do Y," in which Y rewards X, and the failure of X implies the failure of Y.

In contrast, behavioral family therapists who focus on conflict management (Harrell & Guerney, 1976) rather than positive reinforcement advocate the use of interlocking contracts. Interlocking contracts center on issues of concern to both partners. In successful contracting of this kind each partner agrees to one change in behavior which both agree would help resolve the conflict. The full process includes determining the conditions of the contract; additional reinforcements may be included as well to provide incentives beyond those presumed to be intrinsic in the behavioral exchange.

Bob and Lucille constantly argue about disciplining their children. Bob says Lucille is too hard on the children. Lucille says Bob is a "pushover." They contract for a two-week period as follows:
Bob and Lucille both agree not to criticize each other's disciplinary efforts in front of the children. They will discuss such issues after the children are asleep.
Lucille accords child discipline to Bob when they are both present. If Lucille feels Bob is being "too soft," she will leave the room for at least five minutes.
Bob consents to take responsibility for disciplining the children when he and Lucille are together.

There appears to be a difference in strategy and values between the two perspectives. Advocates of increasing positive reinforcement encourage each spouse to behave in ways that are (more) pleasing to his/her spouse whether or not they specifically promote conflict resolution. In fact, it could be argued that such therapists encourage conflict avoidance. For example, while Stuart (1975) emphasizes that couples should communicate accurately, he indicates that optimal communication is less than complete; that is marital partners should not be totally honest about everything. Couples are instructed to use "measured honesty" (e.g., censor messages that might inhibit rather than promote constructive action). Also Stuart encourages couples to decide which of them will assume primary decision-making responsibility in particular content areas.

Georgene will be responsible for running the household (children, household chores, everyday purchases). Roger will oversee the "plantation" (major purchases, investments, finances, politics).

In marked contrast, behavioral family therapists interested in conflict management do not attempt to help couples avoid conflictual areas through prior agreements or censorship, but rather to teach couples a generalized methodology of conflict resolution. Clearly there is a split in the field over this issue. Further research specifically comparing outcomes of these two approaches would be welcome.

Beyond the goals of increasing positive reinforcement or conflict resolution, there appears to be a commitment on the part of operant family therapists to reframe the family problems so that the family members begin to view it not in terms of the negative behavior(s) to be reduced, but in terms of the behavior(s) they wish increased. In addition, family therapists have the family redefine their problem as dyadic, rather than as belonging to one family member. To the extent that operant family therapy aims to refocus family perceptions, it is possible to view attitude change as a precondition to behavior change. However, Hobbs (1962) argues that one's attitude changes as desired behavior increases, with insight the result, not the cause, of behavior change. The issue of defining "insight" and its relationship to behavioral change is not dealt with in the operant family literature, but appears to be of significant importance in identifying what specific treatment procedures are necessary and sufficient to produce behavior change. Which technique or multimodal therapy is best for a client, dyadic unit, or family depends on (a) the client's behavioral assets and deficits, (b) the problem for which counseling was sought, (c) who can be utilized as the principal change agent, and (d) the value of reinforcers available (Hosford and Briskin, 1969; Lazarus, 1974).

THERAPISTS

Role. Therapists assume two major roles in the operant family therapy model. First, they act as direct interveners or change agents. In this role the therapist attempts to change behavior by directly manipulating contingencies and providing reinforcements. There are two major limitations to this. First, the therapist only is available to control contingencies for a brief period; second, the therapist is not part of the natural environment of the family. For these reasons, operant family therapists who function in a direct-service role are concerned with providing means to generalize behavioral changes to the natural setting. A primary means of increasing the likelihood of generalization is to teach family members to act as change agents.

The therapist acts as a teacher/trainer (Coe, 1970; Stuart, 1970) either as a supplement to the direct intervention described above or as a replacement for it. In this role, the therapist teaches behavorial principles to one or more family members. Then the trained family members act as change agents within their families. Thus in this way the operant family therapist is both a teacher and a supplementary source of reinforcement to these selected family members (Liberman, 1970). The advantage of this is that the mechanisms for producing behavioral change are explicitly taught to family members, and therefore have a greater likelihood of being incorporated into the family system.

Another issue regarding the role of the therapist in the operant family literature has to do with the importance of the specific therapist in the therapeutic process. In the operant family therapy field, some writers argue that behavioral change will occur in response to behavioral principles regardless of the individual personality or style of the particular therapist (Stuart, 1969; Hawkins, Peterson, Schweid, & Bijou, 1966).

Others in the field (Engeln et al., 1968; Friedman, 1971; Gambrill, Thomas, & Carter, 1970; LeBow, 1972) suggest that a key element in successful operant family therapy is the building of rapport, or of a relationship, between the therapist and the family. Liberman (1970) writes of the importance of creating and maintaining a positive therapeutic alliance, reporting that the therapist is an effective reinforcer and model to the extent that family members value him and hold him in high regard and warm esteem. While the issue seems far from settled, it appears to be amenable to empirical evaluation. Preliminary work by Truax and Carkhuff (1967) has demonstrated that such concepts as nonpossessive warmth, accurate empathy, and genuine concern can be both operationalized and taught. Recent research by Alexander and his colleagues (1976) suggests that a therapist's relationship skills may play a critical role in enhancing his effectiveness. Future empirical studies may thus focus on whether any of these or similar elements are necessary in the production of behavioral change in families.

Background and training. Most of the behaviorally oriented family therapists are psychologists, though some are from other helping professions. The training of behavioral psychologists usually occurs within an academic setting, typically in a Ph.D. program in clinical and/or counseling psychology. In these graduate programs it is emphasized that the psychologist is an empiricist who must evaluate his intervention. Thus practitioners following a behavioral approach utilize intervention strategies that are amenable to the collection of quantifiable data, and they focus on problem areas that lend themselves to empirical research (e.g., school phobias as opposed to existential crises).

Another group of interveners are natural help givers. This refers to those nonprofessionals who are engaged in the direct production of behavior change. Such people are directly part of the individual's environment (i.e., parents, spouses, teachers). While the predominant pattern has been for professionals to train lay people to act as change agents only within their own families, a number of investigators (Ora & Wagner, 1970; Lindsley, 1966; Patterson, Cobb, & Ray, 1970; Stuart, 1969; 1975) have found that such individuals can effectively teach others to use these skills. The little research that has been done in this area suggests that natural help givers, such as parents who have been trained to act as behavior modifiers, can train other parents to function in this role.

The assumption underlying the use of natural help givers appears to be that deviant behavior is essentially a learning defect and can therefore be changed by any individual who has a knowledge of learning principles. This assumption lessens the need for extensive professional training as a prerequisite to being an effective change agent, and thereby opens the help-giving field to a vast array of natural help givers (e.g., teachers, ministers, family members).

SETTING

Behavioral family therapy occurs both in traditional mental health settings and in academic or university-affiliated facilities, and conforms to specific time limits and frequencies (generally once a week for approximately one hour). Also, behavioral family therapists make much more frequent and consistent use of the family home as the setting for assessment (and sometimes treatment) than do psychoanalytic or systems family therapists.

In terms of natural help givers such as teachers, ministers, and the like, the specific setting is a function of the occupation of the natural help giver. What distinguishes the setting for natural help givers is the fact that it is part of the "natural" community (e.g., school or church), rather than a facility designated as a treatment (mental health) center.

CONSUMER

There are minimal data available to suggest what type of families are involved in behavioral family therapy. However, the model itself suggests that certain characteristics and values would make a family more amenable to such an intervention strategy. For example, when family members are markedly distrustful of mental health professionals, this strategy allows for the family to be its own behavior change agent. In addition, it is possible to have this type of intervention be effective even if only one member of the family (usually a parent) is willing to be trained in behavioral techniques, or to have a paraprofessional from outside the mental health professions serve as the behavior change agent.

Secondly, families who are minimally interested in or accustomed to understanding themselves or others in terms of psychological processes would find this action-oriented approach compatible with their value system. This type of family perceives the problem narrowly, as the specific behavioral concern brought to the therapist, and expects treatment to focus on concrete approaches to ameliorating that specific condition.

On the other hand, this action-oriented approach requires that families learn to delay their usual reactions since they are often required to keep charts and other written materials concerning the frequency, consequence, and so on, of the problem behavior. Families who are willing to keep these written records and perceive the scientific rituals of this approach as medicinal are likely to be the "typical" well-educated, middle-class family that responds well to most intervention strategies. However, the behavioral approach does minimize the need for such families to have a psychological orientation or to be able or willing to talk among themselves about feelings or other intangible psychological aspects of their lives.

Notes

1. Contracting (Weiss et al., 1973; Dardig & Heward, 1976) refers to the process by which family members agree to engage in desirable behaviors in exchange for a reward of positive value.

11

Systems Model
of Family
Therapy

The family as seen by Haley (1963) is involved in an ongoing interrelationship, with a shared past and future. The systems approach focuses on the pattern of interaction that characterizes the *current* relationship—the family's system of communication. The model assumes that the family as a system has properties that cannot be identified with any one member. Therefore it is necessary to examine the properties of the system (family), as opposed to examining the individual system components (family members).

The relationship of the components (family members) in the system (family) is not perceived as linear. Rather, maintenance of the system's functioning is based upon a process of feedback. This process of feedback is not dependent upon cause and effect, but upon a cybernetic or circular model. Thus the family system operates by means of a feedback loop which preserves an internal balance in family interactions. In the family systems model, this internal balance is termed homeostasis. Jackson writes that family homeostasis ". . . implies the relative constance of the internal environment, a constance, however, which is maintained by a continuous interplay of dynamic forces" (1968a). The constancy of family homeostasis does not imply an entity that is unchanging, but rather that the interplay of forces serves to limit and direct behavior change. Family interaction, then, is a ". . . closed information system in which variations in . . . behavior are fed back in order to correct the system's response" (Jackson, 1968a, p. 2).

From this viewpoint, all behavior is seen as purposeful in maintaining the current family system. Thus deviant behavior also serves a function in preserving family homeostasis. Based on the systems approach, Haley (1962) described symptomatic behavior as follows:

> Psychopathology in the individual is a product of the way he deals with his intimate relations, the way they deal with him, and the way other family members involve

him in their relations with each other. Further, the appearance of symptomatic behavior in the individual is necessary for the continued functioning of a particular family system. Therefore, changes in the individual can occur only if the family system changes, and resistance to change in the individual centers in the influence of the family as a group (p. 70).

The implications of the assumptions of the system model for the treatment of deviant behavior are profound. Most other models conceptualize deviant behavior as belonging to an individual. The systems approach perceives deviance in the context of the communications system, and therefore as understandable only within the context of the current family system. Treatment within this model approaches the problem of alleviating deviant behavior by focusing on changing the family system so that the deviant behavior is no longer necessary to preserve homeostasis. Deviant behavior is assumed to be constantly reinforced and maintained by the family system. Therefore the unit of treatment must be the entire family, not just the individual displaying the aberrant behavior. (This does not mean that the entire family must be seen in treatment, but rather that the therapist's interventions are directed and guided by his understanding of the family system.)

Advocates of the systems approach regard neither an individual unit nor a dyadic one (according to Haley [1971], the behavioral family model would be dyadic) as sufficient to explain family interaction. The unit of behavior utilized in the systems model is triadic. Bowen (1971) holds that an "emotional system is composed of a series of interlocking triangles" (p. 185). He suggests that a third person (e.g., family member, friend, therapist) is added into a relationship, or triangled in, in order to lessen tension. Essentially, then, Bowen is suggesting that the third person functions to activate homeostatic mechanisms in order to preserve the family system. The family is viewed as a set of interlocking triads that shift in order to maintain a functional family balance. Since triadic relationship patterns are seen as the key to understanding the family system and deviant behavior, the goal of systems family therapy is to produce change in the current sequence of behavioral patterns among family members.

Insight and awareness of intrapsychic motivations are not prerequisite to change in behavioral sequences (Haley, 1971). If a family system is marked by patterns of covert hostility, the premise of the systems model is not necessarily to make explicit the underlying hostility, but to resolve the relationship difficulties that are causing the hostility (Haley, 1970). This systems premise is in direct opposition to the psychoanalytic view of family therapy treatment, which holds that insight into both the dynamic and genetic causes must be obtained by family members in order for relationship difficulties to be resolved. Insight in the sense of understanding intraindividual motivations is not essential to systems intervention, particularly according to Jackson (1962; Jackson & Weakland, 1961) and Haley (1962, 1970, 1971). However, it appears that insight, when construed as an understanding of the current rules of interaction, may be considered by some system theorists as a necessary condition for producing a system change (Satir, 1967, 1971; Turner & Gross, 1976).

There also are major differences among system theorists and practitioners concerning the role of affect in producing change. At one end of the continuum are Haley and Bowen, who perceive a focus on feelings as irrelevant to change; in the middle is Satir, who views the family's sharing of feelings as a critical part of functional communication but minimizes what the therapist shares in regard to his feelings about himself and family members; at the other end of the continuum are Turner and Gross, who argue that feelings are the main determinants of behaviors and that awareness of feelings about oneself and others can be used to monitor and modify family rules. Turner and Gross suggest that feelings can be categorized into three main areas: hard (e.g., anger, dislike, demand-making, etc.), fragile (e.g., needy, hurt, scared, etc.), and soft (e.g., warmth, love, tenderness, etc.). Turner and Gross assume that families have their greatest difficulty with one particular feeling area. They propose that therapists be able to model for the family the recognition, expression, and intensity of the family's difficult feeling area. Thus to the degree that the therapist cannot recognize, share, or cope with the intensity of particular feelings, he will model ineffective problem-solving skills. (These skills will be described in detail later in this chapter.) Although most system adherents share a belief about the impact of emotions on behavior, the weight given the role of affect separates Turner and Gross's affective rule-altering (ARA) model from other systems models (Turner & Gross, 1976). The ARA model will be described in greater detail later in this chapter.

ASSUMPTIONS OF THE SYSTEMS MODEL

1. "Individuals must relate to one another through patterned behavior or redundancies, and . . . these behaviors can be described as rules" (Jackson, 1967, p. 37).

2. Family systems have properties that are both different and not deducible from any examination of the properties (personalities) of the individual members that comprise it.

3. Symptomatic behavior is a product of the way a person deals with intimate relations, the way others deal with him, and the way others involve him in their (triadic) relationships with each other.

4. The appearance of symptomatic behavior is necessary for the continued functioning of a particular family system.

5. Symptomatic behavior is currently being reinforced by the family system, or it would cease to exist.

6. Historical (genetic) insight and awareness are not causal in producing change in transactional patterns of relationships.

7. Resistance to change in an individual centers around the influence of the family as a group.

GOAL OF TREATMENT

The goal of treatment is the alteration of self-reinforcing and mutually destructive patterns of interaction (Jackson & Weakland, 1961). Essentially, systems family therapy aims at changing the current patterns of behavior among family members (Turner & Gross, 1976); that is, of altering dysfunctional rules.

A review of the systems family literature indicates that therapy is aimed at changing the dysfunctional rules of the current family system, and that such change is process- rather than content-oriented (Turner & Gross, 1976). Jackson (Lederer & Jackson, 1968) defines the goal of family therapy as making explicit the family rules. Satir reflects Jackson's position, contending that although rules are part of every family, in the dysfunctional family the rules constrict growth because they are either too rigid and/or hidden (Satir, 1967). The desired outcome of the systems model of family therapy is to change the family system from a rigid position to one in which self-activated change is possible. Turner and Gross (1976) teach families problem-solving skills that allow them to monitor and modify family rules that interfere with effective functioning. Most system adherents would agree that once dysfunctional family rules are altered, symptomatic behavior will disappear.

Specifically, Satir (1971) defines three goals of systems family therapy:

1. Each member should be able to report congruently, completely, and obviously on what he sees, hears, feels, and thinks about himself and others, in the presence of others.

2. Each person should be related to in his uniqueness so that decisions are made in terms of exploration and negotiation of ideas and feelings rather than in terms of power.

3. Differentness must be openly acknowledged and used for growth (p. 130).

The difficulty with these systems goals is the lack of reliable, objectively-defined outcome criteria. Thus the assessment of therapeutic success often remains a matter of subjective evaluation which is therefore subject to bias and variability.

ASSESSMENT METHODS

Formal assessment procedures (tests, structured tasks) are not typically used in the systems model. Pathological behavior is viewed as an interpersonal problem, and individually-oriented methods of assessment and diagnosis are rejected as irrelevant.

Attempts have been made to develop assessment procedures which would examine behavior in terms of triadic interaction patterns. Such studies have been primarily observational in nature. The basic paradigm (Rabkin, 1965) has been to bring family members together, present them with a more or less structured task to be worked out conjointly, and have observers classify and rate the ensuing behavioral interaction (Loveland, Wynne, & Singer, 1963; Goodrich & Boomer, 1963; Farina, 1960; Watzlawick, 1966).

One form of assessment within the systems framework is the Structured Family Interview developed by Watzlawick (1966). In addition to its function as a diagnostic and evaluative tool, the Structured Interview provides information valuable to the treatment process; that is, information concerning family patterns or rules.

This technique is based on the following assumptions:

1. Important relevant information is largely outside the family's awareness.
2. A family has typical ways of handling stress that are expressed in repetitive interactions (rules).
3. Not only the content, but mainly the specific process of communicating in these repetitive interactions is significant.
4. Rather than to wait for such situations to occur, it is possible to create them deliberately.

The Structured Family Interview consists of completing five tasks, with the therapist either participating with the group or directly observing it through a one-way screen. Each task aims to tap behaviors the family would normally exhibit in its natural environment. The tasks are:

1. Deciding on the main problem.
2. Planning something together.
3. Parents discussing how they met.
4. Discussing and teaching the meaning of a proverb.
5. Identifying faults and placing the blame on the correct person.

The technique, which usually requires at most one hour, has tremendous significance in its ability to reveal the family's patterns of communication: their methods of decision making, the ways they disagree and ways they cover up disagreement, areas of discrepant information, and their use of maneuvers such as scapegoating, favoritism and/or self-blame. In addition the interview and its tasks initiate the realization by the family that the problems it is experiencing are related to it as a family. The Structured Family Interview is a simple way to immediately bring under observation the systems model's main object of therapeutic intervention—the family's patterns of interaction (rules).

A number of difficulties are inherent in interactional, observational diagnostic procedures. Among these are observer inference concerning the behavior being coded and the degree of representativeness of the behavior patterns oberved. The development of procedures for assessing interactional patterns is hampered by the lack of an operational language of interaction; that is, a conceptual system which can simultaneously describe multiple-party interactions (Rabkin, 1965).

Currently assessment within the systems model includes a clinical evaluation of the ongoing family process by the therapist. Specifically the therapist makes an assessment of the current operating rules of the family system (Foley, 1974; Turner & Gross, 1976). The focus of the assessment is on *how* the system is presently interacting; it minimizes *why* the system is as it is (historical causation).

Systems therapists typically perceive diagnosis as inseparable from intervention. They view neither the definition of the communication problem nor the modification or treatment of the family system as separate processes. One reason for this intermingling of asssessment and treatment is that the systems therapist includes himself in the system under examination. The therapist views the family problem in terms of how the family responds to the therapist. Haley (1970) states explicitly that "evaluation of a family is how the family responds to your therapeutic interventions" (p. 232). He argues (1971) that in the ideal case, information-gathering and intervention to produce change occur simultaneously.

One example of simultaneous diagnosis and intervention is the approach used by Turner and Gross (1976) in their "Affective Rule-Altering" model. Turner and Gross argue that feelings are the major determinant of our behavior, and that the more one is unaware of one's feelings, the less one can choose how one will behave. Conversely Turner and Gross argue that the more one is aware of how one is feeling both about oneself and others, the more one can use these feelings to monitor and alter rules that interfere with effective functioning. Turner and Gross teach families a problem-solving method that begins with family members recognizing what feelings (hard, fragile, or soft) are difficult for them to identify and express directly.

In the initial family therapy session, Turner and Gross ask the family to discuss among themselves what they perceive as the problem (this is similar to one of the tasks used in the Structured Interview). After a few minutes Turner and Gross can identify which of the three feeling areas is most difficult for the family by noting which feeling area is omitted, whether certain affective terms are minimized, and what patterns of affective interaction characterize the family (these patterns will be described later in this section).

Turner and Gross argue that every family has specific rules governing the expression of feelings. One way to analyze what rules are in operation for a particular family is to use what Turner and Gross label the "behavior-self-other" format. Briefly, a behavior-self-other statement (b-s-o) consists of a description of what is happening (behavior), how one feels about oneself (self) and how one feels about the other person (other). For example, an irate husband told his wife, "When you ask my permission to say something during our therapy session (behavior) I feel like an ogre, a very old ogre who is ugly and mean (self), and I get angry at you (other) and feel like leaving."

According to Turner and Gross there are three styles that characterize how people share feelings (rules). The first style is the behavior-self (b-s) approach, which consists largely of feeling statements about the self. For example, "When Mary does that I'm disappointed and very scared," or "When Henry tells me that he is upset, I feel so bad and fearful that he'll leave me." For the most part, people who mainly use b-s statements are more adept in the fragile area and have the most difficult time with the hard area. Turner and Gross would argue that the feeling area that would make a person using b-s statement feel vulnerable would be from the hard area, and that when such a person reports being scared, frightened, sad, and so forth, he is using feeling statements that allow him to be comfortable, even if the comfort is a miserable one. On the other hand, some people use a behavior-other (b-o) style, which means that they are most comfortable when using feelings in the hard area. For example, "You son of a bitch, you are an idiot—I can't stand you." Or, "Again dinner is not ready, it is never ready, you are a slob!" People who mainly use b-o statements are comfortable when dealing with feelings from the hard area and are most vulnerable when they must focus on fragile feelings.

Turner and Gross assume that a person's ability to move from one feeling area to another follows a specific sequence. That is, hard feelings must be handled first, then hard combined with fragile, then accented fragile combined with hard, then hard-soft and fragile-soft, and finally accented soft with both hard and fragile. For Turner and Gross, diagnosis consists of the therapist helping family members identify which feeling area is most difficult for them, and thereafter teaching family members how to recognize what they do when they are having these difficult feelings. For example, a couple comes to the first therapy session and is asked by the therapist to discuss with each other what they perceive as the problem. The therapist listens a few minutes and notes that the wife begins to talk first as the husband smiles and looks at her. The husband is a young, boyish-looking individual who is dressed in his work clothes (he works on an assembly line). His appearance is that of an asexual adolescent (he is in his late twenties). The wife is dressed plainly, wears little make-up, and appears much older than her age (she also is in her twenties). The wife too appears asexual and acts parental with her husband by spelling out the problem at first talking for him, prompting him, and so forth. During their initial talk the wife reports that the husband has been using his telescope to look at neighbors. There is lots of smiling between husband and wife, and at no point does either directly express any anger or annoyance with the partner. Both report being concerned about the other and use terms such as worry and scared to describe how they are feeling about themselves and their spouse. This couples communication style would be diagnosed as b-s, with the most difficult feeling area being the hard one. To help them recognize what happens when they get angry, the affective rule-altering therapist might proceed as follows:

They are approximately five minutes into the first session.

Therapist: So you find out that Mike is using the telescope by the noise he makes upstairs. Is it pretty loud—these noises?

Mary: Yes—he seems to be loud enough for me to hear (smiles exchanged between Mike and Mary).

Therapist: So once Mike helps you find him—what happens?

Mary: I go upstairs and I get very upset and he apologizes.

Therapist: And then?

Mary: It happens all over again.

Mike: (Smiling) I don't know why—I want to stop— (Mary smiles).

Therapist: Mary, how do you feel about yourself when you see Mike looking out the window at the neighbors? Attractive—unattractive?

Mary: Unattractive (beginning to cry).

Therapist: How unattractive? Little—lots?

Mary: Very unattractive—I feel awful (sobbing).

Therapist: How old? Young—old?

Mary: I don't know—I guess I feel my age.

Therapist: Well, do you start moving faster? slower?

Mary: Slower, it's so hard to do anything—I just get so tired.

Therapist: Sounds like you feel old.

Mary: Maybe you're right.

Therapist: How sexy do you feel, Mary?

Mary: Not at all sexy.

Therapist: So when Mike does use the telescope you feel unattractive, tired, slow, not sexy. How do you feel about Mike?

Mary: Sorry for him, he must be sick.

Therapist: Do you want to get closer or farther away from Mike?

Mary: Closer.

Therapist: What do you do to get close?

Mike: She cries a lot—and feels real bad.

Mary: (Smiling) Then you go away until I feel better.

Mike: (Smiling) Guess I do.

Therapist: Mike, when Mary is crying and feels bad—do you want to get closer or farther away from her?

Mike: Closer ... but, well, I need time alone.

Therapist: You mean you get farther away. Let's go back and see what happens. Mike, when you are making the noise to let Mary know you are upstairs how long does it take for her to catch on (Smiles)?

Mike: (Smiling) Long time—but I don't really signal her.

Therapist: How do you feel about yourself when Mary comes up and catches you? Boy—man?

Mike: Like a kid with his hands in the cookie jar.

Therapist: How attractive—unattractive?

Mike: Real unattractive—stupid (Smiles).

Therapist: Sexy—not sexy?

Mike: Not sexy (low voice), not attractive (sounds annoyed and looks sad).

Mary: (Smiling) I know we can work it out.

Therapist: Mike, when Mary comes and you feel not sexy, unattractive and like a kid, how do you feel about Mary?

Mike: (Smiles. Long pause) I don't know—I just feel ashamed.
Therapist: Do you want to get closer—farther away from her?
Mike: I guess away.
Therapist: How do you do it?
Mike: I go off to the basement.
Mary: And reads *Penthouse* (smiling).
Therapist: And when Mike goes to read *Penthouse* do you act older—more sad—more tired?
Mary: Yes.

This sequence illustrates how both Mary and Mike express anger: Mary as an old, sexless, unattractive mother and Mike as a stupid, unattractive, sexless adolescent. By having them spell out the sequences of their behavior and their feelings about themselves and their spouse, Mike and Mary will gain insight into their relationship rules. This will enable them to both monitor and modify how they act (relabel their behavior) if they *choose* to do so. Specifically, when they are angry at each other Mary acts older and Mike acts younger. As the first session progressed the therapist would provide the couple with additional tools to modify their mother-son interaction. (This will be discussed in the following section).

TREATMENT

It is impossible to give a homogeneous picture of how systems therapists operate. They begin from a common perspective and share a common goal, but use a wide range of methods. The perspective they share is that dysfunction is a property of the current family system; therefore the system must be the unit of treatment. They further agree that change in the family system is the goal of treatment and that the role of the therapist is to induce this change.

In focusing on the current transactional patterns, the intervener attempts to have the family members interact with each other while he directs and refocuses their interaction. Therapy aims to alter self-reinforcing and mutually-destructive interaction patterns, rather than to examine the content of the interactions. For some system therapists, describing such patterns is explicitly assumed not to be necessary. Jackson and Weakland (1961) report that pointing out repetitious patterns has not been found to be effective in altering transactions (i.e., insight is not necessary or sufficient to produce behavioral change), although they present no data to support their assertion. They argue further that the systems therapist must actively manipulate the system so that the repetition of a pattern of family interaction is either impossible or no longer effective in maintaining the family equilibrium.

There is a wide variety of methods and techniques used by systems therapists to influence the ongoing family system. One such method is relabeling (Jackson, 1967; Jackson & Weakland, 1961). This refers to reframing or reinterpreting messages from family members by the therapist. Essentially the therapist provides the family with a context or interpretation of a message other than the one to which they have become accustomed (for example, labeling Mary and Mike's mother-child behaviors as signs of their being angry, anger being a sign that they care enough to treat each other as worthy opponents). Relabeling, according to Jackson, is ". . . simply taking the motivation that has been labeled in a negative way and labeling it in a positive way" (1967, p. 200). Jackson (1967) illustrates this point as follows: "A will always say, 'Well, I think it's A-X, B-Y,' and B will always say 'No, it's B-Y, A-X.' You can upset the system by saying, 'Well, I think it's C-Q' so that both of them are confounded" (p. 201). The purpose of relabeling, then, is to upset the system, to make an interpretation of events which does not fit within the current family system, so that the system must change to incorporate it.

Another method employed by Jackson (1967) is to prescribe the symptom. In this procedure family members are explicitly instructed to continue a set of behaviors which they define as the problem. As an example of this procedure, Jackson (Ferber, Mendensolin, & Napier, 1972) provides this intervention: "A delinquent stepson who will not mind his new stepmother is asked to agree that no matter how angry she gets, he will pay no attention to her orders—indeed she is not to give any. He will be disciplined only by his father" (p. 194).

The technique of prescribing the symptom appears to serve three purposes. First, it makes explicit to family members the unwritten rules of the current interaction. Since an assumption of the systems theory is that unwritten rules continue to maintain a system precisely because they are unwritten, systems theorists have designed the technique of making such rules explicit to upset the system, thus providing room for change. This process of making explicit the implicit rules of the system appears to parallel in the interpersonal sphere, the process of making conscious the unconscious processes (i.e., insight) in the intrapsychic sphere.

A second effect of symptom prescription is the therapist's implication that behavior is mutable rather than a permanent personality characteristic. For example, when a therapist tells a patient who is complaining of chronic depression that he should be depressed six days next week instead of four, he is also communicating the information that such behavior can be consciously controlled. Placing the therapist in control of the behavior is a third effect of prescribing the symptom. Use of this technique allows the therapist to observe the desired symptomatic behavior. Such behavior does not then act as a resistance to therapy. Haley (1963) regards gaining control of the family system as the key element in producing change, and he believes this third effect to be the most important outcome of symptom prescription.

Prescribing the symptom is actually a specific technique of systems intervention, representing a class of systems intervention methods we call paradoxical instructions. The major goal of these instructions is to place the therapist in control of the family system. He prescribes usual behavior patterns, thereby robbing the unwritten family rules of their power, and provoking change in the system.

Satir (1967) describes systems family therapy techniques in terms somewhat different from Haley's and Jackson's. She emphasizes that the therapist should present a model of clear communication. The therapist's function within the family system is to check out and clarify the messages sent and received by family members. Questioning and clarifying messages appear to reflect two processes: relabeling messages and making explicit the implicit family rules. Thus, although Satir uses a more affective orientation than Haley and Jackson, she also uses the same processes that the latter therapists advocate for effecting system change.

Turner and Gross (1976) also stress that the therapist must present a model of clear communication, but unlike Satir, they argue that the therapist must be able to share his feelings both about himself and the other family members regarding what is happening in the session. Turner and Gross suggest that the therapist model a problem-solving process called contracting. This involves learning how to use one's feelings to monitor and modify family rules. They describe six problem-solving skills involved in contracting: recognition of feelings; sharing of feelings; enrichment (intensity), demand making, negotiation, and monitoring.

To help the client recognize what the feeling area of most difficulty is, the affective rule-altering therapist will (1) request that each family member use "I" rather than "we" when speaking, (2) teach the family members an affective vocabulary, (3) highlight discrepancies between verbal and nonverbal behaviors, (4) highlight patterns between what a person feels and how that affects what they do, and (5) focus on interactions among family members.

The second stage, sharing feelings, uses the b-s-o format discussed previously. The third stage, enrichment, teaches people how to make quality b-s-o statements. By quality, Turner and Gross mean indicating the intensity of the feeling. To help clients learn to express the varying intensities of their feelings, Turner and Gross encourage clients to use whatever imagery best enables them to capture their reactions. Interestingly, Turner and Gross report that most therapists find the client's expression of intensity quite unsettling, and they report that in their training program this is one of the most difficult stages for novice therapists to master. Enrichment often is assumed to be the same process as the analytic concept of abreaction. It differs in that enrichment occurs within an interpersonal (triadic) context and focuses on the feeling about both self and other in regard to a specific behavior. Merely telling a person how frightened or angry one feels is not an example of enrichment. An example of enrichment with Mike and Mary would be as follows:

Therapist: When you say unattractive—how unattractive?
Mary: A little.
Therapist: What kind of animal do you feel like—
Mary: A mouse—
Therapist: What's the mouse like—big—small . . .
Mary: Small—hiding—God, I feel awful.

Therapist: How awful. You say it so gently—Mary, it makes me feel angry at you—I have to pull and I begin to feel like a real ogre.

Mary: (Slightly louder) Well, I don't want you to feel . . .

Therapist: How are you feeling about me right now, Mary—you are getting older, sexless, sounding tired.

Mary: Confused.

Therapist: Goddamn you, Mary—you are punishing me—I feel like punishing you right back—you make me feel so impotent—like a little boy.

Mike: (Smiling—starting to laugh).

Mary: (Smiles).

Therapist: Does this seem familiar to you, Mike? Part of Mary enjoying getting me?

Mike: Yea, guess you lost (Laughter).

Therapist: Mike, you seem to enjoy that. That makes me feel like you'd let me hang and I resent that. In fact, I feel like sharing very little and ignoring you. How about it, Mary; feel familiar?

Mary: (Looking surprised) Yes.

Therapist: How do you feel about yourself when Mike lets you hang?

Mary: Ugly, old, unimportant (Crying).

Therapist: How ugly—old—unimportant—loud, Mary?

Mary: Very—I can't stand it.

Therapist: Mike, not it—tell Mike.

Mary: I don't like you . . . (much softer)

Therapist: Louder—how much don't you like Mike when he leaves you hanging? Do you want to be more or less motherly?

Mary: More—more (still crying, but louder).

The above example focuses on Mary and her reaction to Mike and the therapist as the latter provokes her. Again the goal is to help the person learn the degree to which he feels something and to legitimize its expression. By demanding that family members share their feelings about self and other, one minimizes the attacking and displaying of emotions that are easy for the person and serve little purpose but to create fireworks.

The fourth stage of Turner and Gross's model is demand-making. Each family member is taught to accent his or her preferences, again using a b-s-o format. Once again clients are encouraged to use imagery to enrich their feelings and to help them describe what they want from their spouses, children, and others. Turner and Gross describe this process as saying what you want without censoring so that you can become aware of what preferences you have and how important they are to you. Operationally, Turner and Gross define demand-making as two or more people using b-s-o and saying what they want and how they would feel about themselves and their significant other if that person gave them what they were asking. At this point in time Turner and Gross tell clients not to argue or disagree, but rather both to share how it would make them feel about themselves and the other if they agreed to the demand and to describe how clear and/or interesting the demand was.

In the fifth stage, negotiating, the couples use the b-s-o format to fight for what they want. The goal is for everyone to feel like a winner. This is to be differentiated from compromise, where often people feel like losers. Negotiation continues until all involved parties feel like winners. This means treating each other as worthy opponents and engaging in affective bargaining using quality b-s-o statements.

Once individuals reach agreement, they must set up consequences that will occur both if they follow through with their agreement and if they fail to do so. A consequence differs from a punishment in that it is (a) planned beforehand, and (b) designed so as to have the person who errs do something special but difficult for the person with whom he contracted. In punishment, the person who made the error is told to do something that he does not like, and which may or may not be rewarding to the person with whom he negotiated. Once a positive and negative consequence is established the clients are ready for the sixth and final stage of the contracting process, monitoring.

Monitoring requires that the clients agree on a specific time to review their contracting, and that the consequences are clearly spelled out and agreeable to all parties. If there is disagreement, the contracting process would begin with recognition of feelings and proceed through the other stages until all parties are feeling good about themselves. The contracting process, by permitting monitoring of family rules via feelings, serves not only to alter dysfunctional rules but teaches family members how to modify rules before they become disruptive. Thus contracting as a problem-solving process teaches individuals how to be affective rule-altering monitors of their family system.

The techniques described here are representative examples of systems intervention methods. In the process of intervention with the family, the systems therapist may vary the composition of the family group. In general almost all systems therapists see the whole family at least once to get a total picture. Beyond that, sessions may involve all family members, individuals, marital pairs, or combinations of siblings. The group or subgroup seen is determined by the therapist's view of which group of family members seems most appropriate to the resolution of the problems involved. The systems approach also may be broadened to include additional relatives and friends of the family in the network approach (Attneave & Speck, 1974), and to sessions including a number of families, which is called multiple-family therapy (Laqueur, 1968; Laqueur, LaBurt, & Morong, 1964).

THERAPISTS

Background and training. Systems family therapists represent the various mental health disciplines of social work, psychology, psychiatry, and nursing. No one discipline dominates in numbers or influence. There appears to be an assumption on the part of systems therapists that training in traditional (individually-oriented) intervention procedures and theories does not consequently enhance the effectiveness of a systems therapist. Therefore nonprofessionals have been trained as interviewers. In fact, Haley (1973) argues that nonprofessionals are more easily trained in the family systems approach than are mental health professionals, precisely because the nonprofessionals have not been exposed to the individual orientation. He contends that professionals must unlearn much of what they have been taught about individual psychodynamics and pathology in order to function effectively as systems interveners. To date, however, no comparative study of the effectiveness of mental health professionals and nonprofessionals has been reported in the literature. Thus Haley's assertion that nonprofessionals make more effective systems therapists stands only as an assertion.

Among nonprofessionals, the focus on intensive training in systems theory and methods argues for the use of paraprofessionals rather than volunteers. For both professionals and nonprofessionals, training in the systems approach most frequently takes place in practical and institute settings, instead of academic programs (Stanton [1975] reports on academic departments and internship facilities offering family therapy training). Training and supervision of systems therapists often involves experientially-oriented supervision rather than the more traditional didactic therapy supervision of case consultation (Cohen, Gross, & Turner, 1975). For example, supervision may include phone calls by the supervisor during the session, the supervisor walking in to directly intervene during the session, calling the trainee out of the session to discuss planning on the spot, and feedback sessions immediately after the session which may include the use of videotape playback (Starr, 1972; Haley, 1971; Cohen, Gross, & Turner, 1975).

Role.   Therapists within the system framework view their role as one of controlling and imposing change upon a currently stabilized and dysfunctional family system. The assumed chronic nature of the dysfunctional pattern of relationships leads system therapists to perceive themselves as rule breakers or crisis creators (Minuchin, 1974; Turner & Gross, 1976). By understanding the family's rules and purposefully disrupting the system, the therapist both attempts to produce a crisis and to control the process of crisis resolution in order to effect a more functional system of interaction. The systems approach can be described as intrusive, powerful or controlling, and manipulative. The role of the systems family therapist is twofold. The therapist acts first as an educator and secondly as a controller of the system (Haley, 1963). Clearly, of these two roles, Haley considers the latter the more important, while Turner and Gross (1976) would stress the former.

Other system therapists perceive that their major role is to act as a model of clear communication (Satir, 1967). Turner and Gross (1976) agree with Satir's emphasis; however, they argue that part of clear communication involves the therapist sharing his feelings both about himself and other family members as they interact with each other. They argue that the therapist needs to model the legitimization of all feelings by being able to acknowledge and share his reactions to the family using the b-s-o format. Turner and Gross perceive the role of the systems therapist as both a model of clear communication and an educator.

SETTING

The model setting for family therapy is a traditional mental health facility. Often such facilities have treatment rooms especially designed for video recording and/or are equipped with a one-way mirror. The family home is used infrequently as a therapy setting. Generally sessions last one to one-and-a-half hours, with one or two therapists intervening. Numerous exceptions exist. One such exception is the "pony express" approach (Starr, 1972), in which a team of therapists works with a family over an extended time period. The length of therapy may range from relatively brief intervention (not more than a month or two) to long-term family therapy lasting more than a year.

CONSUMER

The systems approach has been used with a wide variety of families. Though several of the major figures in the field have emphasized the suitability of the systems approach for dealing with lower-class families (Minuchin et al., 1969), the majority of systems practitioners appear to work with middle-class families.

The boundaries of which family types a systems approach may best serve seem to be determined more by social class than any systematic research that suggests how to increase effectiveness by matching the family therapist and intervention approach.

Like the behavioral-family-therapy approach, the systems orientation emphasizes both specific behavioral goals and behavioral accountability. It also stresses brief interventions with an emphasis on the here and now. Thus this approach is not suitable for families or individuals who wish to explore etiological factors or who prefer longer-term therapy which allows for historical exploration of family issues.

The boundaries of this approach are vague and appear overinclusive. Indeed even the requirement that at least a core group within the family be willing to attend therapy sessions is not viewed as a necessity by some systems-oriented therapists.

Part of the reason for this overinclusiveness is the assumption that symptoms indicate crazy rules are preventing family members from meeting their basic needs. Therefore there are crazy rules of interaction, not crazy people.

12

Evaluative
Research

In this chapter we will provide the reader with a status report on research examining the efficacy of family crisis intervention, crisis intervention, and family therapy.

Family Crisis Intervention

This section focuses on research designed to measure the effectiveness of family crisis intervention methods. Specifically, the basic criteria for evaluating the effectiveness of family crisis intervention will be examined, and issues relevant to the evaluation of family crisis intervention programs will be raised. This will be followed by a summary of the kinds of family crisis intervention projects reported in the literature. Three of these studies will be examined in detail, in terms of both their experimental design and theoretical underpinnings. Finally, we will assess the current state of evaluative research in the family crisis intervention field.

CRITERIA OF EFFECTIVENESS

Theoretical formulations about family crisis resolution suggest that family crises follow a predictable sequence leading to enhanced family functioning or to the increased vulnerability of family members to psychiatric disorder. Further, the family crisis intervention framework hypothesizes that family crisis intervention increases the likelihood of a positive outcome, and decreases vulnerability to mental illness. Therefore it appears that the most basic criterion for evaluating the efficacy of family crisis intervention is: does the frequency of a detrimental outcome of a family crisis decrease with its provision, in contrast with matched families in crisis receiving noncontingent attention?

Further, the family crisis intervention framework hypothesizes that the active participation of family members, and the rapid and intense provision of crisis intervention services jointly increase the likelihood of successful crisis solution. Thus the family crisis intervention framework argues that family-oriented crisis intervention produces a greater decrease in the frequency of detrimental outcomes of family crisis situations than does either individually-oriented crisis treatment or a tertiary treatment modality, whether it be individually or family oriented. Therefore a more comprehensive criterion for evaluating family crisis intervention effectiveness is: does the frequency of a detrimental outcome of a family crisis decrease with its provision in contrast with matched families in crisis receiving alternate forms of treatment?

BASIC ISSUES IN EVALUATING
FAMILY CRISIS INTERVENTION EFFECTIVENESS

A comprehensive evaluation of family crisis intervention services should provide answers to the following questions:

1. Do family crisis intervention services decrease the frequency of a negative outcome in the form of psychiatric disturbance relative to matched families in crisis who receive noncontingent attention?
2. Do family crisis intervention services produce a differential effect in post-crisis adjustment compared to other treatment modalities, such as individually-oriented crisis intervention, individual therapy, family therapy, or hospitalization?
   a) Does rapidity of service provision affect outcome?
   b. Does intensity of service provision affect outcome?
   c) Does inclusion of the family in treatment affect outcome?
3. Is it possible to specify under what conditions one model of family crisis intervention is more effective than another?
4. As a result of intervention are families more able, equally able, less able to cope with additional family crises?

RESEARCH IN FAMILY CRISIS INTERVENTION

Reports of family crisis intervention programs are typically descriptive and anecdotal. With few exceptions, such reports do not attempt to tie programs to a specific theoretical base or framework. An overview of the literature in the family crisis intervention field, however, suggests that these program reports may be classified as belonging to one of two categories: family crises involving a psychiatric problem, and family crises involving an interpersonal or social problem.

In the first group of reports, the researchers define populations appropriate for family crisis intervention in terms of one family member exhibiting acute psychiatric symptomatology (e.g., suicide threats or attempts, bizarre behaviors). In other words, these programs are characterized by their focus on families that have an identified patient exhibiting behaviors considered indicative of mental-health problems. The second group of studies focuses on family crises in which psychiatric symptomatology is not present, but in which the family is in disequilibrium. Such crises include family conflicts, life crises (e.g., premature birth), and externally caused crises (e.g., loss of housing). Family crisis intervention programs representing these two foci will be briefly summarized to provide an overview of the kinds of programs attempted in the field to date.

FAMILY CRISIS INTERVENTION PROGRAMS FOCUSING ON PSYCHIATRIC PROBLEMS

Family crisis intervention programs which focus on psychiatric problems provide rapid and intense intervention, including the frequent use of psycho-pharmaceuticals to alleviate acute symptomatology in the identified patient (Becker & Weiner, 1966). Intervention occurs in a number of settings, including the family home, on an immediate (Cameron & Walters, 1965; Gwaltney, 1974) or delayed basis (within 24 to 48 hours; Becker & Weiner, 1966), at an outpatient mental health famility (MacGregor et al., 1964; Ritchie, 1960; Goldstein & Giddings, 1973), and at the admitting office of a psychiatric hospital (Langsley et al., 1968a). Interveners in these programs are exclusively mental health professionals, usually operating as a mental health team that includes some medically trained personnel.

Program reports usually do not specify the dimensions of the presenting problems to which they respond, except with the vague catchall phrases, "psychiatric emergency" or "psychiatric problem" (Cameron & Walters, 1965; Becker & Weiner, 1966; Gwaltney, 1974). For example, MacGregor (1962) discusses the appropriateness of family crisis treatment for families "threatened with the evidence of mental illness in a child" (p. 15), while Langsley and his colleagues (Langsley et al., 1971) report the use of family crisis treatment with families in which one member is acutely psychotic. It appears that these family crisis intervention programs are designed for cases in which the imminent psychiatric hospitalization of a family member is considered likely. Indeed, a number of these reports discuss effectiveness in terms of preventing hospitalization (Cameron & Walters, 1965; Langsley et al., 1968b).

Family crisis intervention programs focusing on psychiatric problems vary in the degree to which treatment methods emphasize an individual or an interpersonal focus. Two prototypical studies that differ on this issue will be reviewed in detail. The first, a family crisis intervention project in Pinellas County, Florida (Cameron & Walters, 1965) provided twenty-four-hour mobile crisis services, as well as post-crisis follow-up, in cases involving a psychiatric emergency. Staffed by medically trained mental health professionals, this general crisis intervention service reported 60 percent of its calls were received from families, or from police in contact with families, in which a member was showing signs of psychiatric disturbance.

Cameron and Walters suggest that assessment and intervention involved both an individual and a family orientation. In their description, current family relationships were portrayed both as a stress agent and as a resource for the individual. The focus of intervention appears to have been on bolstering the defenses of the individual through family-oriented treatment. Further details of assessment and treatment methods are not reported, nor is there any indication of the frequency or duration of post-crisis follow-up contacts. Outcome data are reported in this study in terms of county-wide frequencies of both jail detention and hospital admission of the mentally ill. In a nine-month period, Cameron and Walters report the virtual elimination of jail detention in psychiatric emergencies, as well as a 13.9 percent decrease in first admissions to the local state hospital.

Cameron and Walters make the assumption, based on the above findings, that the provision of this mobile response family crisis intervention program produced this change. Their data are correlational in nature, and do not provide a basis for concluding a cause-and-effect relationship between service provision and the decreases noted. Moreover, their experimental design, which approximates a one group pre-test post-test paradigm, does not control for the possible confounding effects of a number of extraneous variables, including the effects of history, maturation, test reactivity, instrument decay, and statistical regression. Specifically, a vast number of uncontrolled events may have occurred in the community in addition to the provision of family crisis intervention services, and may account for the differences reported. For example, the police may have become more aware of, and concerned with, psychiatric problems (Hawthorne effect). Police awareness of the project also may have resulted in different reporting procedures. In addition changes in the community itself (e.g., economic conditions, additional mental health facilities) may have occurred over the nine-month period. Likewise changes in personnel in the admissions office of the psychiatric hospital may have affected admission rates. Finally, differences in admissions rates may reflect normal fluctuations in hospitalization rates for the population.

Moving from a methodological to a theoretical vantage point, the Cameron and Walters study does not provide any discussion of the theoretical orientation of the project, nor of any of the assumptions underlying the treatment mode. Further, the vagueness with which treatment procedures are described does not allow replication of the study or discrimination of the theoretical framework used. As such, the project demonstrates many of the weaknesses of family crisis intervention research to date. Providing no theoretical perspective and minimal information about treatment procedures, results can be neither replicated nor compared to other projects in the family crisis intervention field purporting to treat similar problems. Such projects, even if they report positive results, provide little direction for future research or practice in the field.

The second family crisis intervention program focusing on psychiatric problems (Langsley et al., 1968b) emphasizes an interpersonal focus in treatment to a much greater extent than the Cameron and Walters study (1965). Developed at the Colorado Psychopathic Hospital, Langsley's approach to family crisis intervention, termed family crisis therapy, involved brief, outpatient, interpersonally-oriented therapy for families in which a member has been adjudged to need immediate psychiatric hospitalization. Family crisis therapy (FCT) was conducted in lieu of such hospitalization.

Families were included in the study only if the identified patient came voluntarily to the hospital seeking admission, lived within a family, and was no more than an hour's drive from the hospital. From this pool of subjects, families were randomly selected for outpatient treatment using FCT (experimental group) or for standard hospital admission (control group; Pittman et al., 1966b). To assure comparability of the two groups, fifteen characteristics of the identified patient (e.g., social class, marital status, diagnosis) and ten features of family composition (e.g., number and relationship of family members living in the same household) were controlled, along with the use of random selection (Langsley, Flomenhaft, & Machotka, 1969).

Intervention using the FCT approach consisted of the following techniques and procedures (Flomenhaft, Kaplan, & Langsley, 1969):

1. *Family oriented interview.* An interview, lasting one to two hours, was promptly conducted with the identified patient, immediate family members, and significant others. The interview served to assess current interactional patterns, points of disruption in the family system, and events provoking the current request for hospitalization. The problem was reframed as a family problem, and medication was prescribed as needed to various family members. The prescription of medication (to family members in addition to, or instead of, the identified patient) appears to be a powerful relabeling technique in itself. Such a procedure would seem to challenge the family's perception that the problem belongs to only one family member. During the initial session tasks were assigned to individuals or the family group for immediate action. Such tasks are described as family oriented, and require a level of family functioning higher than that evidenced in the session (Pittman et al., 1966a). Also a number of baseline measures, including those of individual and family adaptation, and of previous crisis management ability, were obtained at this point.

2. *Twenty-four hour availability* The family was informed that the staff was available on a twenty-four hour basis.

3. *Home visits.* Within twenty-four hours of the initial interview a home visit was made to assess the internal family environment and to make contact with any additional family members.

4. *Therapy sessions.* Family therapy sessions were held on a frequent basis (daily in some cases) for a period of one to three weeks. Treatment was conducted by a team of mental health professionals, using what Pittman (Pittman et al., 1966a) describes as an "authoritarian" approach. This approach seems to refer to the role of manipulator or controller of system functioning described in systems family therapy and systems crisis intervention. The goals of FCT were described as producing change in the current family interaction pattern that was maintaining the crisis, helping the family reinstate

a previous equilibrium or achieve a better one, and maintaining appropriate role functioning during therapy. No attempt was made to alter personality traits, and insight was not seen as a necessary condition for the alleviation of acute symptoms or maladaptive behavior (Langsley et al., 1968b).

5. *Post-crisis referral.* Following the resumption of previous functioning by the identified patient (i.e., symptom alleviation), referral was made when necessary to other social agencies for follow-up counseling, therapy, or other assistance.

6. *Follow-up.* Measures of individual and family adaptation and crisis management ability were repeated six months following the termination of FCT (or in the case of controls, six months following discharge). Subsequent annual follow-ups were planned, but have not been reported in the literature. Follow-up data were collected by a team of professional social workers uninvolved in the FCT project. These social workers also conducted clinical interviews in the families' homes with both experimental and control groups. Having data collected by a team separate from the treatment therapists serves to partially control for therapist bias. There is no suggestion in the research report that a double blind procedure was used, thus leaving open the possibility of experimenter bias effects.

The Langsley group reports outcome data for 105 experimental families and 150 controls (Langsley, Flomenhaft, & Machotka, 1969a; Langsley, Pittman, & Swank, 1969b). For the experimental group, FCT involved an average of 4.2 office visits, 1.3 home visits, 5.4 phone calls, and 1.2 collateral contacts with social agencies. The mean length of time elapsing between initial contact and FCT termination was 24.2 days. Identified patients in the control group were admitted as regular psychiatric patients and received individual, group, and milieu therapy, medication, and other usual forms of treatment. Mean length of hospitalization was 28.6 days.

Evaluative data, reported from baseline to six-month follow-up, includes the following. First, 29 percent of the control group were readmitted to a psychiatric facility in the six-month period, while 13 percent of the experimental group were admitted for treatment (p .001). In those cases requiring hospitalization in the interim period, the hospital stays of those in the control group were three times as long as the experimentals'. This statistically significant finding suggests that FCT procedures did more than delay hospitalization; rather, they appear to have reduced both the likelihood and length of hospitalization for the treated group.

Secondly, members of the control group lost a median of twenty-three days from their usual role functioning, while experimentals averaged a loss of only five days. Third, on the Social Adjustment Inventory (Berger, Rice, Sewall & Lemkau, 1964), the experimentals showed significant improvement on three subindices (family and social relations, social productivity, and self-management) and on the total scale, while the controls showed significant improvement only on the self-management subscale. Differences between the two groups were not statistically significant, but indicate a trend toward improved social functioning by the experimental group. Fourth, both groups showed significant improvement on the Personal Functioning Scale (Langsley, Flomenhaft, & Machotka, 1969). Results on the Social Adjustment Inventory and the Personal Functioning Scale indicate no difference between control and experimental families over the six-month period.

Based on the findings described above, the Langsley group concludes that: the most frequent precipitating factor in family crises is a change in family equilibrium; families treated using FCT function at least as well after six months as do those in which hospitalization occurred, with the FCT group less likely to be admitted to a hospital following initial treatment; intensive crisis-oriented family therapy is most effective where a crisis exists (a recent acute upset in a family resulting from role changes for one or more family members); hospitalization can be avoided by these treatment methods; and FCT is a much less expensive method of treatment than traditional hospitalization (Langsley, et al., 1968b).

The Langsley studies show a significantly greater degree of research sophistication than other family crisis intervention studies. Better controls are evident in their research design, notably a) the inclusion of a control group receiving an alternate form of treatment, b) random selection of families for inclusion in each group, c) the use of additional tests to assure comparability between experimentals and controls, d) the collection of baseline and follow-up data, e) the use of a team distinct from the treatment team to collect data, and f) the use of evaluation scales measuring interactional variables rather than only individually-oriented scales. The failure to use a double blind in data collection becomes increasingly important in evaluating crisis management ability and adaptation levels, as ratings on these variables were made based on experimenters' conclusions regarding subjective data. Further research is needed, particularly to resolve the issue of experimenter bias.

The FCT approach is explicitly defined by Langsley and his colleagues (1968a) as an example of a "system-oriented" family crisis intervention approach, based on the assumption that "symptoms" of a family member are in part an expression of family conflicts (p. 10). Comparison of the treatment procedures reported by the Langsley group to the proposed systems family crisis intervention model developed in Chapter 4 shows no major incongruities. For example, the systems family intervention model indicates that rapid, intense intervention should occur during a period of family disequilibrium, and would be appropriate in cases where a family member is demonstrating acute psychiatric symptomatology. Furthermore, the model indicates that the presenting problem should be redefined as a family problem and that the goal of treatment would be the production of change in family interaction patterns. The Langsley studies conform to this systems framework on all points. As such, the FCT approach provides a relatively "pure" example of the systems model of family crisis intervention.

FAMILY CRISIS INTERVENTION PROGRAMS FOCUSING ON
INTERPERSONAL AND SOCIAL PROBLEMS

Family crisis intervention programs focusing on family conflicts, life crises, and externally caused crises, are of two general types: those that directly provide services by mental health professionals to families in crisis or at risk of crisis, and those that give services indirectly through consultation and training of natural help givers and volunteers.

Direct services from mental health professionals A number of articles have addressed themselves to the normal crises of family life (Rapoport, 1963; Warkentin & Whitaker, 1966; Hill, 1958). Such articles are concerned with identifying the specific points in family life where crises may occur due to a shift in family responsibilities or membership (e.g., birth of a child, loss of income, death in the family). Also a number of researchers have explored family patterns of dealing with these and other crisis situations, such as disaster (Drabek & Boggs, 1968), terminal illness in a child (Kaplan, Smith, Grobstein, & Fischman, 1973), and the addition or loss of a family member (Hadley, Jakob, Milliones, Caplan, & Spitz, 1974).

Bolman (1968) indicates three major forms of family crisis intervention that focus on interpersonal problems and occur at the primary and secondary levels of prevention. The first approach is community-wide intervention. This aims at improving the state of organization of the community, both at the level of environmental quality and that of effective provision of family supportive services. Its goal is to better the community such that families will face fewer crises, and so the impact of those crises which do occur will not be as great. The milestone approach, the second form of family crisis intervention, attempts to intervene directly with families at those points in their lives when normal family crises are likely to occur. Such programs are limited to those publicly visible family crisis points such as school entry, childbirth, and death. An example here might include free clinics for prenatal and early infant care, teaching parents basic childrearing skills, etc. The third approach, intervention with high-risk families, is oriented toward those families identified through clinical and epidemiologic studies to have the highest risk of crisis or of failure to successfully achieve crisis resolution. While Bolman (1968) occasionally points to high-risk subpopulations in the middle socioeconomic class, he concludes that the major portion of high-risk populations is defined by poverty (see Chapter 1, section 1).

Family crisis intervention programs focusing on interpersonal problems predominantly represent a combination of the milestone and high-risk approaches. Typically these studies include a brief description of the specific family crisis being examined, a brief overview of the services rendered, and a number of illustrative case summaries (Brown, Burditt, & Liddell, 1965; Rapoport, 1965). For example, Brody and Spark (1966) report on the provision of family crisis intervention services when family members request institutionalization of an aged family member. Four illustrative cases are presented, but no indication is given of the conditions under which such a request is considered appropriate, the number of cases involved, or the outcome of intervention. From an experimental viewpoint these studies are incomplete and provide no basis for evaluation and comparison.

Indirect services through volunteers and natural help givers. The second major approach to family crisis intervention focusing on interpersonal and social problems is to provide indirect services through training of and consultation with natural help givers and volunteers. The utilization of these help givers appears to be based on two premises representative of the problem-oriented model of family crisis intervention described in Chapter 3. First, family crisis intervention is viewed as a process of applying specific and definable techniques to any behavioral problem. Second, these intervention techniques can be taught in a relatively brief period of time to individuals who have not received extensive training in a mental health discipline. Thus nonprofessional volunteers and help givers such as police, lawyers, and parents are assumed to be potentially effective crisis interveners.

In the family crisis intervention field, mental health professionals have focused extensively on the police officer as a natural help giver. The movement to train and consult with police on family crises has arisen within the last decade as a result of increasing requests from legal authorities for assistance in this area. While conceptually the training of police officers in handling family crises "fits" the problem-oriented model, it would be a mistake to assume that such training grew out of this concept. Mental health professionals involved in the provision of such services have primarily been experts in police-community relations, and did not necessarily have any previous involvement in family therapy, family crisis intervention, or crisis intervention.

The demand for training in family crisis management by legal authorities is a result of the frequency with which violence is associated with family crises. A number of studies have reported on the incidence and factors associated with intrafamilial violence, including homicide (Boudouris, 1971; O'Brien, 1971; Goode, 1971; Whitehurst, 1971; Federal Bureau of Investigation, 1970). In 1958, Wolfgang reported that between 35 percent and 50 percent of all homicides were perpetrated by one family member on another. The greatest number of assaults also are intrafamilial, which has led a number of writers to suggest that the more intimate a relationship, the greater likelihood of aggressive interaction (Malinowski, 1948; Lorenz, 1966). Thus there are numerous studies which support Emil Durkheim's observation that "while family life has a moderating effect upon suicide, it rather stimulates murder."

"Of all social agencies, it is the police who are most likely to be summoned during intrafamilial disputes, especially among the less privileged. A request for such police intercession may be seen as public declaration that acceptable limits of aggression ... are being reached and that unacceptable violence is imminent" (Bard & Zacker, 1971, p. 678). The police request for training in the area of family crises is not merely a selfless attempt to prevent violence among family members. It is also the result of statistics indicating that police responding to family disputes are more likely to be injured or killed than they are in responding to any other category of police work. In fact, on a national basis, 22 percent of all police deaths and 40 percent of all police injuries are sustained as a result of calls to intervene in domestic disputes (Bard, 1969).

Two major approaches have been taken in the training of police officers as family crisis interveners. These are commonly termed the specialist-generalist and the generalist models. The specialist-generalist model is one in which a subgroup of patrolmen is selected for intensive training in family crisis intervention and then assigned to patrol units as specialists who take primary responsibility for handling domestic disturbances in addition to normal patrol duties. Three major projects have been conducted within the specialist-generalist model—in New York City (Bard, 1970), in Louisville, Kentucky (Driscoll, Meyer, & Schanie, 1971, 1973), and in Oakland, California (Radelet, 1973; Oakland Police Department, 1971).

The generalist model is one in which all patrolmen assigned to a particular precinct or area are given training in family crisis intervention. Following training these officers return to their normal tour of duty and handle domestic disputes as part of their normal police function. The generalist approach assumes that a natural part of the police function is to act as a mental health resource, sometimes called a frontline screener, for psychiatric and other social problems (Liberman, 1969). Specifically, it has been estimated that almost 90 percent of police time is spent in dealing with service calls unrelated to crime control or law enforcement (Epstein, 1962). In addition, requests to intervene in family disputes have been found to account for over 50 percent of all police calls nationwide (President's Commission on Law Enforcement and Administration of Justice, 1967). Two major projects utilizing the generalist model have been conducted, one in Richmond, California (Phelps, Schwartz, & Liebman, 1971), and the other in Columbus, Ohio (McGee et al., 1975). Nonprofessional volunteers have also been utilized as family crisis interveners in cases of family disputes. McGee (1974) reports the provision of mobile response to the family home by such volunteers in cases where police and other community members report a family disturbance and request their assistance.

The Bard (1970) study of police intervention in family crises using the generalist-specialist approach will be reviewed in detail as an example of a family crisis intervention study focusing on interpersonal and social problems. The New York project conducted by Bard between 1967 and 1969 under a LEAA grant is a classic study of police training in family crisis intervention. Eighteen officers were selected from a pool of forty-two volunteers to receive extensive training in family crisis intervention skills. Selection procedures are not clearly specified, although Bard indicates an initial screening by precinct commanders, as well as a requirement that officers have not less than three or more than ten years of experience. Additional selection criteria are not indicated

These eighteen officers participated in a 160-hour training course, which included lectures on specific behavioral techniques to be followed in resolving domestic disputes, field trips, role plays of domestic disputes in which officers intervened (Bard & Zacker, 1971), and sensitivity training (Driscoll, Meyer, & Schanie, 1973). The goal of sensitivity training sessions was "gradual modification of personal attitudes and a generalized increase in self-understanding to facilitate the sensitive nature of interpersonal interventions to be attempted" (Bard, 1970, p. 167). Following this period of intensive training the men were assigned in teams to regular patrol assignments. During the twenty-two-month post-training phase, group discussions and weekly consultation sessions were held.

The New York project outlined six evaluative criteria (Bard, 1970), and evaluated officer performance relative to a control precinct. Although median income was similar for both precincts, ethnic composition was radically different—the experimental precinct was 90+ percent Black, the control precinct, 90+ percent Puerto Rican. This factor suggests questionable comparability between the two groups. In any case, in comparison to the control precinct, it was predicted that: a) the number of family dispute calls would decrease, b) the number of repeat calls by trained officers would decrease, c) homicides would be reduced, d) intrafamilial homicides would decrease, e) the number of assaults would decrease, and f) police injuries would decrease.

Bard reports an outcome in the predicted direction on only two of the six measures. Fewer assaults were found in the experimental precinct, and an injury rate of zero was recorded for trained officers, while three untrained officers were injured. While much has been made of these results, even these two positive outcomes remain questionable. First, while the number of assaults decreased, the number of homicides increased, leaving in doubt the effectiveness of the family crisis teams in decreasing violent behavior. Second, the frequencies of police-sustained injuries are too small to be meaningfully or statistically evaluated. At best, then, the New York project provides only equivocal support for the efficacy of this approach.

Bard does not report any theoretical framework or set of assumptions about interpersonal family crises as a basis for the specific training approach or intervention procedures employed in the study. In retrospect, the Bard study appears to reflect a combination of theoretical approaches. Specifically, the notion of using police officers as natural help givers in family crisis intervention would be consistent with a problem-oriented model of family crisis intervention. So too would be the assumption of the Bard study that specific behavioral techniques, which could be easily taught to nonprofessionals, would be effective in dealing with interpersonal disputes among low income families. However, Bard's emphasis on sensitivity training, which focuses on self-examination and awareness, is inconsistent with a problem-oriented approach, and appears more in line with psychodynamically-based approaches (e.g., the psychoanalytic family crisis intervention model). Thus Bard seems to be suggesting that families in crisis can be helped through problem-oriented intervention focusing on behavior change, while changes in the officers being trained in family crisis intervention must include self-exploration, insight, and attitude shifts. Such an admixture of theoretical models is confusing, since the models define the necessary and sufficient elements in the production of change along different, and conflicting, dimensions.

SUMMARY

Family crisis intervention hypothesizes that a) the active participation of family members, and b) the rapid and c) intense provision of crisis intervention services increase the likelihood of successful crisis resolution. Therefore this framework must demonstrate that family-oriented crisis intervention produces a greater decrease in the frequency of detrimental outcomes of family crises than would occur as a result of using other treatment modes.

Review of the literature in the field indicates that the issue of efficacy has rarely been experimentally examined by researchers in the field. Using a systems model, the Langsley studies compare family crisis intervention to hospitalization in cases of acute psychiatric symptomatology, and conclude that this approach to family crisis intervention results in a decreased frequency of future psychiatric hospitalizations for this population. The study, however, is limited by its selection of hospitalization as an alternate form of treatment, since hospitalization is a rather vague treatment mode. Essentially the Langsley studies are the only ones in the field comparing a family crisis intervention approach to another form of treatment. As such their results provide the first bit of evidence in support of family crisis intervention. Additional studies are needed comparing the outcome of treatment using family crisis intervention models with other treatment modalities such as individual crisis intervention and family therapy.

Reports of family crisis intervention programs have been shown to focus on two kinds of family crises: psychiatric emergencies and interpersonal and social problems. Those focusing on psychiatric emergencies have exclusively utilized mental health professionals as interveners, while those focusing on interpersonal and social problems have emphasized the use of nonprofessional volunteers and police officers. This presumption that different classes of interveners are necessary to treat different classes of family crises suggests that researchers in the field have made implicit assumptions about the necessary and sufficient ingredients needed to produce change in specific classes of family crises. Researchers have not attempted to explicitly define the theoretical framework and assumptions underlying their intervention approaches. Each study appears to be done "uniquely," with little regard for previous research in the field, and with no attempt to draw implications for future research efforts. As such, research efforts within the family crisis intervention field do not constitute a consistent, focused research effort. Further, reports of family crisis intervention programs provide a very vague description of sampling and intervention procedures, thus providing a poor base for replication or elaboration in the field. Such studies are therefore not particularly useful in terms of testing the basic issue of the efficacy of family crisis intervention.

The Langsley studies of family crisis therapy are exceptional in the family crisis intervention field in specifying the theoretical assumptions upon which intervention methods were based. Moreover, this group of studies indicates the use of well-controlled sampling procedures, and specifies treatment methods in much greater detail than do other family crisis intervention studies. The studies, then, do provide a basis for replication and comparison with future research in the field. The advantages of the Langsley studies suggest that research which explicitly defines its theoretical basis, develops an internally consistent approach to intervention, and reports its methodology in detail will prove much more advantageous for the future development of the family crisis intervention field.

Crisis Intervention

To date, evaluative research in crisis intervention has focused on validating the principles of crisis theory (Kaplan, 1968), examining the effectiveness of service provision (Bleach, 1973), outcome research (Weakland et al., 1974; Weisman et al., 1969), and evaluating the quality of service providers (McGee, 1974). Before reviewing these studies, it is important to make clear the criteria to be used in measuring the effectiveness of crisis intervention, and to raise questions pertinent to an evaluation of effectiveness. Difficulties in developing adequate research designs also will be examined.

CRITERIA OF EFFECTIVENESS

Theoretical formulations about crisis and crisis resolution suggest that crisis resolution follows a predictable sequence leading either to enhanced functioning or increased vulnerability to psychiatric disorder. Furthermore, this theoretical framework hypothesizes that crisis intervention will increase the likelihood of a positive outcome and decrease vulnerability to mental illness. It appears, therefore, that the basic criterion for evaluating the effectiveness of crisis intervention is that there be a decreased frequency of detrimental outcomes resulting from crisis situations (Kaplan, 1970). At the primary prevention level, for example, decreased frequency of detrimental outcomes are reflected in systemwide frequencies of psychiatric admissions. Comparisons between matched communities as well as pre- and post-intervention designs are possible ways of evaluating crisis intervention.

At the secondary prevention level, decreased frequencies of detrimental outcome should be reflected in terms of individual outcomes of crisis management. A matched group receiving no outside assistance should show higher psychiatric admission rates than a group receiving crisis intervention services. Use of this criterion also suggests that measures of the effectiveness of a particular model of crisis intervention, or of a particular group of interveners, would likewise be based on measures of differential decrease in the frequency of detrimental outcome.

BASIC QUESTIONS IN EVALUATING CRISIS INTERVENTION EFFECTIVENESS

A comprehensive evaluation of crisis intervention services would need to provide answers to a number of questions.

In the area of primary prevention:

1. Does the provision of primary preventive services in the form of a) education, b) information, and c) consultation with natural help givers reduce the system-wide incidence of such detrimental crisis outcomes as mental disorder and suicide?

In the area of secondary prevention:

2. Does the provision of crisis intervention services to individuals in crisis decrease the likelihood of detrimental outcome in the form of psychiatric disturbance over both the short and long term?

3. Does the provision of crisis intervention services to individuals in crisis produce a differential effect in post-crisis adjustment compared to other treatment modalities such as long-term therapy or hospitalization?

4. Is it possible to specify conditions under which one model of crisis intervention is more effective than another?

5. Does immediacy of service provision affect outcome?

6. As a result of treatment are clients more able, equally able, less able to cope with additional crisis situations (i.e., does learning that can be applied to future crisis situations occur as a result of crisis intervention)?

7. Is it possible to specify under what conditions one group of crisis interveners is more effective than another?

DIFFICULTIES IN DEVELOPING ADEQUATE RESEARCH DESIGNS

A number of researchers have outlined the difficulties inherent in developing adequate research designs in crisis intervention. At the primary prevention level, Caplan (1970) illustrates the problems of such research projects by pointing to the sheer volume of consultees and consultants required to study the effects of consultation with ministers on the outcome of bereavement reactions of widows. For example, sample size would need to be extremely large to provide a large enough subsample of crisis resolution failures and to randomize factors other than the main variable. Secondly, clergymen receiving consultation focusing on bereavement reactions must be matched with a similar set of clergymen not receiving consultation. Thirdly, if consultation arouses interest among the consultee group in working with this crisis population, then differences may be more a result of having been given attention than an outcome of the consultation itself. In order to overcome this obstacle, Caplan (1970) suggests that the experimental group be divided into two groups, one to receive consultation; the other, educational seminars. However, this requires an additional increase in sample size.

It must be clear by this time that the projected study is reaching dimensions that render its feasibility highly questionable. It is hard to imagine developing the requisite channels of communication and stability of relationships with so large a group of clergymen and with their congregations with a team of consultants and mental health educators sufficiently large to organize such a program. (pp. 325–326).

While Caplan points to these obstacles as almost insurmountable, a number of alternatives exist. First, selecting a crisis with a higher incidence in the general population—for example, school entry—would provide a larger and more accessible sample. Moreover, it is a sample for which records and data are normally collected and are readily available to the researcher. Further, both populations under study, the clients (children entering school) and the consultees (teachers) are available to the researchers at a specific location during identified time periods. In addition, schools in the same geographical and socioeconomic areas may be matched for comparison of treatment effects. While no research project is known to have specifically examined the effects of consultation on the school entry crisis, it appears amenable to empirical investigation and presents a practical alternative to Caplan's discussion. While Caplan selects a particular design which may indeed strain the limit of research capacity, his analysis cannot be taken as a generalized statement of the impossibility of examining the effectiveness of primary prevention efforts.

At the secondary prevention level, Bleach (1973) points out the inherent problems in evaluating suicide and other crisis telephone services which maintain caller anonymity as a basic tenet of operation. McGee (1974), in attempting to evaluate volunteer effectiveness, lists the following problems in terms of outcome criteria: a) infrequency with which crisis intervention services permit individual workers to maintain a follow-up caseload, b) lack of continuity of care, c) frequent use of multiple interveners, and d) referral of individuals in crisis to other community sources for continued care (p. 275). While both Bleach and McGee note difficulties in evaluating the effectiveness of secondary crisis intervention services, these problems are not of such magnitude as to prevent effective evaluation. For example, despite caller anonymity, one can still utilize such unobtrusive measures as rates of hospital admission, referral use, and callbacks to measure effectiveness. McGee's recitation of difficulties focuses on traditional therapeutic notions of follow-ups and care continuity, while crisis intervention's goal of successful crisis resolution does not necessarily assume either of these processes as essential. Evaluation of effectiveness must focus on the specific outcome of the crisis problems presented; that is, the level of functioning of the individual following crisis resolution.

The following section will examine the evaluative research data currently available in the field of crisis intervention in order to assess the extent to which basic evaluative questions have been addressed.

VALIDATION OF PRINCIPLES OF CRISIS THEORY

Studies have examined the normal patterns of crisis resolution and delineated the specific tasks which must be completed to produce a positive outcome. These studies have in general focused on a particular crisis stimulus, such as reactions to grief (Lindemann, 1944), to premature birth (Kaplan & Mason, 1960), and to surgery (Janis, 1958). It is on the basis of the similarity of the process of successful crisis resolution which these studies present, that Caplan (1964) finds validation for the general principles of crisis theory. Two prototypical studies, Lindemann's (1944) classic work on bereavement reactions and an examination by Kaplan and Mason (1960) of maternal reactions to premature birth, will be discussed.

Lindemann's study of the symptomatology and management of acute grief (1944) is based on data collected through psychiatric interviews with 101 individuals who had lost a family member. In most cases, the deaths were unanticipated, and occurred in the Coconut Grove night club fire, although some of the deaths had occurred under other circumstances and may have been anticipated. Unfortunately Lindemann does not report such characteristics of his study's population as socioeconomic class, closeness of kinship ties, or extent of death anticipation.

In addition to psychiatric interviews, the study involved the collection of medical data. Interviews were designed to elicit descriptions of symptoms and to note changes in mental status over time. Laboratory work included gastrointestinal and metabolic studies. Lindemann does not report the data collected by these two methods, nor does he provide a statistical analysis of his data. He does report however, that based on his data he found five major symptoms that were "pathognomonic of grief" reactions: 1) somatic distress, 2) preoccupation with the image of the deceased, 3) guilt, 4) hostile feelings, and 5) loss of patterns of conduct. He reported a sixth symptom which he believed to be related to pathological reactions to grief. This symptom was "the appearance of traits of the deceased in the behavior of the bereaved, especially symptoms shown during the last illness, or behavior that may have been shown at the time of the tragedy" (p. 142).

On the basis of these interviews and tests, Lindemann goes on to describe the following tasks as necessary for a successful resolution of the death crisis: achieving emancipation from bondage to the deceased, readjustment to the environment from which the deceased is missing, and the formation of new relationships. Through case examples he points to instances in which grief work was not completed, and to its pathological effects. Lindemann's study was the first to present a description of the steps necessary for successful crisis resolution. As such it provides the basic theoretical notions from which Caplan and others developed crisis theory. On this basis Lindemann's study of bereavement reactions remains a classic. Case studies reported by Lindemann support his conclusions regarding both normal and abnormal grief reactions. The study's major weaknesses lie in its failure to concretely specify the population under study and the procedures used in evaluating grief reactions. These issues prevent replication of the study and, more important, leave in question the generalizability of his results.

Kaplan and Mason (1960) studied maternal reactions to premature birth. Like Lindemann, they focus on the generalized process of crisis resolution. Data in this study were collected from a sample of sixty families in which a premature birth occurred. Demographic data on this population are not provided, so that once again it is impossible to assess the generalizability of the findings. Data collection consisted of several interviews during the period from birth of the premature infant until the child had been in the home for two months. Based on an examination of the clinical material from these interviews, the authors concluded that the mother of a premature infant is confronted with a crisis event, and that its successful resolution depends on the completion of specific tasks. These consist of a) anticipatory grief (e.g., the child might die), b) acknowledgement of failure (e.g., I failed to carry to term), c) resuming actively relating to the baby, and d) accepting the child's special needs as a premature infant and accepting the temporary state of those needs (e.g., the child is not normal now, but will be normal soon). Good outcome was "considered one in which the mother sees the baby as potentially normal, gives it realistic care, and takes pride and satisfaction in that care" (pp. 125–126). The authors further report that deviation from the typical pattern correlated with poor outcome of the stress situation.

This study is descriptive in nature, outlining the process of successful crisis resolution in the specific case of premature birth based on a number of clinical interviews. Like the Lindemann study, this report fails to provide data specifying the population examined, procedures used, or data collected. While the conclusions reached support notions of a generalized crisis resolution process involving a set of tasks specific to the crisis stimulus, failure to collect and report systematic data prevents an empirical validation of the generic model.

In a second article, Kaplan (1970) provides data that support the conclusions reached in the Kaplan and Mason article. Based on data collected through interviews with the mothers of premature infants which focused on the crisis tasks identified in the former study (1960), good and poor outcomes of the premature birth crisis were predicted. Follow-up interviews after the child had been in the home for more than two months correlated significantly with these earlier predictions. The reported results of this study support the assumption of the generic model that crisis outcome is dependent on the completion of a set of tasks specific to the crisis stimulus. Kaplan, however, does not provide a detailed description of the methods used to evaluate interview data. The lack of operationally defined procedures for categorizing interview data precludes the possibility of replication.

EFFECTIVENESS OF SERVICE PROVISION

Studies of the effectiveness of service provision have, in general, analyzed demographic data. For example, Bleach (1973) reports on the effectiveness of a telephone crisis line by using such data as number of calls received, length of calls, time and date of call, problem presented, and disposition of call. Jacobson and his colleagues (1965), in evaluating a walk-in crisis center, give data on the number of clients seen, how many of them are ordinarily underrepresented in the mental health structure, the percentage of clients according to diagnosis, the percentage of clients who have acute versus chronic problems, and the number of visits to the clinic. While these studies purport to analyze the effectiveness of their crisis services, they tend to ignore the basic criterion by which such services must be evaluated. Since crisis theory assumes that crisis is a temporary state of disequilibrium leading both to positive and negative outcome, it would seem essential that any study of the efficacy of a crisis service must include as a major variable the outcome of crisis management. None of the variables reported above would be sufficient to indicate that any change had occurred in crisis outcome as a correlate of crisis intervention. Therefore it must be concluded that these studies fail to address the issue of effectiveness of service provision.

OUTCOME STUDIES

Outcome studies are of two general types: subjective assessment and objective evaluation.

Subjective assessment. By far the bulk of outcome data in crisis intervention involves subjective assessment. Studies generally take the form of case descriptions in which client improvement is assessed by the intervener (Normand, Fensterheim, & Schrenzel, 1967; Harris, Kalis, & Freeman, 1963).

For example, Normand, Fensterheim, and Schrenzel (1967) report on the effectiveness of a walk-in clinic at New York Medical College, emphasizing the utility of brief therapy (a maximum of six sessions) for patients from a low-income community. The authors do not provide a further description of client characteristics. This study primarily represents an individual model approach to crisis intervention, with emphasis on both a dynamic formulation of the problem (stressing the personality of the client and how he relates to his environment), and a subsequent action formulation (stressing the treatment strategy). The action formulation primarily focuses on insight attainment and environmental manipulation. The goal of treatment was defined as amelioration of immediate symptoms rather than "cure" or personality change. The authors provide one illustrative case summary leading to a positive crisis resolution to support their conclusion that brief therapy within the individual model is an appropriate and effective treatment mode. In this case study, symptom alleviation was assessed by means of the retrospective, subjective evaluation of the intervener.

The one-shot case-study approach (Campbell, 1957) used by Normand

and his colleagues is a frequent method of reporting the outcome of crisis intervention programs. It is not a true experiment and serves only to generate hypotheses and raise questions testable through the use of more controlled research methods (Paul, 1967).

A study by Weakland, Fisch, Watzlawick, and Bodin (1974) provides a second example of subjective assessment of crisis intervention services, using in this case a one-group pre-test/post-test design (Campbell, 1957). Weakland and his colleagues report on their experience in working with families at the Brief Treatment Center, Palo Alto, California. Their results are based on a sample of 97 cases in which 236 individuals were seen on a conjoint family basis. They describe this population as heterogeneous both sociologically and in terms of presenting problems.

Treatment contact was limited to a maximum of ten one-hour sessions and consisted of a six-stage treatment process. The first stage involved the initial contact between the client(s) and the Brief Treatment Center. In the second stage, the major presenting problem was assessed. Stage three focused on assessing what behaviors were maintaining the problem based on the assumption that "problem behavior persists only when it is repeatedly reinforced in the course of social interaction between the patient and other significant people" (1974, p. 153). These three stages were generally completed in the first session. At the fourth stage, treatment goals were set. An attempt was made to have the client(s) specify a concrete and reasonable goal. Client goals, however, were assessed by the therapy team for appropriateness and were sometimes superceded by the therapists' goals. Goal setting was expected to be completed by the end of the second session.

Phase five included the bulk of intervention contact and consisted of selecting and imposing intervention strategies. In pursuing the goal of behavior change a number of techniques were used:

1. *Interpretation or relabeling.* Behaviors labeled by clients were relabeled by the therapist (e.g., "hostile" became "concerned interest"). Interpretation here differs from the psychoanalytic tradition in that no assumption was made that distortions were being replaced by reality-based insights. Instead, interpretations or relabelings were used only because they might be effective in breaking up a set of behaviors maintaining the crisis.

2. *The use of idiosyncratic characteristics and motivation.* This set of techniques essentially made use of the clients' responses to the therapeutic setting. Characteristics traditionally termed resistances were used as levers to manipulate the client system (e.g., if the family's goal was to defeat the therapists, therapists predicted a worsening of the problems. Thus achieving the family's goal, defeat of the therapist, required positive change in the family's behavior).

3. *Behaviorally-oriented homework assignments.* Assignments were designed to provide continued work on problem behaviors outside the therapy session.

4. *Paradoxical instructions.* This involved "prescribing behavior that appears in opposition to the goals being sought in order actually to move toward them" (p. 158). An example would be the request to worsen a specific symptom or to make it occur more frequently.

The final stage was termination, which occurred either at the tenth session or earlier, if the goals identified in stage four were achieved. Weakland and his colleagues (1974) attempted to use termination to extend their influence on client behaviors beyond the last session. They did this through the use of the various techniques of intervention listed above, and by informing clients terminating early that the remainder of the ten sessions might be used in the future. Clients also were informed that a three-month follow-up interview would take place. This interview, conducted by experimenters otherwise unrelated to the Brief Treatment Center, was highly structured, focusing on a) whether the specific treatment goal had been met, b) the status of the main complaint, c) the occurrence of any additional improvements, and d) the occurrence of any new problems.

Weakland's findings based on 97 cases in which success was defined as symptom removal and subjective assessment of improvement, were as follows: success, 40 percent; significant improvement (symptom alleviation and subjection assessment of improvement), 32 percent; failure, 28 percent. Weakland and colleagues reported that these results are generally comparable to those obtained in longer-term treatment modalities.

The Weakland group makes no attempt to analyze successes in terms of diagnostic categories or type of presenting complaint. They argue that such analyses primarily focus on characteristics of the individual and are therefore antithetical to their approach. While this position is consistent with the systems approach, it suggests the need for systems adherents to develop an interpersonally-oriented schema in which major types of systemic problems may be identified, and differential rates of effectiveness assessed.

The Weakland study, in using a one-group pre-text/post-test design, fails to control for a number of extraneous variables which may equally well account for the differences observed between pretreatment and follow-up. These variables include the effects of history (extra-experimental and uncontrolled stimuli) and maturation (e.g., spontaneous remission). For example, there may be positive results because of other factors involved in the families being in treatment (e.g., placebo and nonspecific attention factors) rather than because of the treatment program itself (Gross & Miller, 1975).

Objective evaluation. Studies of crisis intervention services which make use of objective outcome data are rare in the crisis intervention literature. A study by Weisman, Feirstein, and Thomas (1969) examined the effects of a three-day hospitalization for clients who would ordinarily have been admitted to a regular mental-hospital system, but were instead admitted to the Emergency Treatment Unit at the Connecticut Mental Health Center. Their study is based on follow-up evaluation of the first 100 patients admitted to the unit. Seventy percent of this group were referred from hospital emergency rooms., 11 percent were unscheduled patients who walked in asking for treatment, and 19 percent were outpatients at the mental health center. Seventy-six percent of this population were from the lower socioeconomic class (Hollingshead's class IV and V), 67 percent were female, and 80 percent were caucasian. Additional demographic variables were presented, making this one of the most detailed accounts of a population base in the crisis intervention literature. Major techniques used in treatment consisted of a) time-limited contracts, b) use of multiple intervention teams, c) the maximizing of patient autonomy, d) strong focus on adaptive strengths of the individual, e) use of psychotropic agents, f) early intense family involvement, and g) use of a structured day to minimize regression.

Weisman and his colleagues reported that 82 percent of those admitted to the crisis hospitalization program were returned to the community within three days; 18 percent were referred for further inpatient treatment. An additional 19 percent of those released were readmitted for longer-term care within a year. In summary, over a one-year follow-up period, 63 percent of their clients were neither transferred nor readmitted, but were maintained in the community. On the basis of this datum, Weisman and his colleagues conclude that brief crisis treatment in an inpatient setting is effective in preventing longer-term psychiatric hospitalization in a majority of cases.

Weisman and his colleagues provide only a sketchy description of the criteria used in selecting clients for treatment on the Emergency Treatment Unit (only a limited number of persons with alcohol and drug problems were accepted; unquietable, violent patients were excluded). Beyond this they fail to provide a description of the criteria for inclusion in the treatment group. Further, they fail to report whether ward personnel could choose to reject prospective patients. In any case, selection criteria must be seen as biased toward very acute cases (70 percent from emergency rooms; 11 percent walk-ins). Also, the vague reporting of selection procedures does not permit replication of the experimental conditions and raises the possibility that selection procedures were biased toward those patients most likely to be helped by crisis hospitalization (better prognosis, hospitalization not really required).

If the sample used in the Weisman study is representative of the population of hospitalized patients, then their conclusion that brief crisis treatment is effective in preventing longer-term hospitalization can be considered. Indeed their use of a one-year follow-up procedure controls for the possibility that crisis treatment only delays traditional hospitalization rather than preventing it. Their data suggests that this occurs only in a minority of cases.

EVALUATION OF THE QUALITY OF SERVICE PROVIDERS

Studies in this area have focused on the quality of volunteer service providers. For example, Bleach and Clairborn (1974) evaluated the effectiveness of volunteer telephone crisis workers by using undergraduate callers with a standard script of a mock crisis situation. Calls were made to three crisis phone lines in the community. Tapes of the phone conversations were rated in terms of counseling skills (Truax-Carkhuff scales of empathy, warmth, and genuineness) and information-giving skills (scales developed by Bleach and Clairborn). Based on ratings of these tapes, they reported the following findings: worker skills do not measurably improve as a function of length of time worked, and volunteers who participated in a rigorous training program emphasizing counseling skills scored higher than did volunteers from other programs with a less rigorous training focus. Details of these training programs are not provided.

The experimental conditions used by Bleach and Clairborn effectively approximate a crisis call without violating the basic premise of crisis lines; that is, the confidentiality of callers. This study also controls such variables as the presenting problem and caller differences. The major limitation of the study is the choice of criteria. No measure of external validity of the rating scales is provided, thus leaving open the question of whether the clinical skills of crisis workers were adequately and accurately measured by the scales employed.

Neither a comparison of the effectiveness of crisis workers of various types (professional, paraprofessional, volunteer, and natural help givers) nor an evaluation of the effects of differential training and supervision modes on intervener effectiveness are available.

SUMMARY

A review of the existing research in the field indicates that few definitive studies of the effectiveness of crisis intervention have been completed. In response to the basic questions of intervention effectiveness raised earlier, we conclude:

1. The following issues have not been addressed in any definitive manner in the literature:
   a) the efficacy of primary prevention;
   b) comparative evaluation of the efficacy of the individual, generic, and systems models;
   c) the effects of immediacy of service provision;
   d) the ability of the individual to deal with succeeding crises as a result of crisis intervention;
   e) comparative evaluation of the efficacy of the use of professionals, paraprofessionals, volunteers, and natural help givers.
2. Some tentative beginnings have been made in the area of validating theoretical constructs.
3. Outcome research is not extensive. Case studies are the most common means of reporting the outcome of crisis intervention programs. As such, they provide hypotheses for further testing, but do not of themselves support the

premise that the provision of crisis intervention services reduces detrimental outcome. Outcome studies, which purport to show that crisis intervention services reduce detrimental outcomes (e.g., Weisman et al., 1969), or are at least as effective as longer-term treatment modalities (e.g., Weakland et al., 1974), fail to control for the possible effects of a number of confounding variables.

In summary, a statement made by Litman (1966) in relation to suicide prevention stands as an adequate summary of the current state of crisis intervention research: "Although reputable authorities from all over the world sincerely believe, on the basis of clinical experience, that many persons have been influenced to refrain from self-destruction, one could not now provide strict scientific proof for the prevention of any suicide by psychiatric or other means" (p. 275). Clearly the crisis intervention field has not systematically and critically evaluated the efficacy of providing crisis intervention services to varying populations. Such research efforts seem necessary at both the primary and secondary prevention levels.

Since crisis theory makes the presumption that crises are self-terminating (four to six weeks according to Caplan), research must demonstrate that the provision of crisis intervention services produces some differential effect on the outcome of the crisis resolution process. This suggests that crisis intervention research must compare outcomes of treated groups to matched groups receiving no treatment. At minimum, then, this requires assigning a random sampling of individuals experiencing a particular crisis to either a control or treatment situation.

Beyond this basic design it may be hypothesized that the three models of crisis intervention produce differential effects on crisis management for different populations (e.g., sociological parameters, different crisis events). Analysis of the differential effectiveness of the various models for different populations might involve a series of experiments, in each of which the population would be held constant and individuals assigned to one of the experimental conditions (a multiple X design where x_1 refers to an individual model paradigm; x_2, to a generic model paradigm, and so on). Such research would provide a basis for deciding under what conditions a particular type of crisis intervention is most effective, and therefore would constitute the treatment of choice.

Family Therapy

In this section, evaluative research in family therapy will be examined. In contrast to the crisis and family crisis literature, family therapy provides research paradigms specific to the theoretical model employed. For this reason we will begin by reviewing the research specific to the psychoanalytic, behavioral, and systems models. This will be followed by a general assessment of the current state of evaluative research in the family field.

EVALUATIVE RESEARCH WITHIN THE PSYCHOANALYTIC MODEL

Evaluative research of psychoanalytically-oriented family therapy is minimal. There is no research recorded that was aimed at empirically investigating the theoretical base for psychoanalytic family therapy, nor is there any literature that examines the theoretical basis by which intrapsychic processes have been extended to encompass interpersonal processes.

The most extensive research in psychoanalytic family therapy is outcome research, which relies primarily on the subjective assessment of successful treatment outcome by the therapist (Balint, 1966; Titchner, 1966; Whitaker, 1966; Markowitz & Kadis, 1968; Sonne & Lincoln, 1966). The definition of successful outcome may be variously described as overly broad or undefined. Wynne (1971) describes several criteria that indicate successful outcome: facilitation of individual therapy, altered behavior, increased understanding, and reduction of tension in family relationships. While Wynne includes tension reduction as an outcome criterion, Mitchell (1961) reports that reduction of tension is a necessary antecedent of family therapy. The contradictory nature of these two statements exemplifies the difficulty in the psychoanalytic family field in achieving consensus for outcome criteria.

A study by Kaffman (1963), utilizing symptom alleviation as the criterion of successful treatment, will serve as an example of outcome research within the psychoanalytic model. Kaffman reports on the outcome of short-term analytic treatment with families in which the child was the identified patient. Subjects were selected for treatment from a pool of 70 families referred to a child guidance clinic. Selection procedures are not specified, with the exception of exclusion categories. Families were excluded from treatment in all cases in which the child showed symptoms of severe or chronic (symptoms present and unchanged for several years) psychopathology, retardation, or neurological damage. On this basis, 41 of the 70 families were considered unsuitable for short-term analytic treatment and were referred elsewhere for guidance, residential treatment, or prolonged therapy. Short-term psychoanalytic therapy was attempted with the remaining 29 families.

Diagnostic classification of the presenting problems of these cases basically fell into three categories: primary behavior disorders (8), neurotic traits (9), and psychoneuroses (11). One family was accepted into treatment in which the presenting problem was classified as a schizophrenic reaction. For 20 of the 29 families the presenting problem was considered chronic; that is, it had lasted for several years. Short-term analytic family treatment was limited to three months and approximately fifteen hours of contact with the therapist. No formal testing or assessment procedure is reported, although Kaffman indicates that the first four family sessions were concerned with assessment and involved both conjoint and individual interviews. Diagnostic classifications appear to be derived from the clinical assessment by the therapist. Treatment methods are unspecified, although Kaffman suggests a dual focus on intrapsychic and interactional processes during therapy.

Treatment outcome was evaluated using a five-point scale on which a rating of 1 meant "no objective change in family dynamics. Subjective feeling that problems and symptoms were even worse" (1963, p. 217), and a rating of 5 suggested a "complete disappearance of referral problems. Complete absence of manifest clinical symptoms. Adequate insight positively used to modify or eradicate sources of former difficulties" (p. 218). While the procedure for evaluating outcome is not detailed by Kaffman, he suggests that ratings were made both by the therapist and by family members. Procedures for combining these ratings are not reported. Based on ratings of improvement using the five-point scale, Kaffman reports that 10 families showed total symptomatic improvement; 11 families, considerable improvement; four families, moderate improvement; and three families were unchanged. One family discontinued treatment. He further reports that a follow-up interview six months later, "in most cases" confirmed the degree of improvement which was obtained at termination. No description is provided of the procedures used or the data collected during the follow-up. On the basis of these data Kaffman concludes that "in more than three-quarters of the cases a remarkable improvement was obtained as shown by the total disappearance of the central symptoms and referral problems" (p. 219).

The Kaffman study does not control for the possible confounding effects of a number of variables. For example, having the same people who provide treatment engaged both in the selection of families appropriate for treatment and in the evaluation of outcome effectiveness raises the possibility that therapist expectations biased both the selection of cases and the reported outcome. This issue becomes even more critical since Kaffman reports that the primary basis for exclusion from the treatment group was the severity and chronicity of pathology. He goes on to report that in 20 of the 29 cases, symptoms were of several years' duration. Thus the study violates its own selection criterion in over two-thirds of its cases. The possibility must be raised that the basis for inclusion in the study reflects additional factors unspecified in the study and possibly biased in the direction of increasing successful outcome. The selection criteria reported by Kaffman, therefore, appear vague and are probably unreplicable. Likewise treatment methods are unspecified and therefore also not amenable to replication.

Ratings of change in symptoms following treatment are not operationally defined. For example, it is not clear whether symptom disappearance refers to absence of symptomatic behavior within the sessions, or within the home. Further, it is not clear whether symptom disappearance was ascertained by direct observation of the therapist or by the verbal report of family members. Interpretation of the results of the Kaffman study is further hindered by the failure to provide comparable control groups of families receiving noncontingent attention or another form of treatment. The lack of control groups raises the possibility that positive results could be attributable to factors other than short-term analytic family treatment (e.g., spontaneous remission, nonspecific attention).

Finally, Kaffman's conclusion that total disappearance of the central symptoms was obtained in more than 75 percent of the cases must be questioned in terms of his own reported data that only 10 of the 29 families (34 percent) showed total symptomatic improvement following treatment. While short-term analytic family therapy may be an effective method of treating behavioral and neurotic problems, it must be concluded that the Kaffman study fails to control for the effects of a number of confounding variables and therefore does not provide a substantial support of this hypothesis.

The Kaffman study is representative of research attempted within the psychoanalytic model (e.g., Friedman et al., 1965; Markowitz & Kadis, 1968; Titchner, 1966), and as such demonstrates some of the major methodological problems encountered therein. It must be concluded that the psychoanalytic family therapy model presently lacks supporting evidence, in terms of carefully controlled outcome research, as to its effectiveness as a therapeutic method.

EVALUATIVE RESEARCH WITHIN THE BEHAVIORAL MODEL

Since the operant family approach is based on the collection of baseline data and subsequent measures of the frequency of the target behavior(s), ideally evaluation is built into each intervention. The wealth of evaluative data thus produced is a strong point of the operant family approach. Results are reported in several ways, including the presentation of case studies (Liberman, 1970), self-report methods (verbal reports, self-rating scales), charting of behavior (Knox, 1971; Stuart, 1970), and direct observation and rating of behavior occurrence by the therapist and/or researcher (Hawkins et al., 1966).

Numerous studies indicate successful outcome at treatment termination (Engeln et al., 1968; Stuart, 1970; Straughan, 1964; Walker, Winkel, Peterson, & Morrison, 1965). For illustrative purposes, a prototypical study by Hawkins and his colleagues (1966) will be reviewed. This study was designed to test the notion that operant family therapy in a natural setting (home) with a parent in the role of change agent would produce predicted changes in targeted behaviors of a child. The focus of change was the undesirable behavior of a four-year-old child in relation to his mother, who was to act as the change agent. The experimenters focused on nine undesirable behaviors of the child, including biting his shirt or arm; kicking or biting himself, others, or objects; and removing or threatening to remove his clothing. Treatment consisted of two to three sessions a week for approximately twenty weeks. Treatment was divided into five stages. During the first baseline period (16 sessions), experimenters recorded the pretreatment rate of the targeted behaviors, the child's verbalizations, and the mother's verbalizations. Mean agreement on these three measures between experimenters ranged from correlations of .88 to .96.

During the first experimental period the mother was instructed to positively or negatively reinforce her son's behavior in response to appropriate gestural signals by the experimenter in a prescribed way. After six sessions, a second baseline period (14 sessions) was instituted. No signals were given by the experimenter and the mother was instructed to interact with her son as she had prior to treatment.[1] A second experimental period was instituted wherein the experimental procedure was reintroduced and continued for six sessions. A final follow-up was conducted after a twenty-four-day period of no contact between experimenters and the family. During these final three sessions the mother was instructed to act as she had previous to treatment; no signals were provided.

A sharp decrease in the frequency of the targeted behaviors was noted in the first experimental period. The rate of occurrence of the targeted behaviors increased during the second baseline period, though not to the pretreatment level. The rate of targeted behavior during the second experimental period was comparable to that obtained during the first experimental period. Data obtained during the follow-up indicate that the targeted behaviors remained at a low rate after twenty-four days of no contact between the family and the experimenters. Measures of verbalization over the five treatment phases indicated no change in the child's rate of verbalization. This would suggest that the treatment procedures produced a change in the targeted behaviors but did not generalize to other classes of behavior such as verbalization. On the other hand, the mother's verbalization rates showed significant change in frequency in relation to the child's targetted behaviors. A correlation of .39 was found between mother's verbalizations and child's targeted behavior for baseline periods; while a correlation of −.41 was found for treatment periods (experimental and follow-up). This finding suggests that prior to treatment the mother attended to and thereby reinforced undesirable behaviors while ignoring and extinguishing positive behaviors. Following treatment, the mother's verbalizations showed a reversal in which negative behaviors received less, and positive behavior more, attention.

This study demonstrates many of the elements of the operant family model, and supports the notion that family members can be trained to act as behavior modifiers. Hawkins and his colleagues, however, do not deal with a number of elements that may contribute to the outcome of the study. For example, the effect of the experimenters' presence on both child and parent is ignored. The cueing of responses by the experimenters, paired with their lack of distress when a targeted behavior was displayed, may have served both a modeling and a supportive function for the mother. Likewise these experimenter behaviors may have directly affected the child's behavior. An additional methodological problem exists with regard to the interobserver reliability ratings reported by Hawkins and his colleagues. Since the observers were in a position not only to observe the interactive behavior of the mother and son, but also to observe each also to observe each other's behavior, it is possible that each observer could detect when the other scored a response. On this basis, the obtained reliability scores may be overestimated.

The Hawkins study is an example of the intrasubject replication design that has been used in a number of family therapy studies (Zeilberger, Sampen, & Sloane, 1968; Sherman & Baer, 1969). This approach involves the gathering of baseline bata on the behavior in question, followed by the application of treatment techniques. "The ensuing behavior change is evaluated by withdrawing the treatment element and noting the return of the behavior to or near its pretreatment level" (LeBow, 1972, p. 369). This approach often is called a reversal technique (ABAB design), and its purpose is to indicate that behavior change was due to the application of the specific technique employed rather than to coincidental processes. The difficulty with this approach is that undesirable behaviors must be temporarily reinstated; it is therefore frequently resisted by the family.

While numerous studies of operant family therapy indicate successful outcome at treatment termination, few studies include a follow-up evaluation to assess the stability of those changes. In other words, there is little evidence in the operant family literature as to whether such changes hold up over time. Further, evidence is meager as to whether families incorporate behavioral principles into their family system in such a way that they are able to modify future problem behaviors. Thus, while short term effectiveness is supported by experimental findings, little can be said about the durability of behavior change or the generalization of behavior principles within the family. The importance of the therapist's role is likewise unresolved. In addition, researchers in the field have not attempted to compare the effectiveness of the operant family model to other treatment approaches. Thus there are currently no data to suggest that the operant family model is more or less effective than any other therapeutic paradigm in treating any particular set of symptoms or any specific type of family. Each of these issues is amenable to experimental study and may become a major focus of operant family therapy research in the future.

EVALUATIVE RESEARCH WITHIN THE SYSTEMS MODEL

Little evaluative research has been done by adherents of the systems model. Preliminary studies have attempted to isolate transactional variables which clearly distinguish families with a dysfunctional pattern of interaction (exemplified by a symptom-bearing member) from "normal" families. The Bateson project (Bateson et al., 1956; Bateson, 1961) is one such attempt. This project attempted to develop a descriptive system for families, based on data from therapy sessions with families of schizophrenics. Schizophrenic and nonschizophrenic families were placed in a standard interview situation (including both periods in which an interviewer was present and was absent). As a result of these interview sessions, project planners tried to choose experimental settings in which to measure family behavior. However, in attempting actual experiments with families, Bateson reported that the design was inadequate and concluded that theoretical notions at the transactional level remained so vague that it was relatively impossible to specify the main variable to be measured; furthermore, this kind of experimentation and the sampling problems affecting it had no precedent in the mental health field.

Haley (1962) has approached family systems analysis from a different vantage point, arguing that experimental designs for family research cannot be paralleled with those used in small-group research. He reports that in the latter, the idea is to examine the effect of the experimental setting or context on the behavior of unrelated individuals. The goal of family research, according to Haley, is exactly the opposite—to measure how members of the family *"typically* respond to each other, while attempting to eliminate as much as possible the effect of that particular setting on their performance" (p. 269). In the same article Haley reports the results of a coalition experiment, using a triadic family system in an experimental setting in which points are gained for entering into a coalition with another family member through the use of signals. The signals in this study were visual scores (points) accumulated as a result of pressing buttons. The stated goal of each set of four two-minute sessions was for each individual family member to attempt to win (i.e., have the highest score).

A sample of 60 families participated in the experiment: 30 normal families randomly selected from a high-school directory with no history of psychotherapy and willing to come in for the experiment, and 30 families which included a schizophrenic child and were selected on the basis of their availability. The differences between the groups were in age and sex distribution of children, psychotherapy experience, and educational range of the parents. Haley does not discuss the possible effects of these sampling differences.

Statistically significant findings indicated that family members in the schizophrenic group pressed their buttons less than members of the normal group, spent less time scoring with each other, and had longer periods when no one was scoring. Further, normal family members shared coalitions about equally, while parents of the schizophrenics formed coalitions with each other more than the normal parents, and with their child, less than did normal parents. When asked to plan the winner and loser of each round, families with a schizophrenic tended to predict rather than plan how the round would come out. Moreover, almost all normal families were able to make the winner of the round come out as planned, while half of the schizophrenic group were unsuccessful.

Haley's coalition study (1962) is essentially a pilot study which is of primary significance in supporting the hypothesis that research aimed at isolating and testing interactional variables is possible. However, numerous theoretical and methodological problems exist within it. First, Haley is attempting to measure the "typical" patterns of coalition formation among the two groups of families. He does not, however, present any evidence that the behaviors observed in the experimental context accurately represent typical family patterns. It is equally possible that his findings represent atypical family responses to an unusual situation.

The issue of sampling also appears critical. Haley points out that sampling designs in psychology are typically based on the characteristics of individuals (e.g., sex and age), and that these designs may be inappropriate for selecting a sample of families. He then, however, defines his samples of nonschizophrenic and schizophrenic families along these precise parameters, and further reports that on the basis of these individual characteristics his two samplings are not comparable. Thus there is no indication of comparability between the two samples in terms of either individual or family characteristics.

A second sampling problem concerns the study's bias toward families who are willing to cooperate. This bias may well restrict the generalization of results to a population of volunteer families. Further, it seems unlikely that the two groups could be considered comparable even on the dimension of volunteering. Specifically, it might be assumed that nonschizophrenic families volunteered either to confirm their "health" or to use the experimental setting as an opportunity to seek help with family problems. Families with a schizophrenic child, on the other hand, might view the experimental setting either as a chance to disavow responsibility for their child's pathological behavior or as an opportunity to acquire help for themselves. These differences are likely to have the effect of making the experimental setting, which was designed to be objectively identical for all families, subjectively different for the two groups. Results obtained by Haley thus may be confounded by the different expectations of the two groups.

A third sampling problem has to do with the presumption that schizophrenia is a single entity and that therefore all families in the schizophrenic group were homogeneous on this dimension. Haley's findings in fact suggest that the schizophrenic group was more heterogeneous than the controls in responding to the experimental situation, and it is possible that the results are confounded by the presumption of homogeneity in an actually diverse sample. A similar problem exists with regard to the control group, since it is defined largely by not having a child labeled schizophrenic.

The Haley study is prototypical in its attempt to define and measure interactional variables and is representative of the sampling problems involved. A number of studies of family interaction have been undertaken, including those concerned with decision making (Strodbeck, 1954; Ferreira & Winter, 1965; Bodin, 1969; Farina & Dunham, 1963; Watzlawick, 1966); and behavior (Murrell & Stachowiak, 1967; Ferreira, Winter, & Poindexter, 1966; Winter & Ferreira, 1967).

In addition, a comparatively large amount of family interaction research has been concerned with family communication patterns and family rules of affective expression. In most of these studies families with a schizophrenic or a nonschizophrenic disturbed child were compared to families with normal, healthy children. Although no causality can be inferred from correlations made between patterns of expression and either normal or schizophrenic families, the findings can aid family researchers and therapists in their understanding of the mechanics of the "disturbed" vs. the "healthy" family systems. Later the correlations found in these exploratory studies may be examined for causal relationships through the use of more rigorously designed experiments.

Several of these communication studies have found a relationship between the expression of positive affect and the category of the family, (i.e., schizophrenic vs. normal). Findings indicate that healthy families display more warmth and support (Alexander, 1973a, 1973b; Hetherington, Stouwie, & Ridberg, 1971; Lewis, Beavers, Gosset, & Phillips, 1976; Mishler & Waxler, 1968; Stabenau, Turpin, Werner, & Pollin, 1965). In addition, findings support the notion that healthy families have a friendlier atmosphere and more opportunities for tension release through laughter and humor than do disturbed families (Blum, 1972; Lewis et al., 1976; Mishler & Waxler, 1968; Riskin & Faunce, 1970).

Although all of these studies support the notion of an existing relationship between disturbed or healthy families and communication patterns, some studies have found no difference between the families in terms of their expression of positive affect (Bugental, Love, & Kaswan, 1972; Cheek 1964a, 1964b, 1965; Winter & Ferreira, 1967). Further, a few of these studies have found no significant difference in overt hostility or antagonism when comparing schizophrenic and normal families (Cheek 1964a, 1964b, 1965; Winter & Ferreira, 1967).

While some studies show no evidence of the utility of studying patterns of communication, the majority of results from observation and assessment of family interactions indicate that there are significant differences for affective expression, both positive and negative. There is strong support for the notion that members of normal families express greater negative affect, including anger and dislike (Blum, 1972; Lewis et al., 1976; Mishler & Waxler, 1968; and Riskin & Faunce, 1970). However, displaying extreme negative affect, including hostility, antagonism, disparaging criticism and rejection, has been shown as less likely in a healthy family than a disturbed one (Beakel & Mehrabian, 1969; Blum, 1972; Bugental et al., 1972; Ferreira, 1963; Friedman & Friedman, 1970; Glick, Gross & Pepinsky, 1978; Hetherington et al., 1971; Hutchinson, 1967; Lennard & Bernstein, 1969; Lewis et al., 1976; Riskin & Faunce, 1970; Schulman, Shoemaker, & Moelis, 1962; Stabenau et al., 1965).

As a whole, the family interaction research on patterns of communication indicates that healthy families tend to show a greater amount and variety of affective expression. However, a summary of this area also must consider the several studies in which no significant differences were found between schizophrenic and normal families for either positive or negative affect (Cheek 1964a, 1964b, 1965; Ferreira & Winter, 1965; Winter & Ferreira, 1967).

A major issue which is still to be resolved by systems theorists is the definition of the critical variables to be examined in interactional research. If a critical variable is the system's rules for family interaction as Jackson (1968a), Haley (1971), Satir (1971), and Turner & Gross (1976) argue, then a means must be developed to objectively specify which rule structures result in dysfunction and which define healthy interaction. Until the critical variables are isolated it appears unlikely that the issue of adequately controlled comparison groups can be resolved, since one must wonder what the systems researcher is controlling for (i.e., are socioeconomic class, histories of previous psychiatric hospitalization, or ethnic background relevant dimensions?). Jacob (1975), in an exhaustive review of family interaction studies, has shown that demographic variables, including age of children and parents, sex and birth order of child, social class, religion, and ethnicity, are important determinants of family behaviors and must therefore be controlled. Most critically, it is likely that until such time as a methodology for reliably measuring family interaction is developed, little headway will be made in interactional research.

Like the interaction research described above, studies focusing on family therapy outcome within the systems approach are still in the exploratory stage. One attempt to assess outcome of systems family intervention was conducted by Minuchin and his associates (Minuchin, et al., 1967). Family systems therapy was conducted with twelve families who had one member labeled a juvenile delinquent. A control group of ten families having no children labeled delinquent, and matched on socioeconomic and age factors, was used for comparison. Data collected on these families served as a criterion for "normal" or "nondelinquent" family interaction.

Families with a delinquent child had thirty conjoint sessions and were pre- and post-tested using the Family Interaction Appreciation Test (FIAT) and the Family Task. Both of these instruments measure the actual interaction of the family members rather than focusing on self-report or personality measures (Olson, 1970). Also, interaction patterns in treatment sessions near the beginning and the end of therapy were systematically coded. The Family Task instrument showed little change over the treatment period or in comparison with the normal families. However, the FIAT showed many changes in the predicted direction of the normal families. Minuchin and his colleagues also rated seven of the twelve families as clinically improved as a result of treatment.

A number of methodological problems in the Minuchin study limit the possibility of generalizing about the findings. First, problems in sample selection parallel those encountered in the Haley study, including a bias toward families willing to cooperate, the lack of an operational definition of delinquency, and the possibility that families in the control group might, if followed over time, also demonstrate delinquent behavior. Secondly, the use of a volunteer control group receiving no treatment leaves open the possibility that change in the treatment group was due to factors unrelated to the specific treatment approach such as placebo effects or nonspecific attention (Goldstein, 1962; Umana & Schwebel, 1974; Gross & Miller, 1975).

In addition, Minuchin and his colleagues do not provide an operational definition of improvement (or lack of it) in concluding that seven of the twelve families improved as a result of treatment. In fact they report that the criteria used in deciding whether a family had improved varied from family to family. Thus ratings of clinical improvement rest on the clinical judgment of the treatment team, and may be confounded by therapist bias. A final problem exists in the repeated administration of the FIAT and the Family Task. No control was provided for the possible effects of test reactivity or maturation. Changes in the scores on these instruments, then, may be due to repeated administration rather than to the effects of therapy.

A study by Sigal and his colleagues (Sigal, Rakoff, & Epstein, 1967) examines the interaction of process and outcome variables in a conjoint family setting. The researchers examined the hypothesis that family functioning after a period of conjoint family therapy could be predicted from the amount of interaction and the change in interaction among family members observed in early treatment sessions. Twenty families who meet the criteria of being intact, sufficiently fluent in English for treatment, and in which the identified patient was at least seven years old and not overtly psychotic, received conjoint family therapy for periods ranging from an average of five sessions (defined by Sigal et al., as premature termination) to twenty-five sessions. Ratings based on the family's interaction style were made by the therapist after the second, sixth, and twelfth sessions. The therapists also completed a questionnaire, the Family Category Schema, after each session. Members of the staff not involved in treatment rated therapist reports for change in the family and these ratings were later combined to measure the outcome of treatment. All families in the study also were interviewed prior to treatment, and again fourteen months after treatment began, by other members of the treatment team. After both interviews, questionnaires (including the Family Category Schema) were completed by the interview team and rated by three judges for change in eleven areas (e.g., instrumental problem solving, affective communication). Judges rated change over the fourteen-month time period as follows: no change (0), slight change (1), moderage change (2), great change (3). An interjudge reliability rating of 97 percent was found when a difference of one scale point was permitted. Based on these ratings, five families were included in the poor outcome group, and one was dropped from the study because follow-up could not be completed.

No relationship was found between the success of treatment measured in the fourteen-month follow-up and the interaction scores obtained during the second, sixth, and twelfth sessions. Also, the amount of interaction was found to increase during treatment, but this increase was not found to be related to outcome. The Sigal study is limited by its small N in the poor outcome group.

Of the five families comprising this group, three withdrew from treatment prior to the twelfth session, further decreasing sample size. A second problem is based on having to rely on therapist statements about interaction. Sigal and his colleagues make the assumption that these statements accurately reflect the frequency and type of interaction occurring during the session. The researchers report no attempt to check the validity of these reports (for example, through an objective count of transcribed sessions). In addition to the possibility of inaccuracy, it is possible that therapists were aware of the purposes of the study and that their reports were influenced by this knowledge.

This study clearly indicates the dilemma of systems therapy research. Interaction measures (both in terms of kind and frequency of interaction) fail to reflect differential outcomes of therapy as assessed by therapists. The implication of these results is that the systems model has not as yet developed a reliable system of classifying interaction that is relevant either to notions of improved functioning or to discriminating dysfunctional family interaction patterns from functional or adequate patterns. In a review of family interaction research, Riskin & Faunce (1970) found that many studies professing to measure interaction actually measure general atmosphere or climate. Further, Jacob (1975) reviewed the interaction literature and found that the families' behaviors measured often varied depending upon the task, setting, and presence of an observer. Exploratory studies examining a number of diverse variables (e.g., frequency and kind of coalitions, kind of family rules) over a wide range of families (e.g., socioeconomic and ethnic variables, presence versus absence of diagnosed psychiatric disturbance) are necessary in order to begin to factor out the most fruitful hypotheses.

SUMMARY

One generalization that can be made, based on a survey of family therapy literature, is that few empirical studies of family therapy outcome have been attempted in the field. Further, studies of family therapy outcome which have been reported are primarily of a preliminary and tentative nature. The Group for the Advancement of Psychiatry report (1970), for example, indicates that of 312 family therapists surveyed, only 3 percent were currently involved in research related to this field.

A comprehensive evaluation of family therapy services must provide answers to a number of questions. These are noted below, followed by a summary of the relevant research in the area.

1. What are the critical variables in defining healthy/unhealthy family functioning? Gurman (1973) reviewed marital therapy outcome research and found that while most studies reported favorable outcomes for patients treated with marital therapy, the studies often were methodologically weak, used small samples, and therefore have limited generalizability. Gurman points to the need for marital therapy outcome studies that include a better description of patients (including socioeconomic and educational level), independent judge evaluations

(other than those made by the therapist), behavioral data, and multidimensional assessments. He is especially concerned with the need for interactional testing to assess effects on patterns of behavior among family members (e.g., role behavior, expectations, and conflict).

In a review of the findings of outcomes of marital counseling, Beck (1975) analyzed the research designs of several studies. Like Gurman (1973), she also points to the need for larger patient samples, adequate controls for extraneous factors, more frequent follow-up, and more sophisticated outcome measures. In addition Beck puts extra emphasis on the need for instruments that are less time consuming, less expensive, broader in coverage, and applicable to some degree to the practical setting.

A review of the family therapy outcome literature by Wells, Dilkes, & Trivelli (1972) further assesses the methodological problems associated with this research. These include inappropriate experimental design, selection bias, unreliable or invalid measures, and failure to assess important variables at pre- and post-treatment, and follow-up points.

As pointed out previously, none of the models provide a concrete (objectively defined) statement of the critical variables differentiating healthy families from those that are dysfunctional (likely to produce symptomatic behavior in a family member). Each model points to a particular set of variables, but defines them too loosely to provide a concrete base for evaluation. For example, the psychoanalytic model suggests that current family interaction may be motivated either by present stimuli or by unresolved conflicts from the family members' pasts, and that this differentiates the healthy family from the unhealthy one. However, the model fails to provide specific variables that outline the boundaries of healthy versus unhealthy families.

Behaviorists, on the other hand, suggest that current family interaction predominantly reflects either positive reinforcement principles or negative reinforcement and deceleration principles, and that this differentiates the healthy family from the unhealthy one. This model does not indicate, on an a priori basis, the specific behaviors to be accelerated or decelerated. Systems theorists focus on the family's rules of interaction, suggesting that family rules may be either overt, or covert and rigid, and that this differentiates healthy from unhealthy family systems. This model does not differentiate the effect of various sets of rules (e.g., those affecting the sharing of information and affect, and decision making). These models are no more specific than the psychoanalytic model in outlining a priori the variables which differentiate healthy from unhealthy families.

Each perspective provides a potential base for the development of testable hypotheses and for subsequent research efforts. Cromwell, Olson, & Fournier (1976) in a review of the diagnostic and evaluation techniques, also point to a need for marriage and family therapy research to be carried on more as a science than as an art. They conclude that it is necessary to bridge the gaps between the research, theory, and practice of counseling. They suggest that this union be realized through the use of methods that tap theoretical concepts and dimensions related to the treatment process.

These suggestions agree with those of Framo (1972), who earlier pointed to the need to fill the gap between family researcher and therapist through the use of methods based on clinical theories. Although it is difficult to extract meaningful variables out of clinical complexity, and further to put these subjective concepts into operational form, Framo asserts that family researchers must attempt to test the pre-scientific, clinical theorizing about how the family operates in producing health or pathology in its members. He posits that the difficulties of clinical theory based research will be balanced out by the benefits gained (i.e., an ability to make sense of observational data and the prevention of self-deception on the part of therapists). Yet a review of the literature indicates that attempts to examine family interaction (Bateson et al., 1956) have consistently bogged down at the point of trying to develop objectively defined and reliable measures of interactional variables.

2. Does the provision of family therapy to families with a member exhibiting psychiatric symptomatology produce a differential effect on symptom alleviation when compared to a matched group of families receiving noncontingent attention? Research reported in the family therapy literature has not compared families in treatment to similar families in which treatment is either delayed or withheld. While a number of studies (Kaffman, 1963; Hawkins et al., 1966; Minuchin et al., 1967) purport to show that treated families improve as a result of treatment, they fail to control for the possibility that these changes are unrelated to treatment.

In addition, little if any attention has been paid to deterioration as a result of marital and family therapy. A recent review by Gurman and Kniskern (1977) found that of those studies that allowed for measurement of deterioration, half presented reasonable, or undeniable evidence of such negative effects. In other words, these studies reported that five to ten percent of the treated patients or marital or family relationships worsened as a result of therapy.

Gurman and Kniskern (1977) examined factors that influence the occurrence of deterioration. They found that treatment outcome was not related to the severity or chronicity of the family or marital disorder. However, they did find a relationship between certain therapist styles (e.g., one that is highly confrontive, has poor relationship-building skills, structures and guides early in the treatment sessions, lacks intervention techniques that moderate feedback from others towards members with low ego strength) and deterioration.

In addition, reviewed findings (Gurman & Kniskern, 1977) suggest that there is a relationship between different forms of marital-family therapy and treatment outcome. More specifically this means that deterioration was more common in individual and group-marital therapy than in conjoint or concurrent collaborative therapy. The more involved both spouses or all family members are in the treatment process, the less chance of negative effects or deterioration.

More research concerning treatment outcome needs to be conducted in order to more fully understand the symptom alleviation and/or symptom exacerbation effects of marital and family therapy.

3. Does the provision of family therapy services produce a differential effect on symptom alleviation of a family member compared to other treatment modalities such as individual therapy or hospitalization? This issue has not been addressed in the family therapy literature. It is of particular importance since one of the basic contentions of family therapists is that pathological symptomatology is often a response to family interactions, and is therefore more effectively alleviated through treatment of the family group.

4. Does the provision of family therapy to families produce a differential effect on family interaction patterns when compared to a matched group of families receiving noncontingent attention? This question is critical, as a number of family therapists define treatment success not so much in terms of symptom removal as in terms of changing family interaction style. The difficulty here is that process-oriented research has so far failed to identify the critical interaction variables which would be required to answer this.

5. Does the provision of family therapy services produce a differential effect on family interaction patterns when compared to other treatment modalities such as individual therapy or hospitalization? Since family therapists contend that much of what is labeled deviant behavior is a response to a system of interactions, and further that treatment of the system is necessary to understanding and changing these patterns, they are essentially arguing that family treatment is more effective in changing interaction than is individually oriented treatment. While it would seem critical to test this hypothesis, no research has been reported in the area. As in question 4, such research demands the identification of critical interaction variables.

6. Is it possible to specify conditions under which one model of family therapy is more effective than another? The three models differ in their assumptions about the causes and methods of treatment of family dysfunction. It seems equally possible that the models may differ in their effectiveness in treating different kinds of families or family problems. This issue has not been addressed in the family therapy literature.

7. As a result of family therapy are families more able, equally able, less able to cope with future family problems (i.e., does learning that can be generalized to future family problems occur as a result of family therapy)? This question seems critical in that adherents of all three models of family therapy espouse the goal that family therapy result in fairly permanent changes in family interaction such that new problems are dealt with more effectively as a result of intervention. Research in the family therapy area has not addressed this.

On the whole there has been little in the way of a systematic approach to measuring the outcome of the specific process of engaging in family therapy (Olson, 1970). Parloff's description of the state of family research in 1961, remains accurate today: "The relevant literature is vast, yet very little of it would be classed by the rigorous investigator as research. Most of the contributors to the area have been clinician-naturalists who, having perhaps a Freud-like vision of themselves, have made salutory advances from observation to conclusions with a maximum of vigor and a minimum of rigor" (p. 39). A number of problems exist in the family therapy field which must be considered in order to develop adequate research designs. Ackerman (1958) points to the lack of consensus and precision of many of the descriptive terms, while Rabkin (1965) argues for the development of a language of interaction. Ackerman also acknowledges the need for specification of explicit criteria for testing the validity of hypotheses relevant to notions of therapeutic effectiveness. Boszor-menyi-Nagy (1965) remarks on the need for operationally definable process concepts of psychological health for families.

There seems to be a trend in the family field to focus exclusively on process variables, based on the contention that the critical variables in measuring family interaction must be identified before outcome research can be meaningful. If process-oriented research is the direction of choice, then it appears that a series of exploratory studies should be undertaken, examining a number of diverse variables over a wide range of families. From the data obtained in such studies researchers could then factor out the most fruitful hypotheses for more intensive examination.

Paul (1967) provides an alternative view, arguing for the combination of process- and outcome-oriented research. He points out that it "is precisely through outcome studies with concurrent measurement or manipulation of variables whose influence is unknown that important variables are likely to be identified" (p. 109). Indeed, though researchers in the family therapy field (Rabkin, 1965; Boszormenyi-Nagy, 1965) are arguing for a process-oriented research focus, they are really seeking the identification of interactional variables differentiating healthy from dysfunctional families for the purpose of objectively assessing therapeutic outcome. Thus the process and outcome orientations are inseparable. In fact, if the influence of the relevant interactional variables (process) were known, outcome research would not be necessary since knowledge of the influence of all relevant variables would result in a calculable and nonprobabilistic outcome.

Notes

1. This instruction for the mother to interact with her son as she did prior to treatment appears to differ in intent from other instructions given by the experimenters. Other instructions appear to have been much more specific and tied to identified classes of behavior. This instruction instead appears to be a double-binding command to the mother to ignore the advice of chosen experts and to perform in ways implicitly defined as ineffective while being observed by the experts.

Clearly it is not the intent of the experimenters that the mother in this case actually return to her former mode of behavior. While Hawkins et al., do not provide a rationale for this instruction it may be viewed from a systems model perspective as an example of prescribing the symptom. A more detailed description of symptom prescription and the purposes it serves is provided in chapter 11.

13

Comparative Analyses:
Three Therapeutic Frameworks
and Three Models
of Human Behavior

The purpose of this chapter is twofold. First, we intend to highlight the critical similarities and differences in the three therapeutic frameworks—family crisis intervention, crisis intervention, and family therapy—and summarize the respective payoffs and costs of each framework for both the client and the practitioner. Secondly, we will examine similarities and differences among the three models of human behavior—psychoanalytic, behavioral, and systems—emphasizing the qualitative and quantitative differences among them. We focus only on the differences that have an impact on the consumer and/or the service provider.

Three Therapeutic Frameworks

SIMILARITIES

The three frameworks represent a major philosophical change from long-term individual, traditional psychotherapy. First and foremost is their emphasis on interactional data, on the social context as a critical, if not *the* critical, variable in treatment. Behavior, be it conceptualized as communication or as a function of reinforcement contingencies, is viewed within an interactional framework. No longer is a symptom part of an individual's disease; rather it is construed as a homeostatic mechanism that is reinforced and helps maintain the social context.

Secondly, there is a marked emphasis on growth and prevention. Instead of working with dysfunctional individuals, these frameworks stress man's ability to cope with a rapidly changing society by learning skills which, it is hoped, will help him to adapt better, and will at the very least allow him to return to his previous level of functioning. The accent is both on growth and on preventing dysfunction by working with individuals who are likely to experience a crisis. Figure 13-1 illustrates how each of these frameworks can be viewed in terms of its emphasis on social context and its philosophy of prevention.

To reiterate the general conclusions of the previous chapter, there is no evidence to suggest that one type of treatment is most appropriate for specific problems or consumers. Researchers consistently report outcome data for all three frameworks that is comparable to that reported in the individual psychotherapy outcome literature (Gross & Miller, 1975). This suggests that family crisis intervention, crisis intervention, and family therapy effect similar types of changes with similar populations, and in a shorter period of time. Thus one shared feature of the three frameworks is their tendency to be of shorter duration than individual psychotherapy with no evidence of reduced effectiveness.

Also, all three frameworks are more concerned with growth and/or preventive mental health services than is traditional individual psychotherapy. It is necessary to emphasize that these are differences of degree, and are not absolute.

All three have a here-and-now orientation, with the accent on current functioning. Their goal is to restore the individual and/or family to an asymptomatic state with an effective coping style at least equal to that which existed prior to the time of entering therapy. The focus is more on education-learning than on medical-treating.

Consistent with the educational-learning orientation is the setting of specific behavioral goals which typically acknowledge the importance of social context rather than emphasizing the exploration and/or modification of personality traits. Concurrently a wider range of interactional data beyond the therapist-client relationship is used to effect change. In fact, it is not atypical for

Figure 13-1
Classification of Therapeutic Frameworks

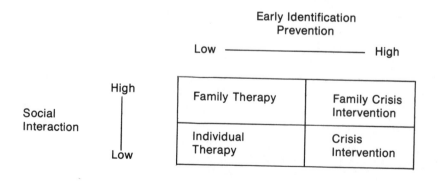

these frameworks to involve social agencies and individuals other than the person identified as the client as part of a treatment program.

DIFFERENCES

The differences among the three frameworks suggest both who and which types of problems will be handled by them respectively. In terms of such factors as brevity of intervention and that the therapist is directive and available, both crisis intervention and family crisis intervention are higher on these dimensions than family therapy (see Table 13-1). The location of both crisis and family crisis units in poorer neighborhoods and/or within community mental health centers suggests that mainly the poor and lower-middle class will utilize these services. Since many private psychiatric facilities do not offer crisis programs, it is likely that middle- and upper-class individuals will be involved in family therapy rather than crisis intervention programs. In fact, it is more likely that such individuals will be involved in individual psychotherapy than in couple or family therapy. This is not to say that any of these approaches could not be effective with other socioeconomic groups; rather it is a description of what currently happens. For example, problems that are viewed as not amenable to traditional therapy are typically assigned to less experienced therapists. Individuals who are perceived as having recalcitrant problems are more likely to be offered crisis intervention approaches than the more "meaningful" psychotherapies. These same crisis-oriented programs are likely to be staffed by less

Table 13-1
Differences Among Frameworks

	High	Middle	Low
Social Group Involvement in Pathology	FT FCI	CI	
Social-Economic Status of Clients		FT FCI	CI
Duration of Psychotherapy	FT		FCI CI
Activity Level of and Availability of Therapist	FCI CI		FT
Prevention of Hospitalization	FCI	FT CI	
Prevention of Future Problems		FT FCI	CI
Utilization of Paraprofessionals	CI	FCI	FT

CI = Crisis Intervention
FCI = Family Crisis Intervention
FT = Family Therapy

experienced individuals, frequently paraprofessionals. Combined with their location it is almost guaranteed that such programs will be offered to the poor, while the wealthier will be left to choose private therapists or private hospitalization.

What is unfortunate is that family crisis intervention does seem particularly suitable for minimizing hospitalization and redefining problems in interactional rather than individual disease terms. Finally, crisis intervention appears most appropriate for single individuals in cases where for the first time one has become dysfunctional as the result of some specific event. Whether the consumer will get the most appropriate treatment seems to be more of a political-economic question than an empirical one of outcome effectiveness.

Three Models of Human Behavior

Once again we reiterate that there are minimal data available to suggest which model is most effective for which problems. What does seem clear is that each one plays a different role for both practitioner and client, with the greatest contrast between the psychoanalytic model and both the behavioral and systems models. It is likely that these theoretical differences are minimized when therapists are more experienced. Thus one would expect experienced therapists to behave alike, regardless of theoretical orientation, while less experienced therapists are more likely to show signs of belonging to one or another theoretical approach.

Table 13-2 outlines some of the major differences and similarities among the models. The major difference is in their respective emphasis on inner and outer man. The psychoanalytic model accents the inner man, relating motivation to unconscious conflict, with personality traits as the key concept. The behavioral model focuses on outer man, stressing the functional relationships between how man behaves and the antecedents and consequents within his environment in maintaining the behavior. The behavioral model construes man in terms of educational-learning factors in much the same manner that the psychoanalytic model addresses the biological drive. Both the psychoanalytic and behavioral approaches perceive man primarily as an individual who is affected by others rather than emphasizing interactional determinants of his behavior. This is not to say that transference and reinforcement contingencies do not deal with interactional factors, but rather that there is a difference in degree that serves to differentiate these models from the systems approach. The primary determinant of behavior for the systems model is interaction. This model perceives the social context as the major factor in determining how an individual will behave. Rather than inner or outer man, the systems approach sees man as a component in a social system whose rules determine how he will behave.

Table 13-2
Comparison of Psychoanalytic,
Behavioral, and Systems Models

	Psychoanalytic	Behavioral	Systems
View of Man	inner	outer/dyadic	social context (triadic)
Behavior	unconscious	reinforcement contingencies	rules
Symptom	underlying conflict	the problem	underlying rules
Crisis	personality	environment	interaction individual & support system
Resolution	working through intrapsychic conflict to build ego strength	altering contingencies	altering rules within social context
Change	slow	rapid	rapid
Focus	intrapsychic conflict	patterns of reinforcement	interaction rules
Outcome	attitudinal	behavioral tasks	behavioral group
Therapist	doctor-expert	educator-trainer	engineer-manipulator
Consumer	patient	student	client
Consumer Skills	verbal	disciplined	action oriented
Role of			
cognition	first	second	third
affect	second	third	second
action	third	first	first

COMBINATION AND COMPARISON OF FRAMEWORKS BY MODEL

Table 13-2 outlines some of the major similarities and differences among the respective models. These aspects of the models hold across the three frameworks, though some factors become more pronounced in certain frameworks. For example, the psychoanalytic model encourages more traditional sex roles than either the behavioral or systems model. This difference does not become evident in either crisis mode of treatment, but it is important in family therapy. This section will examine the payoffs and costs for each model within a specific framework.

Family crisis intervention The major difference among the three models is in terms of the practitioner-consumer relationship. Each model creates a different atmosphere. The psychoanalytic one projects a doctor-patient; the behavioral, an educator-student; and the systems, an engineer-client climate. The choice of model might best be decided in light of which type of environment allows a particular consumer group to learn best. The authors believe that with more experienced therapists the difference in climate will be minimized. Nevertheless the type of practitioner-client relationship will remain a major factor for consumers selecting a mode of treatment.

Both the behavioral and systems approaches are more compatible with clients who are resistant to entering psychotherapy and/or who are unsophisticated and/or antagonistic to a psychological orientation than the psychoanalytic model would be. These models also are less likely to utilize stigmatizing psychiatric diagnoses. For individuals who prefer and/or conceptualize human behavior more in terms of problems in living than in a mental illness framework, the behavioral and system models would be most suitable. On the other hand, individuals who prefer a medical model and who want to address the question "why do I behave as I do" would do best to select a psychoanalytic approach.

Finally, it is likely that individuals who are more verbal and psychologically oriented, which often means that their socioeconomic status is higher, would be attracted to the psychoanalytic framework. The emphasis on insight and understanding, and the intricate and often fascinating mosaic of intrapsychic variables that are postulated to be motivating the individual, makes this model appealing to the intellectual and/or psychologically-oriented person. It is unquestionably the model of choice for those who like a detailed personality theory that can explain a wide range of behaviors and paints a detailed portrait of the individual's psyche. In terms of being colorful, mystical, and deep, the psychoanalytic model would be the model of choice; the systems model would come second; and the behavioral, a distant third.

On the other hand, for individuals who perceive psychological factors as so much fluff and want to keep to the facts, the behavioral model would be the choice. Again, action- rather than psychologically-oriented individuals often are assumed to be synonymous with lower socioeconomic groups. Thus such individuals might do better with the behavioral model. This point needs to be qualified by the fact that individuals who prefer being told what to do—that is, who function best in an authoritarian relationship—might also respond to the psychoanalytic model's role of the therapist as expert rather than the educator role of the therapist within the behavioral model. As we have noted previously, the psychotherapy field is at best characterized by shades of grey rather than any clear-cut distinctions.

Finally, the systems model's emphasis on manipulating people without the client needing to be either psychologically oriented or willing to keep records makes it the model of choice for people who are most antagonistic to mental health-psychotherapy services. As antagonism or reluctance to enter psychotherapy characterizes both action- and psychologically-oriented individuals and probably cuts across social class, it is likely that the systems model would be applicable to a wider range of socioeconomic groups, with the behavioral and psychoanalytic models following respectively.

Crisis intervention. These comparisons and contrasts would be equally applicable to the crisis intervention framework.

Family therapy. The differences also would apply to family therapy. There are several additional differences, however. As noted previously, the psychoanalytic model is most explicit in defining healthy sex roles. In general the model follows a traditional view along the Parsons line with instrumental functions being male, and expressive activities, female. The behavioral and the systems models do not suggest any sex-specific roles, though many adherents of these models write in such a manner as to imply a bias toward traditional roles. Nevertheless, if one prefers to minimize traditional sex roles, the behavioral or systems model might be best. On the other hand, if traditional sex roles are valuable to the individual, a psychoanalytic orientation is likely to be the most compatible of the three models.

Finally, differences in who the client is and how the client is treated become most pronounced in this framework. Both the psychoanalytic and behavioral models are more individually oriented than the systems model. The systems model is more interactional, focusing on family dyads and triads rather than focusing on the therapist and a particular individual in the family. This does not mean that the psychoanalytic and behavioral approaches do not work with couples and/or families, but rather that these models encourage the therapist to be the center of attention while he works with one family member, while the system approach has the therapist commenting and intervening much more as the couple and/or family members are interacting with each other.

In terms of process differences, the previously mentioned practitioner-consumer relationship dichotomy is accented in the family therapy framework, mainly because this therapy lasts longer. Another process difference involves the variable of involvement in, or ownership of, what happens in the session. Both the psychoanalytic and systems models provide the least sense of having the patient/client participate in deciding what will happen in the session, while the behavioral approach offers the client more of an opportunity to determine what happens and how.

Conclusion. In conclusion, we hope that our classification of the respective frameworks and models has been helpful. Clearly the state of the art required this initial step so that we as practitioners and/or researchers can choose in which direction we wish to travel. As clinicians/researchers we found the text's classification schema enabled us to better recognize our underlying assumptions and to appreciate our particular way of defining problems. Without a doubt, the cliché that more research is needed is true. The type of study that is needed most is experimental-outcome oriented, that compares either among frameworks or within frameworks using different models. Studies that address process issues that are not tied to outcome data do not seem helpful in a field flooded with statistically significant correlational findings that yield trivial facts.

Our bias is that practitioners need to have a cognitive map to help direct their interventions. Lacking such a map, evaluation is difficult if not impossible, and without evaluation we are left in a quandary as to the impact of our work as clinicians. For us the systems model of intervention (Chapters 4, 8, and 11) makes the most sense, but our bias is that regardless of what model a practitioner follows, he should know its costs and benefits. We hope that our text has helped in such an assessment.

References

Ackerman, N. W. The family as a social and emotional unit. *Bulletin of Kansas Mental Hygiene Society*, 1937, *12*, 1-3, 7-8.

Ackerman, N. W. Interpersonal disturbances in the family: Some unresolved problems in psychotherapy. *Psychiatry*, 1954, *17*, 359-368.

Ackerman, N. W. *The psychodynamics of family life*. New York: Basic, 1958.

Ackerman, N. W. *Treating the troubled family*. New York: Basic, 1966.

Aguilera, D. C., Messick, J. M., & Farrell, M. S. *Crisis intervention: Theory and methodology*. St. Louis: Mosley, 1970.

Alexander, J. F. Defensive and supportive communication in family systems. *Journal of Marriage and Family*, 1973a, *35*, 613-617.

Alexander, J. F. Defensive and supportive communications in normal and deviant families. *Journal of Clinical and Consulting Psychology*, 1973b, *40*, 223-231.

Alexander, J. F., Barton, G., Schiaro, R. S., & Parsons, B V. Systems-behavioral intervention with families of delinquents: Therapist characteristics, family behavior, and outcome. *Journal of Consulting and Clinical Psychology*, 1976, *44* (4), 656-664.

Alkov, R. A. Life changes and accident behavior. *Approach: A Naval Safety Center Publication*, February, 1975, 18-20.

Allen, K. E. & Harris, F. R. Elimination of a child's excessive scratching by training the mother in reinforcement procedures. *Behavior Research and Therapy*, 1966, *4*, 79-84.

Attneave, C. L., & Speck, R. V. Social network intervention in time and space. In A. Jacobs & W. Spradlin (Eds.), *The group as agent of change*. New York: Behavioral Publications, 1974, pp. 166-186.

Ayllon, T., & Michael, J. The psychiatric nurse as a behavioral engineer. *Journal of Experimental Analysis of Behavior*, 1959, *2*, 323-334.

Azrin, N. H., Naster, B. J. & Jones, R. Reciprocity counseling: A rapid learning-based procedure for marital counseling. *Behavior Research and Therapy*, 1973, *11*, 365-382.

Bachrach, A. J., Candland, D. K., & Gibson, J. T. Group reinforcement of individual response experiments in verbal behavior. In I. A. Berg & B. M. Bass (Eds.), *Conformity and deviation*. New York: Harper, 1961.

Balint, E. Marital conflicts and their treatment. *Comprehensive Psychiatry*, 1966, *7* (5), 403-407.

Bard, M. Family intervention police teams as a community mental health resource. *Journal of Criminal Law, Criminology and Police Science*, 1969, *60* (2), 247-250.

Bard, M. *Training police as specialists in family crisis intervention* (National Institute of Law Enforcement and Criminal Justice). Washington, D. C.: U. S. Government Printing Office, 1970.

Bard, M., & Berkowitz, B. Training police as specialists in family crisis intervention: A community psychology action program. *Community Mental Health Journal*, 1967, *3*, 315-317.

Bard, M., & Berkowitz, B. Family disturbance as a police function. In S. Cohn (Ed.), *Law enforcement science and technology II*. New York: Port City Press, 1969, pp. 565–568.

Bard, M., & Zacker, J. The prevention of family violence: Dilemmas of community intervention. *Journal of Marriage and the Family*, 1971, *33* (4), 677–682.

Barten, H. H. The expanding spectrum of the brief therapies. In H. H. Barten (Ed.), *Brief therapies*. New York: Behavioral Publications, 1971.

Bateson, G. The biosocial integration of behavior in the schizophrenic family. In N. Ackerman et al. (Eds.), *Exploring the base for family therapy*. New York: Family Service Association, 1961, pp. 116–122.

Bateson, G., Jackson, D. D., Haley, J., & Weakland, J. H. Toward a theory of schizophrenia. *Behavioral Sciences*, 1956, *1* (4), 251–264.

Beakel, N. G., & Mehrabian, A. Inconsistent communications and psychopathology. *Journal of Abnormal Psychology*, 1969, *74*, 126–130.

Beck, D. Research findings on the outcomes of marital counseling. *Social Casework*, March 1975, 153–181.

Beck, D. F., & Jones, M. A. *Progress on family problems*. New York: Family Service Association, 1973.

Becker, A., & Weiner, L. Psychiatric home treatment service: Community aspects. In J. H. Masserman (Ed.), *Current psychiatric therapies* (Vol. 6). New York: Grune & Stratton, 1966, pp. 281–289.

Beels, D. C., & Ferber, A. Family therapy: A view. *Family Process*, 1969, 8, 280–318.

Berger, D, Rice, G., Sewall, L., & Lemkau, P. Post-hospital evaluation of psychiatric patients: The social adjustment inventory method. *American Psychiatric Association, Psychiatric Studies and Projects #15*, 1964.

Berman, A. L. Experiential training for crisis intervention. In G. A. Specter & W. L. Clairborn (Eds.), *Crisis intervention*. New York: Behavioral Publications, 1973, pp. 95–106.

Berman, A. L., & McCarthy, B. W. The university counseling center as a training-consultation center. Paper presented at the meeting of the American Psychological Association, Washington, D.C., September 1971.

Berman, G. S., & Haug, M. R. New careers: Bridges or ladders? *Social Work*, 1973, *18* (4), 48–58.

Bernstein, B. Social structure, language and learning. *Educational Research*, 1961, *3*, 163–176.

Bibring, G. L., Dwyer, T. F., Huntington, D. S., & Valenstein, A. F. A study of the psychological processes in pregnancy and of the earliest mother-child relationship. In R. S. Eissler and others (Eds.), *The psychoanalytic study of the child* (Vol. 16). New York: International Universities Press, 1961.

Bijou, S. W., Peterson, R. F., & Ault, M. H. A method to integrate descriptive and experimental field studies at the level of data and empirical concepts. *Journal of Applied Behavior Analysis*, 1968, *1*, 175–191.

Blau, T. H. Psychologist views the helper. In C. Grosser, W. E. Henry & J. G. Kelly (Eds.), *Nonprofessionals in the human sciences*. San Francisco: Jossey Bass, Inc., 1969, pp. 183–192.

Bleach, G. Strategies for evaluation of hotline telephone crisis centers. In G. A Specter & W. L. Clairborn (Eds.), *Crisis intervention*. New York: Behavioral Publications, 1973, pp. 109–113.

Bleach, G., & Clairborn, W. Initial evaluation of hotline telephone crisis centers. *Community Mental Health Journal*, 1974, *10* (4), 387–394.

Bloom, B. L. Strategies for the prevention of mental disorders. In G. Rosenblum (Ed.), *Issues in community psychology and preventive mental health*. New York: Behavioral Publications, 1971, pp. 1–20.

Blum, R. H. *Horatio Alger's children*. San Francisco: Jossey-Bass, 1972.

Bodin, A. M. Family interaction: A social-clinical study of synthetic, normal, and problem family triads. In W. D. Winter & A. J. Ferreira (Eds.), *Research in family interaction*. Palo Alto: Science & Behavior, 1969, pp. 125–127.

Bolman, W. M. Preventive psychiatry for the family: Theory, approaches and programs. *American Journal of Psychiatry*, 1968, *125*, 458–472.

Boszormenyi-Nagy, I. The concept of schizophrenia from the perspective of family treatment. *Family Process*, 1962, *1*, 103–113.

Boszormenyi-Nagy, I. The concept of change in conjoint family therapy. In A. S. Friedman et al. (Eds.), *Psychotherapy for the whole family*. New York: Springer, 1965.

Boszormenyi-Nagy, I. From family therapy to a psychology of relationships: Fictions of the individual and fictions of the family. *Comprehensive Psychiatry*, 1966, 7 (5), 408–423.

Boszormenyi-Nagy, I. Relational modes and meanings. In G. H. Zuk & I. Boszormenyi-Nagy (Eds.), *Family therapy and disturbed families*. Palo Alto: Science and Behavior, 1967, pp. 58–73.

Boszormenyi-Nagy, I., & Framo, J. L. (Eds.) *Intensive family therapy: Theoretical and practical aspects*. New York: Harper & Row, 1965.

Boudouris, J. Homicide and the family. *Journal of Marriage and the Family*, 1971, *33* (4), 667–676.

Bowen, M. A. Family psychotherapy. *American Journal of Orthopsychiatry*, 1961, *31*, 40–60.

Bowen, M. The use of family theory in clinical practice. *Comprehensive Psychiatry*, 1966, 7, 345–374.

Bowen, M. The use of family theory in clinical practice. In J. Haley (Ed.), *Changing families*. New York: Grune & Stratton, 1971.

Bowen, M., Dysinger, R. H., Brodey, W. N., & Basamania, B. Study and treatment of five hospitalized family groups each with a psychotic member. Paper presented at the Annual Meeting of the American Orthopsychiatric Association, Chicago, March 1957.

Brandt, L. W. Studies of "dropout" patients in psychotherapy: A review of findings. *Psychotherapy: Theory, Research and Practice*, 1956, *2*, 6–12.

Brewer, R. E., & Brewer, M. B. Attraction and accuracy of perception in dyads. *Journal of Personality and Social Psychology*, 1968, *8*, 188–193.

Brody, E. M., & Spark, G. Institutionalization of the aged: A family crisis. *Family Process*, 1966, *5*, 76–90.

Brown, H. F., Burditt, V. B., & Liddell, C. W. The crisis of relocation. In H. J. Parad (Ed.), *Crisis intervention: Selected readings*. New York: Family Service Association, 1965.

Bugental, D., Love, L., Kaswan, J., & April, C. Videotaped family interaction: Differences reflecting the presence and type of child disturbance. *Journal of Abnormal Psychology*, 1972, *79*, 285–290.

Burgess, A. W., & Lazare, A. *Community mental health: Target populations*. Englewood Cliffs, N. J.: Prentice-Hall, 1976.

Burhenne, R. Personal communication. Emergency Services, Columbus Area Community Mental Health Center, Columbus, Ohio, 1974.

Cameron, W. R., & Walters, V. The emergency mental health service: An important contribution to preventive medicine. *Southern Medical Journal*, 1965, *58*, 1375–1379.

Campbell, D. T. Factors relevant to the validity of experiments in social settings. *Psychological Bulletin*, 1957, *54* (4), 297–312.

Caplan, G. *An approach to community mental health*. New York: Grune & Stratton, 1961.

Caplan, G. *Principles of preventive psychiatry*. New York: Basic, 1964.

Caplan, G. *The theory and practice of mental health consultation*. New York: Basic, 1970.

Caplan, G. *Support systems and community mental health lectures on concept development*. New York: Behavioral Publications, 1974.

Carkhuff, R. R. *The art of problem solving: A guide for developing problem-solving skills for parents, teachers, counselors and administrators*. Amherst, Mass.: Human Resource Development Press, 1973.

Cheek, F. The "schizophrenic mother" in word and deed. *Family Process*, 1964a, *3*, 155–177.

Cheek, F. A serendipitous finding: Sex roles and schizophrenia. *Journal of Abnormal and Social Psychology,* 1964b, *69,* 392–400.

Cheek, F. The father of the schizophrenic. *Archives of General Psychiatry,* 1965, *13,* 336–345.

Clark, E. Round-the-clock emergency psychiatric services. In H. J. Parad (Ed.), *Crisis intervention: Selected readings.* New York: Family Service Association, 1965, pp. 261–273.

Coe, W. C. A family operant program. Paper presented at the meeting of the Western Psychological Association, Los Angeles, 1970.

Cohen, M. Cognitive performance of culturally-different children: Deficiency or difference? Unpublished manuscript, Department of Psychology, The Ohio State University, 1974.

Cohen, M., Gross, S. J., & Turner, M. A note on a developmental model for training family therapists through group supervision. *Journal of Marriage and Family Counseling,* 1976, *2* (1), 48.

Coleman, M. D. Emergency psychotherapy. In J. Masserman (Ed.), *Progress in psychotherapy* (Vol. 5). New York: Grune & Stratton, 1960.

Conway, J. B., & Bucher, B. D. Transfer and maintenance of behavior change in children: A review and suggestions. In E. J. Mash, L. A. Harmerlynck, & L. C. Handy (Eds.), *Behavior modification and families.* New York: Brunner/Mazel, 1976, 119–159.

Cromwell, R. E., Olson, D. H. L., & Fournier, D. G. Diagnoses and evaluation in marital and family counseling. In D. H. L. Olson (Ed.), *Treating relationships.* Lake Mills, Iowa: Graphic, 1976.

Dardig, J. C., & Heward, W. L. *Sign here: A contracting book for children and their parents.* Kalamazoo, Mich.: Behaviordelia, 1976.

Demarest, E., & Leider, A. Transference in group therapy: Its use by co-therapists of opposite sexes. *Psychiatry,* 1954, *17,* 187–202.

DeRisi, W. J., & Butz, G. *Writing behavioral contracts: A case simulation practice manual.* Champaign, Ill.: Research Press, 1975.

Drabek, T. E., & Boggs, K. S. Families in disaster: Reactions and relations. *Journal of Marriage and the Family,* August, 1968, 443–451.

Driscoll, J. M., Meyer, R. G, & Schanie, C. F. *Police training in family crisis intervention.* Louisville, Kentucky: University of Louisville, 1971.

Driscoll, J. M., Meyer, R. G., Schanie, C. F. Training police in family crisis intervention. *Journal of Applied Behavior Science,* 1973, *9* (1), 62–82.

Dublin, L. I. Suicide prevention. In E. S. Schneidman. (Ed.), *On the nature of suicide.* San Francisco: Jossey-Bass, 1969.

Durlak, J. A. The use of nonprofessionals as therapeutic agents: Research, issues, implications. Doctoral dissertation, Vanderbilt University, 1971.

Durlak, J. A. Myths concerning the nonprofessional therapist. *Professional Psychology,* 1973a, *4* (3), 300–304.

Durlak, J. A. Some myths concerning the nonprofessional therapist. An extended report of same-titled article from *Professional Psychology,* 1973b, pp. 1–13.

Engeln, R., Knutson, J., Laughy, L., & Garlington, W. Behavior modification techniques applied to a family unit—A case study. *Journal of Child Psychology and Psychiatry,* 1968, *9,* 245–252.

Epstein, C. *Intergroup relations for police officers.* Baltimore, Md.: Williams & Wilkins, 1962.

Erikson, E. *Identity and the life cycle, selected papers.* New York: International Universities Press, 1959.

Erikson, E. *Childhood and society* (2nd ed.). New York: Norton, 1963.

Farina, A. Patterns of role dominance and conflict in parents of schizophrenic patients. *Journal of Abnormal Social Psychology,* 1960, *61,* 31–38.

Farina, A., & Dunham, R. M. Measurement of family relationships and their effects. *Archives of General Psychiatry,* 1963, *9,* 64–73.

Feallock, R., & Miller, L. K. The design and evaluation of a worksharing system for experimental group living. *Journal of Applied Behavior Analysis*, 1976, 9 (3), 277–288.

Federal Bureau of Investigation. *Uniform Crime Reports—1969*. Washington, D.C.: U.S. Government Printing Office, 1970.

Fenichel, O. *The psychoanalytic theory of neurosis*. New York: Norton, 1945.

Ferreira, A. Family myths and homeostasis. *Archives of General Psychiatry*, 1963, 9, 457–463.

Ferreira, A., & Winter, W. Family interaction and decision-making. *Archives of General Psychology*, 1965, 13, 214–233.

Ferreira, A. J., & Winter, W. D. Stability of interactional variables in family decision making. *Archives of General Psychiatry*, 1966, 14 (4), 352–355.

Ferreira, A. J., Winter, W. D., & Poindexter, E. J. Some interactional variables in normal and abnormal families. *Family Process*, 1966, 5, 60–75.

Flomenhaft, K., & Kaplan, D. M. Clinical significance of current kinship relationships. *Social Work*, 1968, 13, 68–75.

Flomenhaft, K., Kaplan, D. M., & Langsley, D. G. Avoiding psychiatric hospitalization. *Social Work*, 1969, 14 (4), 38–45.

Foley, V. D. *An introduction to family therapy*. New York: Grune & Stratton, 1974.

Framo, J. L. (Ed.). *Family interaction: A dialogue between family researchers and family therapists*. New York: Springer, 1972.

Frank, J. D., Gleidman, L. H., Imber, S. D., Stone, A. R., & Nash, E. H. Patients' expectancies and relearning as factors determining improvement in psychotherapy. *American Journal of Psychiatry*, 1959, 115, 961–968.

Fried, M. Grieving for a lost home. In L. J. Duhl (Ed.), *The urban condition*. New York: Basic, 1963.

Friedman, A. S. Family therapy as conducted in the home. *Family Process*, 1962, 1, 132–140.

Friedman, A. S., Boszormenyi-Nagy, I., Jungreis, J. E., Lincoln, G., Mitchell, H. E., Sonne, J. C., Speck, R. V., & Spivack, G. *Psychotherapy for the whole family*. New York: Springer, 1965.

Friedman, C., & Friedman, A. Characteristics of schizophrenic families during a joint family story-telling task. *Family Process*, 1970, 9, 333–354.

Friedman, P. H. Personalistic family and marital therapy. In A. Lazarus (Ed.), *Clinical behavior therapy*. New York: Science House, 1971.

Gambrill, E. D., Thomas, E., J., & Carter, R. D. Procedure for socio-behavioral practice in open settings. In E. J. Thomas, R. D. Carter & E. D. Gambrill (Eds.), *Utilization and appraisal of socio-behavioral techniques in social welfare*. Ann Arbor, Mich.: Office of Research Administration, University of Michigan School of Social Work, 1970.

Glass, A. J. Psychiatry in the Korean campaign: An historical review. *United States Armed Forces Medical Journal*, 1953, 4, 1563–1583.

Glass, A. J. Psychotherapy in the combat zone. *American Journal of Psychiatry*, 1954, 110, 725–731.

Glick, B. R. A social exchange approach to support-giving in marital interaction: Implications for marital conflict theory and research. Unpublished manuscript, Ohio State University, 1974.

Glick, B. R., Gross, S. J., & Pepinsky, H. B. Self-esteem, the perception of support during marital conflict and marital satisfaction. Unpublished manuscript. The Ohio State University, 1979.

Goffman, E. *Asylums*. New York: Anchor, 1961.

Goldiamond, I. Self-control procedures in personal behavior problems. *Psychological Reports*, 1965, 17, 851–868.

Goldstein, A. P. *Therapist-patient expectancies in psychotherapy*. New York: Pergamon, 1962.

Goldstein, S., & Giddings, J. Multiple-impact therapy: An approach to crisis intervention with families. In G. A. Specter & W. L. Clairborn (Eds.), *Crisis Intervention*. New York: Behavioral Publications, 1973.

Goode, W. J. Force and violence in the family. *Journal of Marriage and the Family,* 1971, *33* (4), 624–636.

Goodrich, D. W., & Boomer, D. S. Experimental assessment of modes of conflict resolution. *Family Process,* 1963, *2,* 15–24.

Gottman, J., Notarius, C., Gonso, J., & Markman, H. *A couple's guide to communication.* Champaign, Ill.: Research Press, 1976.

Greene, C. N. The development of role consensus and its effect on evaluation of performance and satisfaction within the managerial dyad. *Dissertation Abstracts International,* 1970, *31* (2-A), 514.

Gross, S. J., & Miller, J. A research strategy for evaluating the effectiveness of psychotherapy. *Psychological Reports,* 1975, *37,* 1011–1021.

Grosser, C. F. Local residents as mediators between middle-class professional workers and lower-class clients. *Social Service Review,* 1966, *60,* 56–63.

Group for the Advancement of Psychiatry. *The field of family therapy.* Report #78. American Psychiatric Association, 1970, pp. 525–644.

Grunebaum, H., Christ, J., & Neiberg, N. Diagnosis and treatment planning for couples. *International Journal of Group Psychotherapy,* 1969, *19,* 185–202.

Guerin, P. J. (Ed.). *Family therapy: Theory and practice.* New York: Gardner Press, 1976.

Guerin, P. J., & Pendagast, M. A. Evaluation of family system and genogram. In P. J. Guerin (Ed.), *Family therapy: Theory and practice.* New York: Gardner Press, 1976, 450–464.

Gurman, A. S. The effects and effectiveness of marital therapy: A review of outcome research. *Family Process,* 1973, *12,* 145–170.

Gurman, A. S., & Kniskern, D. P. Enriching research on marital enrichment programs. *Journal of Marriage and Family Counseling,* 1977, *3* (2), 3–11.

Gwaltney, B. A. Management review protocol indicator #1. Unpublished manuscript, Ventura County Mental Health Department Service, Ventura, Calif. 1974.

Hadley, T. R., Jakob, T., Milliones, J., Caplan, J., & Spitz, D. The relationship between family development crisis and the appearance of symptoms in a family member. *Family Process,* 1974, *13* (2), 207–214.

Haley, J. Family experiments: A new type of experimentation. *Family Process,* 1962, *2* (1), 265–293.

Haley, J. *Strategies of psychotherapy.* New York: Grune & Stratton, 1963.

Haley, J. Approaches to family therapy. *International Journal of Psychiatry,* 1970, *9,* 233–242.

Haley, J. *Changing families: A family therapy reader.* New York: Grune & Stratton, 1971.

Haley, J. Untitled article. In A. Ferber, M. Mendelsohn, & A. Napier (Eds.), *The book of family therapy.* Boston: Houghton, Mifflin, 1973.

Hall, A., & Fagen, B. Definition of a system. *General Systems Yearbook I,* 1956.

Hansell, N. *The person in distress; on the biosocial mechanics of adaptation.* New York: Behavioral Publications, 1976.

Harrell, J., & Guerney, B. G., Jr. Training married couples in conflict negotiation skills. In D. H. L. Olson (Ed.), *Treating relationships.* Lake Mills, Iowa: Graphic, 1976.

Harris, M. R., Kalis, B. L., & Freeman, E. H. Precipitating stress: An approach to brief therapy. *American Journal of Psychotherapy,* 1963, *17,* 465–471.

Hausman, W., & Rioch, D. Military psychiatry: A prototype of social and preventive psychiatry in the United States. *Archives of General Psychiatry,* 1967, *16,* 727–739.

Havighurst, R. J. *Human development and education.* New York: Longmans, 1953.

Hawkins, R. P., Peterson, R. F., Schweid, E., & Bijou, S. W. Behavior therapy in the home: Amelioration of problem parent-child relations with the parent in a therapeutic role. *Journal of Experimental Child Psychology,* 1966, *4,* 99–107.

Hetherington, E. M., Stouwie, R. J., & Ridberg, E. H. Patterns of family interaction and child-rearing attitudes related to three dimensions of juvenile delinquency. *Journal of Abnormal Psychology,* 1971, *78* (2), 160–176.

Hill, R. Generic features of families under stress. *Social Casework*, 1958, *39*, (2–3), 139–150.

Hobbs, N. Sources of gain in psychotherapy. *American Psychologist*, 1962, *17*, (10), 741–747.

Holland, C. J. Elimination by the parents of fire-setting behavior in a seven year-old boy. *Behavior Research and Therapy*, 1969, *7*, 135–137.

Hollingshead, A. B., & Redlich, F. C. *Social class and mental illness*. New York: Wiley, 1958.

Hosford, R. E., & Briskin, A. S. Changes through counseling. *Review of Educational Research*, 1969, *39* (2), 189–207.

Hutchinson, J. Interaction patterns in families of severely disturbed and normal adolescents. Doctoral dissertation, University of Chicago, 1967.

Jackson, D. D. The question of homeostasis. *Psychiatric Quarterly Supplement*, 1954, *31*, (1), 79–90.

Jackson, D. D. Schizophrenia, *Scientific American*, 1962, *207* (2), 65–78.

Jackson, D. D. Family rules: Marital quid pro quo. *Archives of General Psychiatry*, 1965, *12*, 589–594.

Jackson, D. D. Aspects of conjoint family therapy. In G. H. Zuk & I. Boszormenyi-Nagy (Eds.), *Family therapy and disturbed families*. Palo Alto: Science and Behavior, 1967, p. 28–40.

Jackson, D. D. (Ed.). *Communication, family and marriage (Vol. 1)*. Palo Alto: Science and Behavior, 1968a.

Jackson, D. D. The question of family homeostasis. In D. Jackson (Ed.), *Communication, Family and Marriage*. Palo Alto: Science and Behavior, 1968b.

Jackson, D. D., & Weakland, J. H. Conjoint family therapy: Some considerations on theory, technique and results. *Psychiatry*, 1961, *24*, 30–45.

Jacob, T. Family interaction in disturbed and normal families. *Psychological Bulletin*, 1975, *82*, 33–65.

Jacobson, G. F., Strickler, M., & Morley, W. E. Generic and individual approaches to crisis intervention. *American Journal of Public Health*, 1968, *58* (2), 338–343.

Jacobson, G. F., Wilner, D. M., Morley, W. E., Schneider, S., Strickler, M., & Sommer, G. J. The scope and practice of an early access brief treatment psychiatric center. *American Journal of Psychiatry*, 1965, *121*, 1176–1182.

Jacobson, N. S., & Martin, B. Behavioral marriage therapy: Current status. *Psychological Bulletin*, 1976, *83* (4), 540–556.

Janis, I. *Psychological stress*. New York: Wiley, 1958.

Janis, I., & Gilmore, J. The influence of incentive conditions on the success of role playing in modifying attitudes. *Journal of Personality and Social Psychology*, 1965, *1*, 17–27.

Kaffman, M. Short-term family therapy. *Family Process*, 1963, *2* (2), 216–234.

Kalis, B. L. Crisis theory: Its relevance for community psychology and direction for development. In D. Adelson & B. L. Kalis (Eds.), *Community psychology and mental health*. Scranton, Pa.: Chandler, 1970.

Kanfer, F. H. & Saslow, G. Behavioral diagnoses. In C. M. Franks (Ed.), *Behavior therapy: Appraisal and status*. New York: McGraw-Hill, 1969, pp. 417–444.

Kaplan, D. M. Observations on crisis theory and practice. *Social Casework*, 1968, *49*, 151–155.

Kaplan, D. M. Problem conception and planned intervention. In P. H. Grosser & L. N. Grosser (Eds.), *Families in crisis*. New York: Harper & Row, 1970, pp. 273–290.

Kaplan, D. M. & Mason, E. A. Maternal reactions to premature birth viewed as an acute emotional disorder. *The American Journal of Orthopsychiatry*, 1960, *30* (3), 539–552.

Kaplan, D. M., Smith, A., Grobstein, R., & Fischman, S. E. Family mediation of stress. *Social Work*, 1973, *18* (4), 60–73.

Knox, D. *Marriage happiness: A behavioral approach to counseling*. Champaign, Ill.: Research Press, 1971.

Koegler, R. R. Brief-contact therapy and drugs in outpatient treatment. In G. J. Wayne & R. R. Koegler (Eds.), *Emergency psychiatry and brief therapy*. Boston: Little, Brown, 1966, pp. 139–154.

Koegler, R. R., & Cannon, J. A. Treatment for the many. In G. J. Wayne & R. R. Koegler (Eds.), *Emergency psychiatry and brief therapy*. Boston: Little, Brown, 1966, pp. 93–105.

Komorita, S. S., Sheposh, J. P., & Braver, S. L. Power, the use of power, and cooperative choice in a two-person game. *Journal of Personality and Social Psychology*, 1968, *8*, 134–142.

Koos, E. L. *Families in trouble*. New York: King's Row, 1946.

Langsley, D. G., Kaplan, D., Pittman, F., Machotka, P., Flomenhaft, K., & DeYoung, C. *The treatment of families in crisis*. New York: Grune & Stratton, 1968a.

Langsley, D. G., Pittman, F., Machotka, P., & Flomenhaft, K. Family crisis therapy—results and implications. *Family Process*, 1968b, *7* (2), 145–157.

Langsley, D. G., Flomenhaft, K., & Machotka, P. Follow-up evaluation of family crisis therapy. *American Journal of Orthopsychiatry*, 1969a, *39* (5), 753–759.

Langsley, D. G., Pittman, F., & Swank, G. E. Family crises in schizophrenics and other mental patients. *The Journal of Nervous and Mental Disease*, 1969b, *149* (3), 270–276.

Langsley, D. G., Machotka, P., & Flomenhaft, K. Avoiding mental hospital admission: A follow-up study. *American Journal of Psychiatry*, 1971, *127* (10), 1391–1394.

Laqueur, H. P. General systems theory and multiple family therapy. In J. H. Masserman (Ed.). *Current Psychiatric Therapies* (Vol. 8). New York: Grune & Stratton, 1968, pp. 143–148.

Laqueur, H. P., LaBurt, H. A., & Morong, E. Multiple family therapy: Further developments. *The International Journal of Social Psychiatry*, 1964, Congress Issue, 70–80.

Lazarus, A. A. Some clinical applications of autohypnosis. *Medical Proceedings*, 1958, *14*, 848–850.

Lazarus, A. A. *Daily living: Coping with tensions and anxieties: Relaxation Exercises I, II and III*. Chicago: Instructional Dynamics, 1970.

Lazarus, A. A. *Behavior therapy and beyond*. New York: McGraw-Hill, 1971.

Lazarus, A. A. Multimodal behavioral treatment of depression. *Behavior Therapy*, 1974, *5*, 549–554.

Lazarus, A. A. (Ed.) *Multimodal behavior therapy*. New York: Springer, 1976.

LeBow, M. D. Behavior modification for the family. In G. D. Erickson & T. P. Hogan (Eds.), *Family therapy: An introduction to theory and technique*. Monterey, Ca.: Brooks/Cole, 1972, pp. 347–376.

LeBow, M. D. *Approaches to modifying patient behavior*. New York: Appleton-Century-Crofts, 1976.

Lederer, W., & Jackson, D. D. *Mirages of marriage*. New York: Norton, 1968.

Lennard, H. L., & Bernstein, A. *Patterns in human interaction: An introduction to clinical sociology*. San Francisco: Jossey-Bass, 1969.

Levine, R. Treatment in the home. *Social Work*, 1964, *9*, 19–28.

Levy, L. The role of a natural mental health service delivery system in dealing with basic human problems. In G. Specter (Ed.), *Crisis intervention*. New York: Behavioral Publications, 1973, pp. 18–27.

Levy, L., & Rowitz, L. Ecological attributes of high and low rate mental hospital utilization areas in Chicago. *Social Psychiatry*, 1971, *6*, 20–28.

Lewis, J. M., Beavers, W. R., Gosset, J. T., & Phillips, V. A. *No single thread: Psychological health in family systems*. New York: Brunner/Mazel, 1976.

Liberman, R. Police as a community mental health resource. *Community Mental Health Journal*, 1969, *5*, 111–120.

Liberman, R. P. Behavioral approaches to family and couple therapy. *American Journal of Orthopsychiatry*, 1970, *40* (1), 106–118.

Lidz, T. *The family and human adaptation*. New York: International Universities Press, 1963.

Lidz, T., Cornelison, A. R., Fleck, S. & Terry, D. The intrafamilial environment of the schizophrenic patient. I. The father. *Psychiatry*, 1957, *20* (4), 329–342.

Lidz, T., & Fleck, S. Schizophrenia, human interaction and the role of the family. In D. D. Jackson (Ed.), *The etiology of schizophrenia*. New York: Basic, 1960.

Lieb, J., Lipsitch, I. I., & Slaby, A. E. *The crisis team*. Hagerstown, Md.: Harper & Row, 1973.

Lindemann, E. Symptomatology and management of acute grief. *American Journal of Psychiatry*, 1944, *101*, 141–148.

Lindsley, O. R. An experiment with parents handling behavior at home. *Johnstone Bulletin*, 1966, *9*, 27–36.

Litman, R. E. The prevention of suicide. In J. H. Masserman (Ed.), *Current psychiatric therapies* (Vol. 6). New York: Grune & Stratton, 1966, pp. 268–276.

Loeffler, F., & Weinstein, H. M. The co-therapist method: Special problems and advantages. *Group Psychotherapy*, 1954, *6*, 189–192.

London, P. The end of ideology in behavior modification. *American Psychologist*, 1972, *27* (10), 913–920.

Lorenz, K. *On aggression*. New York: Harcourt, Brace, 1966.

Lorr, M., Katz, M. M., & Rubenstein, E. A. Prediction of length of stay in psychotherapy. *Journal of Consulting Psychology*, 1958, *22*, 321–327.

Lovaas, O. I., Freitag, G., Gold, V. J., & Kassorla, I. C. Experimental studies in childhood schizophrenia: Analysis of self-destructive behavior. *Journal of Experimental Child Psychology*, 1965, *2*, 67–84.

Loveland, N., Wynne, L., & Singer, M. The family Rorschach: A new method for studying family interaction. *Family Process*, 1963, *2*, 187–215.

Lovibond, S. H. The mechanism of conditioning treatment of enuresis. *Behavior Research and Therapy*, 1963, *1*, 17–21.

MacGregor, R. Multiple impact psychotherapy with families. *Family Process*, 1962, *1*, 15–29.

MacGregor, R., Ritchie, A. M., Serrano, A. C., & Schuster, F. P. *Multiple impact therapy with families*. New York: McGraw-Hill, 1964.

Madsen, C. K., & Madsen, C. H. *Parents/children/discipline: A positive approach*. Boston, Mass.: Allyn & Bacon, 1972.

Magoon, T. M., & Golann, S. E. Nontraditionally trained women as mental health counselors/therapists. *Personnel and Guidance Journal*, 1966, *44*, 788–793.

Malinowski, B. An anthropological analysis of war. *Magic, science and religion*. Glencoe, Ill.: Free Press, 1948.

Markowitz, M., & Kadis, A. L. Short-term analytic treatment of married couples in a group by a therapist couple. In B. F. Riess (Ed.), *New directions in mental health* (Vol. 1). New York: Grune & Stratton, 1968, pp. 50–68.

McColsky, A. S. Models of crisis intervention: The crisis counseling model. In G. A. Specter & W. L. Clairborn (Eds.), *Crisis intervention*. New York: Behavioral Publications, 1973, pp. 50–63.

McGee, D. H., Harris, D., Spitzner, J. H., Jackson, E., Lane, C., Momburg, P. W., Murphy, T. J., Rawlings, M. M., & Umana, R. A report to the Columbus Division of Police from the Family Crisis Unit: Current status and recommendations for continued action. Unpublished manuscript, Columbus Area Community Mental Health Center, Columbus, Ohio, 1975.

McGee, R. K. *Crisis intervention in the community*. Baltimore, Md.: University Park Press, 1974.

Menninger, W. C. *Psychiatry in a troubled world*. New York, Macmillan, 1948.

Meyer, H. J., Jones, W., & Borgatta, E. F. The decision by unmarried mothers to keep or surrender their babies. *Social Work*, 1956, *1* (2), 103–109.

Michener, C. W., & Walzer, H. Developing a community mental health volunteer system. *Social Work*, October 1970, 60–67.

Mintz, E. E. Transference in co-therapy groups. *Journal of Consulting Psychology*, 1963, *27*, 34–39.

Minuchin, S. *Families and family therapy*. Cambridge, Mass.: Harvard University Press, 1974.

Minuchin, S., Montalvo, B., Guerney, B. G., Rosman, B. L., & Schumer, F. *Families of the slums*. New York: Basic, 1967.

Minuchin, S., & Barcai, A. Therapeutically induced family crisis. In J. Masserman (Ed.), *Science and psychoanalysis*. New York: Grune & Stratton, 1969.

Mishler, E. G., & Waxler, N. E. *Interaction in families*. New York: Wiley, 1968.

Mitchell, C. A casework approach to disturbed families. In N. Ackerman, F. Beatman, & S. Sherman (Eds.), *Exploring the base for family therapy*. New York: Family Service Association, 1961, pp. 68–82.

Mitchell, H. E. Application of the Kaiser Method to marital pairs. *Family Process*, 1963, *2* (2), 265–279.

Monat, A., & Lazarus, R. S. (Eds.). *Stress and coping: An anthology*. New York: Columbia University Press, 1977.

Murphy, L. P. *Personality in young children*. New York: Basic, 1956.

Murrell, S. A., & Stachowiak, J. G. Consistency, rigidity, and power in the interaction of clinic and non-clinic families. *Journal of Abnormal Psychology*, 1967, *72*, 265–272.

Nakhla, F., Folkart, L., & Webster, J. Treatment of families as in-patients. *Family Process*, 1969, *8*, 79–96.

Neuhaus, R. H., & Neuhaus, R. H. *Family crises*. Columbus, Ohio: Merrill, 1974.

Newman, C. L. The constructive use of police authority with youth and families in crisis. *Police*, 1968, *12* (5).

Nolan, J. D. Self-control procedures in the modification of smoking behavior. *Journal of Consulting and Clinical Psychology*, 1968, *32*, 92–93.

Normand, W. C., Fensterheim, H., & Schrenzel, S. A systematic approach to brief therapy for patients from a low socioeconomic community. *Community Mental Health Journal*, 1967, *6f*, 349–354.

Notman, M. T., & Nadelson, C. C. The rape victim: Psychodynamic considerations. *American Journal of Psychiatry*, 1976, *133* (4), 408–413.

Oakland Police Department. Family crisis intervention program. Unpublished information bulletin. Oakland, Calif. January 1971.

O'Brien, J. Violence in divorce-prone families. *Journal of Marriage and the Family*, 1971, *33* (4), 692–698.

O'Leary, K. D., O'Leary, S., & Becher, W. C. Modification of a deviant sibling interaction pattern in the home. *Behavior Research and Therapy*, 1967, *5*, 113–120.

Olson, D. H. Marital and family therapy: Integrative review and critique. *Journal of Marriage and the Family*, 1970, *32* (4), 501–538.

Olson, D. H. (Ed.). *Treating relationships*. Lake Mills, Iowa: Graphic, 1976.

Ora, J. P., & Wagner, L. I. Contextual variables in oppositional child training. Paper presented at the meeting of the Southeastern Psychological Association, Louisville, Kentucky, 1970.

Papp, P. Family choreography. In P. J. Guerin (Ed.), *Family therapy, theory and practice*. New York: Gardner Press, 1976, 465–477.

Parad, H. J. Preventive casework: Problems and implications. In H. J. Parad (Ed.), *Crisis intervention: Selected readings*. New York: Family Services Association, 1965, pp. 284–298.

Parloff, M. B. The family in psychotherapy. *Archives of General Psychiatry*, 1961, *4*, 445–451.

Patterson, G. R. An application of conditioning techniques to the control of a hyperactive child. In P. Ullman & L. Krasner (Eds.), *Case studies in behavior modification*. New York: Holt, 1965, 370–375.

Patterson, G. R., & Brodsky, G. D. A behavior modification program for a child with multiple problem behaviors. *Journal of Child Psychology and Psychiatry*, 1966, *7*, 277–295.

Patterson, G. R., McNeal, Hawkins, & Phelps. Reprogramming the social environment. *Child Psychology and Psychiatry*, 1967, *8*, 181–195.

Patterson, G. R., Ray, R. S., & Shaw, D. A. Direct intervention in families of deviant children. *Oregon Research Institute Research Bulletin*, 1968, *8* (9).

Patterson, G. R., Cobb, J., & Ray, R. A social engineering technology for retraining aggressive boys. In H. Adams & L. Unikel (Eds.), *Georgia Symposium in Experimental Clinical Psychology*, 2. New York: Pergamon, 1970a.

Patterson, G. R., & Reid, J. B. Reciprocity and coercion: Two facets of social systems. In C. Neuringer & J. Michael (Eds.), *Behavior modification in clinical psychology*. New York: Appleton-Century-Crofts, 1970b.

Patterson, M. L. An arousal model of interpersonal intimacy. *Psychological Review*, 1976, *83* (3), 235–245.

Paul, G. L. Strategy of outcome research in psychotherapy. *Journal of Consulting Psychology*, 1967, *31* (2), 109–118.

Phelps, L. G., Schwartz, J. A., & Liebman, D. A. Training an entire patrol division in domestic crisis intervention technique. *Police Chief*, July 1971.

Pittman, F. S., DeYoung, C. D., Flomenhaft, K., Kaplan, D. M., & Langsley, D. G. Techniques of crisis family therapy. In J. Masserman (Ed.), *Current psychiatric therapies*, 6. New York: Grune & Stratton, 1966a, pp. 187–196.

Pittman, F. S., Langsley, D. G., Kaplan, D., DeYoung, C., & Flomenhaft, K. Family therapy as an alternative to hospitalization. In I. M. Cohen (Ed.), *Family structure, dynamics and therapy. Psychiatric Research Report #20.* Washington, D.C.: American Psychiatric Association, 1966b, pp. 188–195.

President's Commission on Law Enforcement and Administration of Justice. *The challenge of crime in a free society.* Washington, D.C.: U.S. Government Printing Office, 1967.

Rabkin, L. Y. The patient's family: research methods. *Family Process*, 1965, *4*, 105–132.

Radelet, L. A. Conflict management and crisis intervention–Oakland, California. In *The police and the community: Studies.* Beverly Hills. Glencoe, 1973, pp. 281–287.

Rahe, R. H., McKean, J. D., Jr., & Arthur, R. J. A longitudinal study of life-change and illness patterns. *Journal of Psychosomatic Research*, 1967, *10*, 355–366.

Rapoport, L. The state of crisis: Some theoretical considerations. *Social Services Review*, 1962, *36* (2), 211–217.

Rapoport, L. Working with families in crisis: An exploration in preventive intervention. In H. J. Parad (Ed.), *Crisis intervention: Selected readings.* New York: Family Services Association, 1965, pp. 129–139.

Rapoport, R. Normal crises, family structure and mental health. *Family Process*, 1963, *2* (1), 68–80.

Raush, H. L., Barry, W. A., Hertel, R. K., & Swain, M. A. *Communication, conflict and marriage.* San Francisco: Jossey-Bass, 1974.

Reese, E. D. *The analysis of human operant behavior.* Dubuque: Brown, 1966.

Reichard, S., & Tillman, C. Pattern of parent-child relationships in schizophrenia. *Psychiatry*, 1950, *13* (2), 247–257.

Reid, J. B. & Hendriks, A. F. Preliminary analysis of the effectiveness of direct home intervention for the treatment of predelinquent boys who steal. In L. A. Hamerlynck, L. C. Handy & E. J. Mash (Eds.), *Behavioral change: Methodology, concepts and practice.* Champaign, Ill.: Research Press, 1973.

Riskin, J., & Faunce, E. Family interaction scales. I. Theoretical framework and method. II. Data analysis and findings. III. Discussion of methodology and substantive findings. *Archives of General Psychiatry*, 1970, *22*, 504–537.

Ritchie, A. Multiple-impact therapy: an experiment. *Social Work*, 1960, *5* (3), 16–21.

Rose, S. D. A behavioral approach to the group treatment of parents. *Social Work*, 1961, *14*, 21–29

Rosenberg, P. P., & Fuller, M. I. Human relations seminar: A group work experiment in nursing education. *Mental Hygiene*, 1955, *34*, 406–432.

Rotter, G. S., & Tinkleman, V. Anchor effects in the development of behavior rating scales. *Educational and Psychological Measurement*, 1970, *30* (2), 311–318.

Rubenstein, E. A., & Lorr, M. A. A comparison of terminators and remainers in outpatient psychotherapy. *Journal of Clinical Psychology*, 1956, *12*, 345–349.

Safer, D. J. Family therapy for children with behavior disorders. *Family Process*, 1966, *5*, 243–255.

Sager, C. J., & Kaplan, H. S. (Eds.). *Progress in group and family therapy*. New York: Brunner/Mazel, 1972.

Salzinger, K., Feldman, R. S., & Portnoy, S. Training parents of brain-injured children in the use of operant conditioning procedures. *Behavior Therapy*, 1970, *1*, 4–32.

Satir, V. *Conjoint family therapy* (2nd ed.). Palo Alto: Science and Behavior, 1967.

Satir, V. The family as a treatment unit. In J. Haley (Ed.), *Changing families*. New York: Grune & Stratton, 1971.

Schaefer, H. H., & Martin, P. L. *Behavioral therapy*. New York: McGraw-Hill, 1969.

Schneidman, E. Crisis intervention: Some thoughts and perspectives. In G. A. Specter & W. L. Clairborn (Eds.), *Crisis intervention*. New York: Behavioral Publications, 1973, pp. 9–15.

Schulman, R., Shoemaker, D., & Moelis, I. Laboratory measurement of parental behavior. *Journal of Consulting Psychology*, 1962, *26*, 109–114.

Semrad, E. V., & Zaslow, S. L. Assisting psychotic patients to recompensate. *Mental Hospital*, 1964, *15*, 361.

Sheehy, G. *Passages: Predictable crises of adult life*. New York: E. P. Dutton & Co, Inc., 1976.

Sherman, J. A., & Baer, D. M. Appraisal of operant therapy techniques with children and adults. In C. M. Franks (Ed.), *Behavior therapy: Appraisal and status*. New York: McGraw-Hill, 1969.

Sigal, J. J., Rakoff, V., & Epstein, N. B. Interaction in early treatment sessions as an indication of therapeutic outcome in conjoint family therapy. *Family Process*, 1967, *6*, 215–226.

Silber, E., Hamburg, D., Coelho, G., Murphy, E., Rosenberg, M., & Pearlin, L. Adaptive behavior in competent adolescents—coping with the anticipation of college. *Archives of General Psychiatry*, 1961a, *5*, 354–365.

Silber, E., Hamburg, D., Coelho, G., Murphy, E., Rosenberg, M., & Pearlin, L. Competent adolescents coping with college decisions. *Archives of General Psychiatry*, 1961b, *5*, 517–577.

Sonne, J. C., & Lincoln, G. Heterosexual co-therapy team experiences during family therapy. *Family Process*, 1965, *4*, 177–197.

Sonne, J. C., & Lincoln, G. The importance of a heterosexual co-therapy relationship in the construction of a family image. In I. M. Cohen (Ed.), *Family structure, dynamics and therapy. Psychiatric Res ch Report #20*. Washington, D.C.: American Psychiatric Association, 1966, pp. 196–205.

Speck, R. V. Family therapy in the home. *Journal of Marriage and the Family*, 1964, *26*, 72–76.

Specter, G. A., & Clairborn, W. L. *Crisis intervention*. New York: Behavioral Publications, 1973.

Sprey, J. The family as a system in conflict. *Journal of Marriage and the Family*, 1969, *31*, 699–706.

Sprey, J. Extramarital relationships. *Sexual Behavior*, 1972, *2* (8), 34–40.

Stabenau, J., Turpin, J., Werner, M., & Pollin, W.A. A comparative study of families of schizophrenics, delinquents, and normals. *Psychiatry*, 1965, *28*, 45–59.

Stanton, A. H., & Schwartz, M. S. *The mental hospital*. New York: Basic, 1954.

Stanton, M. D. Family therapy training: Academic and internship opportunities for psychologists. Unpublished paper. Philadelphia Child Guidance Clinic, Philadelphia, 1975.

Starr, S. Personal communication. Family Study Unit, Palo Alto Veterans Administration Hospital, Palo Alto, California, 1972.

Steeves, J. M., Martin, G. L., & Pear, J. J. Self-imposed time-out by autistic children during an operant training program. *Behavior Therapy*, 1970, *1*., 371-381.

Stern, S., Moore, S., & Gross, S. J. The confounding of personality and social class characteristics in research on premature termination. *Journal of Counsulting and Clinical Psychology*, 1975, *43*, 341-344.

Stewart. W. A. Urban Negro speech: Sociolinguistic factors affecting English teaching. In R.. Shuy (Ed.), *Social dialects and language learning*. Champaign, Ill.: National Council of Teachers of English, 1964, pp. 10-18.

Stewart, W. A. Continuity and change in American Negro dialects. *Florida Foreign Language Reporter*, 1968, *6*, 3-18.

Stierlin, H. The adaptation of the "stronger" person's reality. *Psychiatry*, 1959, *22*, 143-152.

Stierlin, H. Family dynamics and separation patterns of potential schizophrenics. In Y. Alanen and D. Rubinstein (Eds.), *Proceedings of the Fourth International Symposium on Psychotherapy of Schizophrenia*. Amsterdam: Excerpta Medica, 1972, pp. 156-166.

Stierlin, H. Family theory: An introduction. In A. Burton (Ed.), *Operational theories of personality*. New York: Bruner/Mazel, 1974.

Stierlin, H. *Psychoanalysis and family therapy: Selected papers*. New York: Aronson, 1977.

Stierlin, H., Levi, L. D., & Savard, R. J. Parental perceptions of separating children. *Family Process*, 1971, *10*, 411-427.

Straughan, J. H. Treatment with child and mother in the playroom. *Behavior Research Therapy*, 1964, *2*, 37-41.

Strodbeck, F. L. The family as a three-person group. *American Sociological Review*, 1954, *19*, 23-29.

Strupp, H. H. Some critical comments on the future of psychoanalytic therapy. *Bulletin of the Menninger Clinic*, 1976, *40* (3), 238-247.

Stuart, R. B. Operant-interpersonal treatment for marital discord. *Journal of Consulting and Clinical Psychology*, 1969, *33* (6), 675-682.

Stuart, R. B. Token reinforcement in marital treatment. In P. H. Glasser & L. N. Glasser (Eds.), *Families in crisis*. New York: Harper & Row, 1970, pp. 172-181.

Stuart, R. B. Operant-interpersonal treatment for marital discord. In J. M. Steadman, W. F. Patton, & K. F. Walton (Eds.), *Clinical studies in behavior therapy with children, adolescents and their families*. Springfield, Ill.: Thomas, 1973, pp. 311-323.

Stuart, R. B. Behavioral remedies for mental ills: A guide to the use of operant-interpersonal techniques. In T. Thompson & W. Docken (Eds.), *International Symposium on Behavior Modification*. New York: Appleton, 1975.

Thibaut, J. W., & Kelley, H. H. *The social psychology of groups*. New York: Wiley, 1959.

Thomas, C. S. & Weisman, G. K. Emergency planning: The practical and theoretical backdrop to the emergency treatment unit. *International Journal of Social Psychiatry*, 1970, *16*.

Titchner, J. L. The problem of interpretation in marital therapy. *Comprehensive Psychiatry*, 1966, *7* (5), 321-337.

Titchner, J. L. Family system as model for ego system. In G. H. Zuk & I. Boszormenyi-Nagy (Eds.), *Family therapy and disturbed families*. Palo Alto: Science and Behavior, 1967, pp. 96-105.

Titchner, J. L., & Golden, M. Predictions of therapeutic themes from observation of family interaction evoked by the rescaled differences technique. *Journal of Nervous and Mental Disease*, 1963, *136*, 464-474.

Torrance, E. P. *Constructive behavior: Stress, personality and mental health*. Belmont, Calif.: Wadsworth, 1965.

Truax, C. B., & Carkhuff, R. R. *Toward effective counseling and psychotherapy: Training and practice*. Chicago: Aldine, 1967.

Truax, C. B., & Lister, J. L. Effectiveness of counselors and counselor aides. *Journal of Counseling Psychology,* 1970, *17,* 331–334.

Turner, M. B. & Gross, S. J. An approach to family therapy: An affective rule-altering model. *Journal of Family Counseling,* 1976, 50–56.

Tyhurst, J. S. The role of transition states—including disasters—in mental illness. In *Symposium on preventive and social psychiatry.* Washington, D.C.: Walter Reed Army Institute of Research, 1957, 149–169.

Ulrich, R., Stachnik, T., & Mabry, J. (Eds.). *Control of human behavior* (Vol. II), Glenview, Ill.: Scott Foresman, 1970.

Umana, R. F., & Schwebel, A. I. Academic and behavioral change in tutored inner-city children. *Community Mental Health Journal,* 1974, *10* (3), 309–318.

vonBertalanffy, L. *General systems theory.* New York: Human relations, 1968.

Wagner, M. K. Parent therapists: An operant conditioning method. *Mental Hygiene,* 1968, *52,* 452–455.

Wahl, C. W. Some antecedent factors in the family histories of 392 schizophrenics. *American Journal of Psychiatry,* 1954, *110* (9), 668–676.

Wahler, R. G. Behavior therapy for oppositional children: Love is not enough. Paper presented at the meeting of the Eastern Psychological Association, Washington, D.C., 1968.

Wahler, R. G. Oppositional children: A quest for parental reinforcement control. *Journal of Applied Behavior Analysis,* 1969, *2,* 159–170.

Walder, L. O., Cohen, S. I., Breiter, D. E., Daston, P. G., Hirsch, I. S., & Leibowitz, J. M. Teaching behavioral principles to parents of disturbed children. In B. G. Guerney, Jr. (Ed.), *Psychotherapeutic agents: New roles for non-professionals, parents and teachers.* New York: Holt, 1969.

Walker, R. G., Winkel, G. H., Peterson, R. F., & Morrison, D. C. Mothers as behavior therapists for their own children. *Behavior Research and Therapy,* 1965, *3,* 113–134.

Warkentin, J., & Whitaker, C. Serial impasses in marriage. In I. M. Cohen (Ed.), *Family structure, dynamics and therapy. Psychiatric Research Report #20.* Washington, D.C.: American Psychiatric Association, 1966, pp. 73–77.

Watzlawick, P. A structured family interview. *Family Process,* 1966, *5,* 256–271.

Weakland, J. H., & Jackson, D. D. Patient and therapist observations on the circumstances of a schizophrenic episode. *American Medical Association Archives of Neurology and Psychiatry,* 1958, 79 (4), 554–574.

Weakland, J. H., Fisch, R., Watzlawick, P., & Bodin, A. M. Brief therapy: focused problem resolution. *Family Process,* 1974, *13* (2).

Weisman, G., Feirstein, A., & Thomas, C. Three-day hospitalization: a model for intensive intervention. *Archives of General Psychiatry,* 1969, *21,* 620–629.

Weiss, R. L., Hops, H., & Patterson, G. R. A framework for conceptualizing marital conflict: A technology for altering it, some data for evaluating it. In F. W. Clark and L. A. Hamerlynk (Eds.), *Critical issues in research and practice: Proceedings of the fourth banff international conference on behavioral modification.* Champaign, Ill.: Research Press, 1973.

Wells, R., Dilkes, T., & Trivelli, N. The results of family therapy: A critical review of the literature. *Family Process,* 1972, *11,* 189–207.

Wetzel, R. J., Baker, J., Roney, M., & Martin, M. Outpatient treatment of autistic behavior. *Behavior Research and Therapy,* 1966, *4,* 169–177.

Whaley, D. L., & Malott, R. W. *Elementary principles of behavior.* New York: Meredith, 1971.

Whitaker, C. A. Family treatment of a psychopathic personality. *Comprehensive Psychiatry,* 1966, 7 (5), 397–402.

Whitaker, C. A., Malone, T. P., & Warkentin, J. Multiple therapy and psychotherapy. In F. Fromm-Reichmann & J. L. Moreno (Eds.), *Progress in therapy.* New York: Grune & Stratton, 1956.

Whitehurst, R. N. Violence potential in extramarital sexual responses. *Journal of Marriage and the Family*, 1971, *33* (4), 683–691.

Winder, A., & Hersko, M. The effect of social class on the length and type of psychotherapy in a V. A. Mental Health Clinic. *Journal of Clinical Psychology*, 1955, *11*, 77–79.

Wing, J. K. Institutionalism in mental hospitals. In T. Scheff (Ed.), *Mental illness and social process*. New York: Harper & Row, 1967.

Winter, W. D., & Ferreira, A. J. Interaction process analysis of family decision-making. *Family Process*, 1967, *6*, 155–172.

Wolf, M. M., Risley, T. R., & Mees, H. L. Application of operant conditioning procedures to the behavior problems of an autistic child. *Behavior research and therapy*, 1964, *1*, 305–312.

Wolff, T. Undergraduates as campus mental health workers. *Personnel and Guidance Journal*, 1969, *48*, 294–304.

Wolfgang, M. *Patterns of Criminal Homicide*. Philadelphia: University of Pennsylvania Press, 1958.

Wynne, L. C. Some guidelines for exploratory conjoint family therapy. In J. Haley (Ed.), *Changing families*. New York: Grune & Stratton, 1971, pp. 96–115.

Young, L. *Out of wedlock: A study of the problems of the unmarried mother and her child*. New York: McGraw-Hill, 1954.

Zeilberger, J., Sampen, S., & Sloane, H. Modification of a child's problem behaviors in the home with the mother as therapist. *Journal of Applied Behavior Analysis*, 1968, *1*, 47–53.

Zuk, G. H. Family therapy. *Archives of General Psychiatry*, 1967, *16*, 71–79.

Zuk, G. H., & Rubinstein, D. A review of concepts in the study and treatment of families of schizophrenics. In I. Boszormenyi-Nagy & J. Framo (Eds.), *Intensive family therapy*. New York: Harper & Row, 1965.

SUBJECT INDEX

Behavioral Change Techniques, 107
Behavioral Crisis Intervention, 77
  Assumptions of, 78
  Goals of, 78
  Assessment Methods in, 78
  Treatment Methods in, 79
  Help Givers, 80
  Role of Help Givers, 81
Behavioral Family Therapy, 99
  Assumptions, 101
  Goals of, 104
  Assessment Methods, 105
  Treatment Methods, 106
  Help Givers, 111
  Role of Help Givers, 110
  Setting, 112
  Consumers, 112
Bereavement Reactions, 19
Communications Theory, 13
Comparative Analysis, 171-179
  Three Therapeutic Frameworks, 171
  Three Models of Human Behavior, 174
  Frameworks by Model, 175
Conflict and Self Esteem, 2
Crisis
  Definition of 1, 21
  as a choice point, 4
  as a temporary event, 6
  Types of, 57
  Effects of individual differences, 59
  Characteristic behaviors in, 65
Crisis Intervention, 18

Historical Development, 18-20
Theoretical Framework, 20
Models of, 21
Treatment goals of, 22
Treatment methods in, 22
Consumers, 23
Setting of, 24
Help givers in, 24
Role of Help givers, 27
Models of, 69
(also see Individual, Behavioral, and Systems Crisis Intervention)
Crisis-prone families, 1-2, 3
Crisis Response, 62
Crisis Resolution
  Phases of, 3-4
  Process of, 4
Crisis Theory
  Assumptions, 3, 4, 21
Evaluative Research in Crisis Intervention, 143-153
  Criteria of effectiveness, 143
  Validation of principles of crisis theory, 146
  Service provision, 148
  Outcome studies, 148
  Quality of service providers, 151
Evaluative Research in Family Crisis Intervention 10, 131-143
  Criteria of effectiveness, 131-132
  With Psychiatric Problems, 133-137
  With Interpersonal and Social Problems, 138-142

Evaluative Research in Family Therapy, 153
Psychoanalytic model, 154
Behavioral model, 156
Systems model, 158
Summary, 164

Family
as system, 10-11, 12
Schizophrenia in, 11-12

Family Crisis
Definition of, 1
Precipitating factors, 1
Necessary conditions for 1, 2
Normal, typical, 2
Effect on family behavior, 4-5

Family Crisis Intervention
Goals of, 6
Assumptions of, 6
Assessment in, 7
Treatment Methods in, 7
Role of the Intervenor, 8
Help Givers, 8
Population Receiving Services, 9
Typical Setting of, 9
Models of (See Psychoanalytic, Problem-Oriented, and Systems Family Crisis Intervention).

Family Therapy, 10
Historical development 10-13
as a new perspective on psychopathology, 13
Theoretical framework, 13
Differences from individual treatment, 14
Models of, 15
(also see Psychoanalytic, Behavioral, and Systems Family Therapy)
Treatment goals in, 15
Treatment methods, 15
Consumers, 16
Setting of, 16
Help givers in, 17
Role of therapist in, 18

Help Seeking
in crisis, 4, 5-6

Individual Crisis Intervention, 71
Assumptions of, 71
Goals of, 72
Assessment Methods, 72
Treatment Methods, 72
Help Givers, 74
Setting of, 74
Consumers of, 75

Intervenors
Kind of, and likelihood of seeing families in crisis, 5
Natural help givers, 5, 9, 27, 139-142
Police Officers as Natural Help Givers, 9, 139-142
Effectiveness of professionals vs nonprofessionals, 24, 27, 138-139
and choice of intervention approach, 31

Intervention Approaches
Community wide, 2-3, 24
Milestone, 3, 5
High-risk, 3, 23
Normal Crises, 2,3
Primary Prevention, 80

Problem-oriented Family Crisis Intervention, 43
Assumptions of, 44
Goals of, 45
Assessment Methods in, 45
Treatment Methods in, 47
Help Givers in, 50
Role of Help Givers in, 51
Setting of, 51
Consumers in, 51

Problem-solving Skills
Insufficiency in crisis, 1
Use of novel approaches, 4

Psychoanalytic Family Crisis Intervention, 35
Assumptions of, 36
Goals of, 37
Assessment Methods, 37
Treatment Methods, 38
Help Givers in, 38
Role of Help Givers in, 39

Setting of, 40
Consumers in, 40
Psychoanalytic Family Therapy, 89
Assumptions and goals, 91
Assessment Methods, 92
Treatment Methods, 93
Role of Therapist, 95
Setting, 96
Consumers, 96
Appropriateness of, 96-97
Socioeconomic Status
and crisis proneness, 3
and likelihood of receiving help in crisis, 5
and effectiveness of family therapy, 16
and effectiveness of crisis intervention, 23
Stress
as motivator in crisis, 3-4
and individual differences, 60-65
Support Systems, 1, 3

Symptomatology, the functional value of, in family therapy, 30
Systems Crisis Intervention, 83
Assumptions of, 84
Goals of, 84
Assessment Methods, 85
Treatment Methods in, 85
Help Givers, 86
Role of Help Givers, 87
Setting, 87
Consumers, 87
Systems Family Crisis Intervention, 53
Assumptions of, 53
Goals of, 54
Assessment Methods, 54
Treatment Methods in, 54
Help Givers in, 55
Role of Help Givers, 55
Setting of, 55
Consumers in, 55
Synthesis of family therapy and crisis intervention, 28-33

AUTHOR INDEX

Ackerman, N .W., 11, 13, 89, 93, 168
Alkov, R. A., 59
Arthur, R. J., 59
Ault, M. H., 105
Azrin, N. H., 102, 103, 104
Balint, E., 93
Barcai, A., 32
Bard, M., 140, 141
Barry, W. A., 2
Bateson, G., 11, 13, 158, 159
Beck, D. F., 16, 165
Beels, D. C., 14
Berman, G. S., 25
Bijou, S. W., 105
Bleach, G., 145, 148, 151, 152
Bodin, A. M., 149
Bolman, W. M., 2, 3, 138
Boszormenyi-Nagy, I., 98, 168
Bowen, M., 11, 12, 116
Brody, E. M., 138
Burgess, A. W., 57, 58
Cameron, W. R., 133, 134
Caplan, G., 1, 3, 4, 6, 21, 22, 57, 58,
   66, 78, 144, 145
Carkhuff, R. R., 111
Christ, J., 96
Clairborn, W., 151, 152
Coleman, M. D., 74
Cowen, M, 40, 97
Cromwell, R. E., 165
Dilkes, T., 165
Dublin, L. I., 26
Durlak, J. A., 26
Erikson, E., 57, 90
Fagen, B., 10

Faunce, E., 164
Feirstein, A., 150
Fensterheim, H., 148
Ferber, A., 14
Fisch, R., 149
Fournier, D. G., 165
Framo, J. L., 166
Freud, S., 91
Friedman, A. S., 92, 95, 96
Gilmore, J., 103
Gonso, J., 45
Gottman, J., 45
Gross, S. J., 32, 86, 87, 117, 118, 120,
   121, 125, 126, 128, 129, 162
Grosser, C. F., 25
Group for the advancement of Psychiatry,
   The, 16, 17
Grunebaum, H., 96, 97
Guerin, P. J., 85, 89
Gurman, A. S., 164, 165, 166
Haley, J., 11, 115, 117, 120, 124, 125,
   128, 159, 160, 162
Hall, A., 10
Hansell, N., 62, 64, 66, 67
Haug, M. R., 25
Hawkins, R. P., 157, 158
Hertel, R. K., 2
Hill, R., 1
Hobbs, N.,110
Hops, H., 103
Jackson, D. D., 11, 12, 116, 117, 118,
   123, 124, 125, 162
Jacob, T., 164
Jacobson, G. F., 19, 148
Jacobson, N. S., 102

Janis, I., 103
Jongs, M. A., 16
Jones, R., 102, 103
Kadis, A., L., 95
Kaffman, M., 94, 96, 97, 154, 155, 156
Kaplan, D. M., 79, 146, 147
Kniskern, D. P., 166
Knox, D., 46, 106
Langsley, D. G., 83, 84, 133, 136, 137, 142, 143
Lazare, A., 57, 58
Levy, L., 27
Liberman, R. P., 101, 111
Lidz, T., 11, 12, 91, 96
Litman, R. E., 153
Lincoln, G., 95
Lindemann, E., 19, 21, 78, 146, 147
MacGregor, R., 133
Malone, T. P., 11
Malott, R. W., 49
Markman, H., 45
Martin, B., 102
Mason, E. A., 146, 147
McClosky, A. S., 25, 26
McGee, R. M., 26, 140, 145
McKean, J. D. Jr., 59
Michner, C. W., 26, 32
Minuchin, S., 16, 162, 163
Mitchell, C. A., 95, 154
Markowitz, M., 95
Nadelson, C. C., 58
Naster, B. J., 102, 103
Neiberg, N., 96
Normand, W. C., 148
Notarius, C., 45
Notman, M. T., 58
Olson, D. H., 13, 17, 165
Papp, P., 85
Paterson, G. R., 103
Paul, G. L., 168

Pendergast, M. A., 85
Peterson, R. F., 105
Pittman, F. S., 135
Rabkin, L. Y., 168
Rahe, R. H., 59
Raush, H. L., 2
Reichard, S., 11
Riskin, J., 164
Rowitz, L., 27
Satir, V., 2, 118, 125, 162
Schrenzel, S., 148
Schwartz, M.S., 83
Sigal, J. J., 163, 164
Sonne, J. C., 95
Spark, G., 138
Stanton, A. H., 83
Stierlin, H., 90, 91, 94
Stuart, R. V., 47, 102, 103, 104, 108, 109
Swain, M.A., 2
Thomas, C., 150
Tillman, C., 11
Titchner, J. L., 90, 91, 92, 93, 94
Torrance, E. P., 59
Trivelli, N., 165
Truax, C. B., 111
Turner, M. B., 32, 86, 87, 117, 118, 120, 121, 125, 126, 128, 129, 162
Wahl, C. W., 11
Walters, V., 133, 134
Walzer, H., 26
Watzlawick, P., 119, 149
Weakland, J. H., 11, 12, 123, 149, 150
Weisman, G., 150, 151
Weiss, R. O., 103, 104
Wells, R., 165
Whaley, D. L., 49
Whitaker, C., 11, 95
Wynne, L. C., 96, 97, 154
Zuk, G. H., 89